Accounting and Financial Reporting Guide for Christian Ministries

Evangelical
Accounting Com

Accounting and Financial Reporting Guide for Christian Ministries

Sponsoring Groups

Christian Management Association

P.O. Box 4090
San Clemente, CA 92674

Phone: (949) 487-0900
Fax: (949) 487-0927
Email : cma@cmaonline.org

Evangelical Council for Financial Accountability

440 West Jubal Early Drive, Suite 130
Winchester, VA 22601

Phone: (540) 535-0103
Fax: (540) 535-0533
Email : info@ecfa.org

Evangelical Fellowship of Mission Agencies

4201 North Peachtree Road, Suite 300
Atlanta, GA 30341

Phone: (770) 457-6677
Fax: (770) 457-0037
Email : efma@xc.org

Interdenominational Foreign Mission Association
of North America

P.O. Box 398
Wheaton, IL 60189-0398

Phone: (630) 682-9270
Fax: (630) 682-9278
Email : ifma@aol.com

Canadian Council of Christian Charities

1-21 Howard Avenue
Elmira, Ontario N3B 2C9
Canada

Phone: (519) 669-5137
Fax: (519) 669-3291
Email : mail@cccc.org

Evangelical Joint Accounting Committee

Chair:

>Gregory B. Capin, CPA; Capin Crouse LLP

Members:

>Bill Altman, CPA; Evangelical Council for Financial Accountability
>Ed Anderson, MBA, CPA; Compassion International
>Marjorie Barham, CA, CMA; SIM International
>Dan Busby, MS, CPA; Evangelical Council for Financial
>>Accountability
>James Canning, MBA, CPA; World Vision International
>James E. Fuoss, CPA; International Teams
>Scott Holbrook, MBA, CPA; Gospel Missionary Union
>Richard Karppinen, MBA; Teen Challenge of Arizona
>Richard F. Larkin, MBA, CPA; Lang Group Chartered
>Dale A. Overholt, CPA; Capin Crouse LLP
>Randy Thomann, CPA; Bethel College and Seminary

Committee Consultants:

>Richard F. Capin, CPA, Retired; Capin Crouse LLP
>Eldon J. Howard, MPA; SIM International
>Ronald C. Knechtel, CA, CMA; Canadian Council of Christian
>>Charities
>Kimberly Smith, CA; Kimberly Smith & Associates

With special recognition and great appreciation to:

>Jim Fuoss, Richard Karppinen, and Dick Larkin for their invaluable
>contribution to this project, including significant time and
>efforts as members of the editorial subcommittee.

Table of Contents

Preface xv

Introduction xvii

Chapter 1 — Accounting for Christian Ministries 1

Financial Statements 3
Ministry Accomplishments 5
Accrual Basis of Accounting....................................... 6
Materiality 8
Fund Accounting.. 8
Other Comprehensive Bases of Accounting 9

Chapter 2 — Financial Statements and Reporting 13

Required Financial Statements.................................... 15
 Statement of Financial Position 15
 Statement of Activities 18
 Statement of Functional Expenses 20
 Statement of Cash Flows....................................... 21
 Notes to Financial Statements 22
Comparative Financial Statements............................. 22
Financial Management 24
 Internal Control.. 25
 Cash Management 27
 Ratios 28

Chapter 3 — Net Assets 31

Net Assets and Fund Accounting............................... 33
Classes of Net Assets... 33
Permanently Restricted Net Assets 37

Temporarily Restricted Net Assets 38

Unrestricted Net Assets 40

Reclassification (Transfer) of Net Assets 41

Other Changes in Net Assets 44

    Accounting Changes and Extraordinary Items 44

    Prior Period Adjustments 45

    International Currency Translations 46

    Return of Contributions 46

Chapter 4 — Revenue 47

Contributions 49

    Accounting Principles... 51

    Distinguishing Contributions from Purchases/Sales
        Transactions 51

    Contributions Made 53

    Contributions Received 53

    Unrestricted Support 54

    Donor Restricted Support 54

    Permanently Restricted Support 55

    Temporarily Restricted Support 56

    Change in Temporarily Restricted Net Assets 58

    Direct and Other Designated Gifts 60

        Honoraria and Expense Reimbursements 60

        Personal Gifts.. 61

        Special Fund-Raising Events 61

    "Pass-through" Gifts: Cash and Gifts-in-Kind 63

    Promises to Give 68

        Intentions to Give 69

        Conditional Promises 70

        Unconditional Promises 70

    Discounting of Pledges 77

    Deferred Gifts 78

    Legacies and Bequests 79

    Endowments.. 79

    Donated and Contributed Services 79

    Valuing Contributed Services 82

Donated Materials and Facilities (Gifts-in-Kind)..................... 83
Below Market Rate Loans 89
Earned Income 89
Income Earned on Investments 89
Gains and Losses on Investments... 89
Revenue from Sales of Goods and Services 91
Tax Matters Related to Support and Revenue 92
Tax Rules Related to Charitable Giving 93
Support-Raising 94
Tax Reporting Related to Remittances to Personnel 97
Unrelated Business Income 97
Unrelated Business Activity 98
Debt-Financed Income...100
Managing Unrelated Business Income 102
Sales Tax Requirements..103
Private Foundation Status 103

Chapter 5 — Expenses 105

Functional Classification of Expenses 109
Program Services 110
Supporting Activities...111
Management and General Activities 112
Fund-Raising Activities..114
Membership Development Activities 116
Allocation of Expenses 117
Accounting for Costs Involving Fund-Raising 119
Accounting for Joint Activities 119
Purpose 119
Audience..126
Content..127
Allocation Methods..128
Incidental Activities...128
Disclosures 129
Furloughs, Sabbaticals, and Study Leaves 131
Natural Classification of Expenses..132
Grants (Including Support to Affiliated Organizations) 133

Costs Related to Sales of Goods and Services 137
   Reductions in Amounts Charged for Goods and Services ..137
Advertising Costs 138
Investment Expenses 139
Postemployment Expenses 139
Start-up Activities 141
Internal Use Software 141
Losses..143

Chapter 6 — Accounting for Investments and Property and Equipment 145

Investments...147
   Basis of Recording at Acquisition 148
   Carrying Value of Investments 148
   Unrealized and Realized Gains and Losses.........................149
   Investment Pools 153
Property and Equipment..154
   Reporting of Property and Equipment 155
   Capitalization Policy 156
   Depreciation 157
   Classification of Property, Equipment, and Depreciation 159
   Property Held in Other Countries...159

Chapter 7 — Annuities, Trusts, and Similar Gifts 161

Accounting for Split-Interest Gifts 164
   Lead Interests..165
   Accounting for Lead Interests 166
   Perpetual Trusts Held by a Third Party 169
   Accounting for Perpetual Trusts Held by a Third Party 170
   Remainder Interests 171
   Accounting for Remainder Interests 174
   Charitable Gift Annuities 176
   Accounting for Charitable Gift Annuities 176
   Pooled Income Funds and Net Income Unitrusts 177

Accounting for Pooled Income Funds and Net Income
  Unitrusts..178
Custodian (Agency) Funds 180
Revocable Trusts and Other Agreements.....................180
Life Insurance 181
Life Estates 181

Chapter 8 — Related Organizations 183

Criteria to Determine if Consolidation is Required or
  Permitted 190
Affiliation or Joint Ministries Agreements 192
Developing Organizations..193
Revenue-Producing Operations 193
Operations in Other Locations and Countries 194
For-Profit Entities 195
Consolidated Financial Statements and Disclosures..............195
Mergers of Not-for-Profit Organizations 196

Chapter 9 — Canadian Principles and Practices 199

Principles for Registered Charities 201
Principles for Charitable Gifts....................................202
Accounting Practices 203
  Special Trust Funds 204
  Contingent Beneficial Interest in a Special Trust 205
  Consolidation of Special Trusts 206
  Accounting for Revenue.......................................208
  Endowment Funds 210
  Unrestricted Revenue..212
  Administered Revenue 212
  Fund Accounting 214
  Inter-fund Transfers 216
  Pledges..217
  Gifts-in-Kind 217
  Notional Revenues 217

Life Insurance 218

Bibliography 219

Appendix A — Glossary 223

Appendix B — Accounting for Support and Revenue
Supplemental Information 233

Exhibit 1 — Purchase of Goods or Services vs.
Restricted Grants..233
Exhibit 2 — Purpose—Restricted or Not 237
Exhibit 3 — Bona Fide Pledge 241
Exhibit 4 — Conditional or Restricted...................................247
Exhibit 5 — True Recipient of Donated Services 253
Exhibit 6 — Contributed Services Requiring Specialized
Skills...257
Exhibit 7 — Need to Purchase Services.................................261

Appendix C — Illustrative Financial Statements 267

Exhibit 1 — Large Christian Organization 268
Exhibit 2 — Small Ministry
Exhibit 2a — Full Accrual 296
Exhibit 2b — Modified Cash Basis 303
Exhibit 2c — Cash Basis..309
Exhibit 2d — Comparative Information 314
Exhibit 3 — Religious Broadcaster 320
Exhibit 4 — Camp/Conference Center 331
Exhibit 5 — Church 346
Exhibit 6 — Rescue Mission 355
Exhibit 7 — School..365

Appendix D — Illustrations of an Investment Pool 371

Appendix E — Internal Controls 375

Basic Controls..376
Policies and Procedures..376

Budgets 376
Control Over Cash and Other Receipts 377
Control Over Cash Disbursements..............................378
Control Over Investments..379
Other Areas of Control 381
Fidelity Insurance 382
Foreign Operations 382

Appendix F — Functional Allocations 383

Typical Categories of Program Services........................385
Typical Functional Allocations..................................387

Appendix G — AICPA Flowcharts for Reporting of Related Entities 391

Appendix H — Sample Joint Ministries Agreement 395

Appendix I — Cash Basis Financial Statements 407

Specific Aspects of Cash Basis Reporting.....................408
Fixed Assets and Depreciation..................................408
Investments 408
Other Modifications 408
Statement of Cash Flows..409
Other Footnote Disclosures in Cash Basis Statements........409

Appendix J — Flowchart for Distinguishing Contributions from Agency Transactions 413

Appendix K — Flowchart for Accounting for Split-Interest Gifts 417

Significant Changes in the 2001 Edition 419

Index 431

Preface

*" . . . we are anxious that no one should find fault with
the way we are handling this large gift. God knows we
are honest, but I want everyone else to know it too. That
is why we have made this arrangement."*
2 Corinthians 8:20, 21 (Living Bible)

The Apostle Paul makes it clear that great care needs to be taken in the administration of gifts, including their receipt and disbursement.

He was concerned that:

- qualified people handle the funds

- the work involve several people

- the results of the work be reported back to the contributors

- reports be provided that were honorable in the sight of men

In the recent past we have witnessed scandals in the Christian community and broader nonprofit sector. Many of these scandals involved financial improprieties which have caused great embarrassment. They have also resulted in greater scrutiny of Christian ministries by regulators, Congress, the media, the public, and donors. The impact of these scandals will continue for many years.

This Guide has been prepared to assist Christian ministries in accounting for and reporting their varied activities in conformity with generally accepted accounting principles (GAAP). While emphasizing conformity with GAAP, the Evangelical Joint Accounting Committee (EJAC) recognizes that an even higher level of public accountability is mandated by the Scriptures, which we recognize as authoritative. The Bible exhorts Christians to keep their fiscal behavior beyond reproach. We trust the *Accounting and Financial Reporting Guide for Christian Ministries* will assist ministries in achieving this goal.

Furthermore, this Guide seeks to increase uniformity in accounting and financial reporting among Christian ministries in order to assist users in understanding financial reports. It draws together, interprets, and applies current authoritative accounting standards, making recommendations which apply specifically to this growing, significant segment of the not-for-profit sector. Its development draws heavily on the excellent work done by various entities during the past twenty years. Where significant reliance is placed on these works or where they are quoted directly, specific references are given.

Introduction

In a desire to enhance the accounting, reporting, and accountability of Christian ministries and to recognize the unique environment within which these organizations function, the Christian Management Association (CMA), the Evangelical Council for Financial Accountability (ECFA), the Evangelical Fellowship of Mission Agencies (EFMA), and the Interdenominational Foreign Mission Association of North America (IFMA), in cooperation with the Canadian Council of Christian Charities, appointed the Evangelical Joint Accounting Committee (EJAC) to address the development of the *Accounting and Financial Reporting Guide for Christian Ministries*. Included on the EJAC are chief financial officers from major ministries, public accounting practitioners, consultants, and chief executive officers from the sponsoring agencies. This present Guide is a result of their efforts. It is the intent of EJAC and its sponsoring associations that this Guide establish industry standards for Christian ministries.

The 1987 edition of *Accounting and Financial Reporting Guide for Christian Ministries* presented the conceptual framework discussed in Financial Accounting Standards Board (FASB) Concepts Statement No. 6, *Elements of Financial Statements,* as well as the standards in the American Institute of Certified Public Accountants (AICPA) SOP 78-10, *Accounting Principles and Reporting Practices for Certain Nonprofit Organizations*. Many of the provisions presented recognized that FASB Concepts Statement No. 6 was a conceptual document and that formal accounting standards had not been promulgated by FASB. The 1994 edition presented two newly promulgated FASB accounting standards (FASB Statements No. 116 and 117) including provisions that differed from those previously set forth in SOP 78-10, the primary document cited in the 1987 Guide and its predecessor, *Accounting and Financial Reporting Guide for Missionary Organizations* (1979).

Subsequent to the issuance of the 1994 edition of *Accounting and Financial Reporting Guide for Christian Ministries*, the AICPA issued its *Audit and Accounting Guide, Not-for-Profit Organizations* (June 1, 1996) which replaced SOP 78-10 and accounting guides for voluntary health and welfare organizations and colleges and universities. EJAC incorporated any clarifications and changes resulting from this document in the 1997 edition of its guide.

In 1998 the AICPA issued SOP 98-2, *Accounting for Costs of Activities of Not-for-Profit Organizations and State and Local Governmental Entities That Include Fund Raising*, which superseded SOP 87-2, *Accounting for Joint Costs of Informational Materials and Activities of Not-for-Profit Organizations That Include a Fund-Raising Appeal*. In 1999 the FASB issued its Statement No. 136, *Transfers of Assets to a Not-for-Profit Organization or Charitable Trust That Raises or Holds Contributions for Others*. In addition, staff of the AICPA's Accounting Standards Team has released various nonauthoritative questions and answers (Q&As), commonly referred to as Technical Practice Aids (TPAs), pertaining to not-for-profit organizations. (The TPAs have not been approved, disapproved, or otherwise acted upon by AcSEC or any other senior technical committee of the AICPA. They are not sources of established accounting principles as described in SAS No. 69, *Present Fairly in Conformity with Generally Accepted Accounting Principles*.) Though TPAs are not authoritative GAAP, their conclusions are reflected herein because we consider them to be useful and relevant guidance that should be followed. EJAC has incorporated any clarifications and changes resulting from these documents in this edition of the Guide.

This Guide includes excerpts from:

- Financial Accounting Standards Board (FASB) Publications:

    - *Transfers of Assets to a Not-for-Profit Organization or Charitable Trust That Raises or Holds Contributions for Others* (FASB Statement No. 136, June 1999)

    - *Accounting for Certain Investments Held by Not-for-Profit Organizations* (FASB Statement No. 124, November 1995)

    - *Financial Statements of Not-for-Profit Organizations* (FASB Statement No. 117, June 1993)

- *Accounting for Contributions Received and Contributions Made* (FASB Statement No. 116, June 1993)

- *Elements of Financial Statements*, (FASB Concepts Statement No. 6, December 1985)

- The American Institute of Certified Public Accountants (AICPA) Publications:

  - *AICPA Audit and Accounting Guide, Not-for-Profit Organizations* (*AICPA NPO Guide 2000*)

  - *Accounting for Costs of Activities of Not-for-Profit Organizations and State and Local Governmental Entities That Include Fund Raising* (SOP 98-2, March 1998)

  - *Reporting of Related Entities by Not-for-Profit Organizations* (SOP 94-3, September 1994)

EJAC recommends that all affected organizations obtain copies of FASB Statement Nos. 116, 117, 124, 136, and the AICPA *Audit and Accounting Guide, Not-for-Profit Organizations,* which incorporates SOP 98-2. FASB Statements may be ordered from the Order Department, Financial Accounting Standards Board, 401 Merritt 7, P. O. Box 5116, Norwalk, Connecticut 06856-5116 (www.fasb.org). AICPA publications may be ordered from the AICPA Order Department at 1-888-777-7077 (www.aicpa.org).

Organizations should note that they cannot obtain an "unqualified" (or clean) opinion from their auditors if the requirements of these standards are not applied, unless the organization prepares its financial statements on a comprehensive basis of accounting other than GAAP (see paragraphs 1-16 to 1-20, *Other Comprehensive Bases of Accounting*).

EJAC believes its recommendations contained in this Guide that go beyond those explicitly included in authoritative FASB or AICPA literature are consistent with current GAAP for not-for-profit organizations, including Christian ministries. However, failure to follow EJAC recommendations does not necessarily indicate a GAAP departure. FASB Statement Nos. 116, 117, 124, 136, the AICPA *Audit and Accounting Guide, Not-for-Profit Organizations,* and SOP 98-2 are currently recognized by the accounting profession as constituting GAAP for U.S.-based Christian ministries. Readers should note that future FASB and AICPA pronouncements may clarify and/or change these provisions.

Many areas discussed in this Guide are also the subject of related regulatory tax pronouncements that change from time to time. Readers should research current tax laws and regulations for applicable tax and regulatory treatments or consult competent professional counsel.

The main purpose of this Guide is to bring together into one publication the primary authoritative accounting literature pertinent to reporting by Christian ministries in such a way as to facilitate easy reference to that literature. The Guide also provides EJAC's recommendations on issues that are not specifically covered by authoritative accounting literature, as well as issues where alternative treatments are permissible under that literature. EJAC hopes this Guide will be a useful resource to financial executives of Christian ministries and their auditors, as well as other professionals serving such organizations. Additionally, the Guide includes a summary of Canadian tax and accounting principles and compares and contrasts them to U.S. standards.

Chapter 1

Accounting for Christian Ministries

Contents

FINANCIAL STATEMENTS **3**

MINISTRY ACCOMPLISHMENTS 5

ACCRUAL BASIS OF ACCOUNTING............................ 6

MATERIALITY 8

FUND ACCOUNTING 8

OTHER COMPREHENSIVE BASES OF ACCOUNTING
(OCBOA) 9

Accounting for Christian Ministries

FINANCIAL STATEMENTS

1-1.   The purpose of financial statements is to provide information that meets the needs of users, including individual and church contributors, foundations, creditors, suppliers, governmental bodies, constituent organizations, beneficiaries of the organizations, the governing board, management, individual members, and employees of the organization. Good stewardship is demonstrated in part by relevant and reliable reporting to the users of the financial statements. Care should be taken by Christian ministries to clearly identify the users of their financial statements to be certain that the reporting objectives are satisfied. These users are broadly categorized as internal or external.

1-2.   Financial statements for internal users are generally prepared monthly to inform management and the board about an organization's performance against budget, prior periods, or other benchmarks. Financial statements for internal users are usually much more detailed than financial statements prepared for external use, and they may include a variety of additional analyses or other information beyond that contained in the basic financial statements. It is important that internal financial statements reconcile to and correlate with external statements and that when differences exist, they be explained and understood.

1-3.   General purpose financial statements for external users such as donors, creditors, and governmental bodies normally include only the basic financial statements and notes required by generally accepted accounting principles (GAAP). They may be included with other information, such as an annual report to donors, members, or the general public. In communications with certain users, financial information is often provided in other forms such as specific project results, condensed or selected financial information, tax reports, and trend analysis. To ensure consistency between such information and general purpose audited financial statements, the organization's independent auditors should read the information.

1-4.   Financial statements discussed in this Guide inform external users of the statements about the financial resources of the organization and its stewardship in carrying out the ministry objectives. They do not provide all the information that management or members of the governing board need to meet their fiduciary responsibilities and to effectively manage the charitable resources.

Paragraphs 4 and 5 of FASB Statement No. 117 provide the following regarding the purpose of a set of financial statements:

4.   The primary purpose of financial statements is to provide relevant information to meet the common interest of donors, members, creditors, and others who provide resources to not-for-profit organizations. Those external users of financial statements have common interests in assessing (a) the services an organization provides and its ability to continue to provide those services and (b) how managers discharge their stewardship responsibilities and other aspects of their performance.

5.   More specifically, the purpose of financial statements, including accompanying notes, is to provide information about:

a.   The amount and nature of an organization's assets, liabilities, and net assets

b.   The effects of transactions and other events and circumstances that change the amount and nature of net assets

c.   The amount and kinds of inflows and outflows of economic resources during a period and the relation between the inflows and outflows

d.   How an organization obtains and spends cash, its borrowing and repayment of borrowing, and other factors that may affect its liquidity

e.   The service efforts of an organization

MINISTRY ACCOMPLISHMENTS

1-5.   The true value of services provided by a Christian ministry cannot be measured solely by the amounts shown on financial statements. The primary purpose of the financial statements, therefore, should be to report how resource inflows and outflows have been used to accomplish the ministry's objectives and to reflect the total resources available to carry out these objectives in future periods.

1-6.   The financial objectives of a ministry are to obtain and utilize resources in order to meet spiritual, emotional, physical, and other needs in accordance with the organization's purposes. The goal is not to increase the organization's net assets in order to reward owners, as is common in a business enterprise. On the contrary, the intent, at times, may be to deplete most or even all of the net assets available in order to meet the organization's nonfinancial objectives. The intent may also be to increase net assets in order to be able to carry out new or existing ministries in the future.

Paragraphs 18 and 19 of FASB Concepts Statement No. 6 provide the following:

18.   In contrast to business enterprises, not-for-profit organizations do not have defined ownership interests. . . . A not-for-profit organization is required to use its resources to provide goods and services to its constituents and beneficiaries . . . and generally is prohibited from distributing assets as dividends to its members, directors, officers, or others. Thus, not-for-profit organizations have operating purposes that are other than to provide goods or services at a profit or profit equivalent, and resource providers do not focus primarily on profit as an indicator of a not-for-profit organization's performance.

19.   Instead, providers of resources to a not-for-profit organization are interested in the services the organization provides and its ability to continue to provide them. Since profit indicators are not the focus of their resource-allocation decisions, resource providers need other information . . . about the amounts and kinds of inflows and outflows of resources during a period and the relations between them and information

about service efforts and, to the extent possible, service accomplishments.

1-7.   Many ministry accomplishments can be monetarily presented. EJAC also encourages ministries to publish annual reports, which often report on ministry accomplishments such as churches established, students educated, homeless fed and clothed, and patients treated. FASB Statement No. 117, paragraph 27, Note 6, states that, generally, reporting that kind of information is feasible only in supplementary information, management explanations, or by other methods of financial reporting. This information is usually set forth separately from the financial statements because its inclusion would require that auditors verify its accuracy. Paragraph 14.10 and 14.11 of the *AICPA NPO Guide 2000* further discusses the reporting of nonmonetary information.

ACCRUAL BASIS OF ACCOUNTING

1-8.   GAAP requires that financial statements be presented on the accrual basis of accounting. The accrual basis of accounting is widely accepted as providing an appropriate record of all an entity's transactions over a given period of time. For example, goods and services purchased should be recorded as assets or expenses at the time the liabilities arise (which is normally when the title of the goods passes or when the services are received), rather than when payment is made. Purchase orders and commitments outstanding at the reporting date are not recorded as liabilities at that time; however, significant commitments should be disclosed in the notes to the financial statements.

1-9.   Some Christian ministries prepare internal financial statements on the cash basis throughout the year and, through adjustments at the end of the year such as recording the changes in inventories, accounts payable, and accrued liabilities, prepare external financial statements on the accrual basis. This provides the advantage of simpler daily record-keeping on the cash basis, interim reports focused upon cash management, and acceptable accrual basis annual financial reports.

1-10.   Financial statements prepared at year end on the accrual basis may differ significantly in content and format from those prepared on a cash basis. If this is the case and the costs do not outweigh the benefits, the organization should consider keeping its books on a modified cash or accrual basis so that interim reports to management and the board will be more consistent with the results reported at year end. Another alternative is to provide a schedule reconciling between the internal and external financial statements. It should also be noted that accrual information may be an important tool for management to properly plan and direct the financial affairs of the organization.

1-11.   Although GAAP requires the accrual basis of accounting for fair presentation of the financial position and results of operations of an organization, financial statements presented on a cash basis or other comprehensive basis of accounting can still be considered to be in conformity with GAAP if the resulting financial statements are not materially different from those prepared on an accrual basis. (See Appendix C, Exhibit 2, Sample Small Ministry, for an example of alternative treatments.)

Paragraphs 145 and 140 of FASB Concepts Statement No. 6 provide the following:

> 145. Accrual accounting uses accrual, deferral, and allocation procedures whose goal is to relate revenues, expenses, gains, and losses to periods to reflect an entity's performance during a period instead of merely listing its cash receipts and outlays. . . .

> 140. Thus, accrual accounting is based not only on cash transactions but also on credit transactions, barter exchanges, nonreciprocal transfers of goods or services, changes in prices, changes in form of assets or liabilities, and other transactions, events, and circumstances that have cash consequences for an entity but involve no concurrent cash movement. By accounting for noncash assets, liabilities, revenues, expenses, gains, and losses, accrual accounting links an entity's operations and other transactions, events, and circumstances that affect it with its cash receipts and outlays. Accrual accounting thus provides information about an entity's assets and liabilities and

changes in them that cannot be obtained by accounting for only cash receipts and outlays.

MATERIALITY

1-12. Factors that should be considered in determining whether amounts are material to the financial statements of a not-for-profit organization are similar to factors that should be considered in determining whether amounts are material to the financial statements of a for-profit entity: The omission or misstatement of an item is material if, in the light of surrounding circumstances, the magnitude of the item is such that it is probable that the judgment of a reasonable person relying upon the financial statements would have been changed or influenced by the inclusion or correction of the item. In determining whether departures from GAAP are material, both qualitative and quantitative factors should be considered, such as dollar effects, significance of the item, pervasiveness of a misstatement, and the impact of a misstatement on the financial statements taken as a whole. The quantitative factors should be determined from benchmarks such as total assets, total revenue, and changes in net assets. The *AICPA NPO Guide 2000* does not specify at what level materiality determinations for not-for-profit entities should be made. EJAC recommends, however, that materiality be determined at the level of the individual net asset classes (as defined in paragraphs 3-2 and following) presented in the financial statements. Further guidance is provided in the *AICPA NPO Guide 2000,* paragraphs 2.37 to 2.38.

FUND ACCOUNTING

1-13. Some donors stipulate that their gifts be used for particular purposes. When Christian ministries receive resources that are provided by donors for particular purposes, "fund accounting" is commonly used to classify amounts relating to specific objectives or programs.

1-14. Fund accounting is a convention used to segregate resources that are restricted or designated for particular purposes. Accounting literature defines each fund as an "accounting entity established for the purpose of accounting for resources used for specific activities or objectives in accordance with special regulations, restrictions, or limitations." Each fund group (one or a group of similar funds) has assets, liabilities, and a fund balance (equity or net assets), as well as its own revenue and expense accounts. Thus, a fund group is a self-balancing set of accounts. In other words, a trial balance can be obtained for each fund group since it is represented by both balance sheet and income statement accounts. A separate fund within a fund group may only have its own support, revenue, expenses, and net asset accounts. Although separate accounts are maintained for each fund, the usual practice in preparing financial statements is to group funds that have similar characteristics.

1-15. Funds or managed fund groups can contain one or more "classes" of revenues and net assets. Accordingly, care must be taken to account for both the funds and for the proper use of donor restricted amounts. (See Appendix C, Exhibit 4, Sample Camp/Conference Center.)

OTHER COMPREHENSIVE BASES OF ACCOUNTING (OCBOA)

1-16. Some Christian ministries prepare their financial statements on a basis of accounting other than GAAP, such as the cash or modified accrual basis. This may be acceptable when resource providers (such as foundations or financial institutions) or oversight agencies do not require GAAP financial statements. (ECFA standards require statements that are prepared in conformity with GAAP.)

1-17. Auditors may audit financial statements prepared on OCBOA and render opinions on them, as they do GAAP financial statements. Any exceptions from GAAP, however, must be identified in the opinion letter or notes to the financial statements.

1-18. For example, Christian ministries that are not required to provide GAAP statements may choose to prepare, and have audited, financial statements on the cash or modified cash basis. An organization may choose to adopt modified cash basis policies and recognize only contributions received (but not promises to give or contributed services) but depreciate buildings and equipment. (See Appendix C, Exhibit 2, Sample Small Ministry for a comparison of these methods.)

1-19.   Although this Guide is directed primarily at provisions to conform with GAAP, it may also be useful in assisting ministries in adopting policies that are the most meaningful and cost efficient for their circumstances, even though not in conformity with GAAP. A ministry should carefully consider the requirements and needs of its financial statement users.

1-20.   AICPA Auditing Interpretation No. 14 of Section 623, *Evaluating the Adequacy of Disclosure in Financial Statements Prepared on the Cash, Modified Cash, or Income Tax Basis of Accounting*, (AICPA *Professional Standards*, AU section 623.88), provides, in part, as follows:

> .90   If cash, modified cash, or income tax basis financial statements contain elements, accounts, or items for which GAAP would require disclosure, the statements should either provide the relevant disclosure that would be required for those items in a GAAP presentation or provide information that communicates the substance of that disclosure. That may result in substituting qualitative information for some of the quantitative information required for GAAP presentations. . . .

> .91   If GAAP sets forth requirements that apply to the presentation of financial statements, then cash, modified cash, and income tax basis statements should either comply with those requirements or provide information that communicates the substance of those requirements. The substance of GAAP presentation requirements may be communicated using qualitative information and without modifying the financial statement format. For example:

>> a.   Information about the effects of accounting changes, discontinued operations, and extraordinary items could be disclosed in a note to the financial statements without following the GAAP presentation requirements in the statement of results

of operations, using those terms, or disclosing net-of-tax effects.

b. Instead of showing expenses by their functional classifications, the income tax basis statement of activities of a trade organization could present expenses according to their natural classifications, and a note to the statement could use estimated percentages to communicate information about expenses incurred by the major program and sup-porting services. A voluntary health and welfare organization could take such an approach instead of presenting the matrix of natural and functional expense classifications that would be required for a GAAP presentation, or, if information has been gathered for the Form 990 matrix required for such organizations, it could be presented either in the form of a separate statement or in a note to the financial statements.

c. Instead of showing the amounts of, and changes in, the unrestricted, temporarily and permanently restricted classes of net assets (which would be required for a GAAP presentation), the income tax basis statement of position of a voluntary health and welfare organization could report total net assets or fund balances, the related statement of activities could report changes in those totals, and a note to the financial statements could provide information, using estimated or actual amounts or percentages, about the restrictions on those amounts and on any deferred restricted amounts, describe the major restrictions, and provide infor-mation about significant changes in restricted amounts.

.93   If GAAP would require disclosure of other matters, the auditor should consider the need for that same disclosure or disclosure that communicates the substance of those requirements . . .

Though OCBOA statements may reflect non-GAAP accounting policies, all disclosures under GAAP are still required. EJAC recommends that GAAP provisions for disclosure and treatment of accounting changes, the presentation of functional expenses, and the financial statement format provisions of FASB Statement No. 117 be used for cash basis financial statements. For more specific information on the application of GAAP to cash basis financial statements, see Appendix I.

Chapter 2

Financial Statements and Reporting

Contents

■ REQUIRED FINANCIAL STATEMENTS......................... 15

    Statement of Financial Position (also referred to
       as a Balance Sheet) 15

    Statement of Activities (also referred to
       as a Statement of Revenues and Expenses) 18

    Statement of Functional Expenses......................... 20

    Statement of Cash Flows 21

    Notes to Financial Statements 22

■ COMPARATIVE FINANCIAL STATEMENTS 22

■ FINANCIAL MANAGEMENT 24

    Internal Control 25

    Cash Management 27

    Ratios 28

Financial Statements and Reporting

REQUIRED FINANCIAL STATEMENTS

2-1.   According to FASB Statement No. 117, paragraph 6, a complete set of financial statements of a not-for-profit organization shall include:

- a statement of financial position as of the end of the reporting period (also referred to as a *balance sheet*)

- a statement of activities for the reporting period (also referred to as a *statement of revenues and expenses*)

- a statement of functional expenses required for voluntary health and welfare organizations and encouraged for all others as a separate statement, schedule, or note (paragraphs 5-34 and 5-35 discuss the statement of functional expenses)

- a statement of cash flows for the reporting period

- accompanying notes to the financial statements

2-2.   This Guide uses the terms *statement of revenues and expenses* and *statement of activities* because they are both used by many not-for-profit organizations. Other terms also used include statement of changes in net assets; statement of income; and *statement of revenue, expenses, and changes in net assets.* FASB Statement No. 117 does not prescribe specific titles for this statement.

Statement of Financial Position (also referred to as a *Balance Sheet*)

2-3.   The primary purpose of the statement of financial position, including accompanying notes to the financial statements, is to provide relevant information about an organization's assets, liabilities, and net assets (available funds or fund balances). This includes information about liquidity, financial flexibility, and the interrelationship of an organization's assets and liabilities. Information regarding such disclosure requirements is set forth in FASB Statement No. 117, paragraphs 9 to 12.

2-4.   Liquidity is the measure of an organization's ability to turn noncash assets into cash in order to pay obligations when due.

Paragraph 12 of FASB Statement No. 117 provides the following:

12.   Information about liquidity shall be provided by one or more of the following:

a. Sequencing assets according to their nearness of conversion to cash and sequencing liabilities according to the nearness of their maturity and resulting use of cash

b. Classifying assets and liabilities as current and non-current, as defined by *Accounting Research Bulletin No. 43,* Chapter 3A, "Working Capital—Current Assets and Current Liabilities"

c. Disclosing in notes to financial statements relevant information about the liquidity or maturity of assets and liabilities, including restrictions on the use of particular assets

2-5.   The net assets shall be further broken down, or separated, into the following three classes:

Net Assets:
    Permanently restricted
    Temporarily restricted
    Unrestricted

Permanent or temporary restrictions are based upon the existence or absence of donor-imposed restrictions (either explicit or implied) regarding a contribution's use which were made by donors at the time the contribution was made. Restrictions normally apply to the use of net assets and not to the use of specific assets. Paragraph 3-4 discusses this further.

Factors to consider in determining whether donor-imposed restrictions were explicitly made or implied by donors at the time the contribution was made include, but are not limited to, the following:

- Restrictions stipulated explicitly by the donor in a written or oral communication accompanying the contribution

- Circumstances surrounding receipt or solicitation of the asset—for example, making a gift to a capital campaign whose stated objective is to raise funds for a new building

- The period in which contribution payments are due

- Indications about which period(s) the donor intended to support

Chapter 3 includes additional information concerning classes of net assets.

2-6.   Any restrictions as to the use of material specific assets should be disclosed in the financial statements or notes to the financial statements. Examples of such restrictions are assets held in separate trusts or legally required bond sinking funds and specific assets, the use of which has been limited by the donor. EJAC recommends that such restricted assets (including cash and cash equivalents) be presented separately from other assets and sequenced based on their availability for operating activities.

Paragraph 3.03 of the *AICPA NPO Guide* provides, in part, as follows:

Assets need not be disaggregated on the basis of the presence of donor-imposed restrictions on their use; for example, cash available for unrestricted current use need not be reported separately from cash received with donor-imposed restrictions that is also available for current use. [Footnote 4: Assets other than cash may also be restricted by donors. For example, land could be restricted to use as a public park. Generally, however, restrictions apply to net assets, not to specific assets.] However, cash or other assets either (a) designated for long-term purposes or (b) received with donor-imposed restrictions that limit their use to long-term purposes should not be aggregated on a statement of financial position with cash or other assets that are available for current use. For example, cash that has been received with donor-imposed restrictions limiting its use to the acquisition of long-lived assets should be reported under a separate caption, such as "cash restricted to investment in property and equipment," and displayed near the section of the statement where property and equipment is displayed. The kind of asset should be described in the notes to the financial statements if its nature is not clear from the description on the face of the statement of financial position.

2-7.   The statement of financial position may be presented in one column or may be disaggregated into more than one column. (See Appendix C, Exhibit 1.) If multiple columns are used, they are not required to be by class (permanently restricted, temporarily restricted, or unrestricted). EJAC believes that organizations will generally not disaggregate by class, but that a more meaningful presentation may be by managed fund groups. Examples of managed fund groups are (1) operating, plant, life income, and endowment; (2) expendable, plant, and nonexpendable; each presented as a separate column with a total column. Each column may include permanently restricted, temporarily restricted, and/or unrestricted net assets. Totals, however, are required for assets, liabilities, and net assets.

Statement of Activities (also referred to as a *Statement of Revenues and Expenses*)

2-8.   The purpose of the statement of activities is to provide information about the sources of revenue of the organization and how resources were used.

Paragraph 17 of FASB Statement No. 117 provides the following concerning the purpose and focus of a statement of activities:

> 17. . . . The information provided in a statement of activities, used with related disclosures and information in the other financial statements, helps donors, creditors, and others to (1) evaluate the organization's performance during a period, (2) assess an organization's service efforts and its ability to continue to provide services, and (3) assess how an

organization's managers have discharged their stewardship responsibilities and other aspects of their performance.

2-9.   The statement of activities must present the change in permanently restricted, temporarily restricted, unrestricted, and total net assets for the reporting period. Since donor-imposed restrictions affect the types and levels of service a not-for-profit organization can provide, whether an organization has maintained these classes of net assets may be more significant than whether it has maintained net assets in the aggregate. For example, if total net assets remained unchanged in a period solely because permanently restricted endowment contributions compensated for a decline in unrestricted net assets, users of the report might not notice that the organization had failed to maintain sufficient net assets to pay for activities in the next fiscal period. *(Canadian ministries, see 9-26.)*

2-10.   Organizations may present their revenues and expenses in single or in multiple columns as illustrated in Appendix C of FASB Statement No. 117. If an organization has significant amounts of activity in permanently or temporarily restricted net assets during the year, EJAC recommends that the multicolumn format be used because it is more easily understood. However, an organization with little activity in the restricted classes may find that it can more clearly present its operations or activities in a single column as long as the above disclosures are met. (See Appendix C, Exhibit 2, Sample Small Ministry.)

2-11.   Not-for-profit organizations are required to disclose their expenses by functional classifications, such as major classes of program services and supporting activities. If the components of total program expenses are not evident from the details provided on the face of the statement of activities (for example, if cost of sales is not identified as either program or supporting services), the notes to the financial statements should disclose total program expenses and provide information about why total program expenses disclosed in the notes do not agree with the statement of activities. (*AICPA NPO Guide 2000,* paragraph 13.32). In addition, the financial statements should disclose total fund-raising expenses. EJAC recommends that total general and administrative and any other major supporting services also be disclosed. Additional categories of program services may also be used as appropriate. A more detailed explanation of these requirements is found in Chapter 5 of this Guide. *(Canadian ministries, see 9-6.)*

2-12.   An important distinction to be made in the statement of activities is between revenues and expenses on one hand and gains and losses on the other.

Revenues and expenses are incurred in carrying out activities that constitute the entity's ongoing major or central operations (FASB Concepts Statement No. 6, paragraph 80). Gains and losses are increases or decreases in net assets resulting from transactions which are only peripheral or incidental to the entity's operations (FASB Concepts Statement No. 6, paragraph 83). Examples which usually result in gains or losses are the sale of investments, changes in the fair value of investments, disposition of fixed assets, changes in actuarial valuations, changes in foreign exchange rates, lawsuits, thefts, and natural catastrophes. This is also discussed in paragraph 13.17 to 13.19 of the *AICPA NPO Guide 2000.*

There are three reasons for making this distinction:

- revenues and expenses may not be reported net (except for investment management expenses); gains and losses may be netted,

- losses may be reported in a restricted class of net assets; expenses may not, and

- it may be helpful (although not determinative) in distinguishing between items which will be reported as operating income or expenses and those which are nonoperating.

Statement of Functional Expenses

2-13.   The statement of functional expenses provides information about the nature and amount of costs associated with each of the program services and supporting activities (administration, fundraising, etc.) carried out by the organization. This information may be required to meet the standards of the Better Business Bureau, certain foundations, and similar organizations. Christian ministries qualifying as voluntary health and welfare organizations must provide a statement of functional expenses as a basic statement. A statement of functional expenses is also required on IRS Form 990, Return of Organization Exempt From Income Tax, and on many state forms. (Paragraphs 5-34 and 5-35 discuss the statement of functional expenses further.) *(Canadian ministries, see 9-6.)*

EJAC recommends that not-for-profit organizations, other than voluntary health and welfare organizations, also provide information about expenses by their natural classification (e.g., salaries, rent, utilities) either in a separate statement, schedule, or in the notes to the financial statements. This is also encouraged but not required by FASB Statement No. 117.

Statement of Cash Flows

2-14. The primary purpose of the statement of cash flows is to provide information about the cash receipts and disbursements of an organization over a period of time and the extent to which resources were obtained from or used in operating, investing, or financing activities during the period (FASB No. 95 and FASB No. 117).

2-15. There are two ways of presenting cash flows from operations: the direct and indirect methods. In the direct method, the statement starts by listing all sources of cash from operations during the period and deducts all operating outflows of cash to arrive at the net cash flow for operations. The indirect method begins with the change in net assets for the period and adjusts backwards to reconcile the change in net assets to net cash flows from operations. As stated in FASB Statement No. 117, paragraph 147, "The Board . . . concluded that, consistent with Statement 95, not-for-profit organizations should be encouraged to use the direct method of reporting net cash flows from operating activities and allowed to use the indirect method." EJAC recommends that organizations use the direct method of reporting net cash flows from operating activities. Examples of both of these methods are presented in Appendix C: Exhibit 1, Sample Large Christian Organization.

2-16. FASB Statement No. 95 as originally written did not contemplate certain types of transactions only pertaining to not-for-profit organizations. In order to apply FASB Statement No. 95 to not-for-profit organizations, the FASB amended its definition of financing cash flows in paragraph 30d of FASB Statement No. 117 to include the following:

> Receipts from contributions and investment income that by donor stipulation are restricted for the purposes of acquiring, constructing, or improving property, plant, equipment, or other long-lived assets or establishing or increasing a permanent endowment or term endowment.

EJAC considers this definition to include split-interest gifts such as annuities and trust agreements.

2-17. The statement of cash flows may use either a single column or multicolumn presentation.

(Note: For further information regarding the statement of cash flows, see FASB Statement No. 95, *Statement of Cash Flows,* or FASB Statement No. 117, paragraphs 29 to 30.)

Notes to Financial Statements

2-18. GAAP requires certain disclosures in the financial statements or notes thereto; however, organizations may wish to provide additional information to assist readers in better understanding the financial statements. Notes to the financial statements should include the nature of the organization (related organizations, purpose, tax status, type of activities, etc.) and significant accounting policies. Other notes generally include information about the maturity of pledges, property and equipment, investments, notes and mortgages payable, employee benefit plans, allocation of expenses, commitments and contingencies, and related party transactions.

COMPARATIVE FINANCIAL STATEMENTS

2-19. Comparative financial statements showing more than one reporting period generally provide more meaningful information to the reader than single period statements and are strongly recommended, even though not specifically required.

2-20. If multicolumn financial statements are used, some organizations prefer to present only summarized total-all-funds information (in a single column) for each prior period presented because of space considerations and to avoid possible confusion that a second set of multicolumn statements might cause. This is appropriate if the prior year's report was audited in multicolumn format and proper disclosures are made. (See Appendix C, Exhibit 4, Sample Camp/Conference Center.)

Paragraphs 3.20 and 3.21 of the *AICPA NPO Guide 2000* provide, in part, as follows:

> 3.20. Not-for-profit organizations sometimes present comparative information for a prior year or years only in total rather than by net asset class. Such summarized information may not include sufficient detail to constitute a presentation in conformity with GAAP. If the prior year's financial information is summarized and does not include the minimum information required by FASB Statement No. 117 and this Guide . . . , the nature of the prior-year information should be described by the use of appropriate titles on the face of the financial statements and in a note to the financial statements. The use of appropriate titles includes a phrase such as "with summarized financial information for the year ended June 30, 19PY," following the title of the statement or column headings that indicate the summarized nature of the information. Labeling the prior-year summarized financial information "for comparative purposes only" without further disclosure in the notes to the financial statements would not constitute the use of an appropriate title.

> 3.21. An example of a note to the financial statements that describes the nature of the prior-period(s) information would be as follows:

>> The financial statements include certain prior-year summarized comparative information in total but not by net asset class. Such information does not include sufficient detail to constitute a presentation in conformity with generally accepted accounting principles. Accordingly, such information should be read in conjunction with the organization's

financial statements for the year ended June 30, 19PY, from which the summarized information was derived.

FINANCIAL MANAGEMENT

2-21. Although the purpose of this Guide is primarily for use in preparing external financial reports, this section provides information highlighting the importance of internal financial reporting for proper management control.

2-22. Whereas external financial reporting is prescribed by GAAP, management reports are tailored to the needs of the individual organization. There are no specific requirements regarding the nature or frequency of financial reports prepared for internal purposes. Good management practice requires that such reports be of such frequency and in sufficient detail to help ensure that the organization's management, including the governing board, is provided with sufficient and timely information to facilitate appropriate decision making regarding the organization's affairs.

2-23. Financial reports are generally prepared on a monthly basis; however, not all financial statements may be needed each month. For example, in small organizations the balance sheet may be prepared only quarterly, whereas the statement of activities is prepared monthly. In very large organizations, weekly or even daily financial reports may be needed to monitor important items such as cash flow, donations, or special projects.

2-24. The form and content of financial statements prepared for management purposes may also differ from that used for external reporting purposes. Internal reports should contain all information necessary to properly manage the organization by providing appropriate tools for evaluating past performance and planning for the future. Generally, management reports will show more detailed revenue, expense, and budget information about specific activities or departments, whereas such information may be combined for external reporting purposes.

2-25. Over the long run, total expenditures must not exceed total revenues. Generally, responsibility for the management of individual departments and projects is delegated to supervisors and managers.

Internal accounting reports should follow the management structure of the organization. Revenues should be credited to and traceable costs charged against the appropriate responsibility center. Shared costs should be allocated.

2-26. The operating budget is the primary financial plan of the organization. Periodic comparison of actual revenues and expenditures by program or function to the budget is essential. Management should prepare and regularly update projections of revenues and expenditures for the fiscal year, taking into account such factors as any seasonal or unusual cycles of revenues or expenditures (i.e., shared tuition, Christmas offerings, etc.). Management should respond to any projected deficits by revising short-run plans and adjusting budgets if necessary. Plans should be adjusted and revised budgets prepared for the board's consideration when it appears that revenue or expenditure budgets will not be met.

2-27. Periodic budgets (quarterly, monthly, weekly) should project the revenues and expenditures anticipated for that period. Monthly budgets often are not the annual budget divided by twelve because revenues of nonprofits often have a seasonal cycle, and some significant expenditures may be made only annually or quarterly.

2-28. Comparisons with prior years or other periods are generally helpful but may be of limited use in a period of change in the structure of responsibility centers or differing operating plans.

Internal Control

2-29. Effective internal control is critically important to the proper conduct of organizations. (See Appendix E for further information on internal control.) AICPA Statement on Auditing Standards No. 78, *Consideration of Internal Control in a Financial Statement Audit,* amends Statement on Auditing Standards No. 55 to recognize the definition and description contained in Internal Control–Integrated Framework (the COSO report). Internal control is defined as:

> . . . a process—effected by an entity's board of directors, management, and other personnel—designed to provide reasonable assurance regarding the achievement of objectives in

the following categories: (a) reliability of financial reporting, (b) effectiveness and efficiency of operations, and (c) compliance with applicable laws and regulations.

2-30.   Five interrelated components of internal control are identified as:

- *Control environment* sets the tone of an organization, influencing the control consciousness of its people. It is the foundation for all other components of internal control, providing discipline and structure.

- *Risk assessment* is the entity's identification and analysis of relevant risks to achievement of its objectives, forming a basis for determining how the risks should be managed.

- *Control activities* are the policies and procedures that help ensure that management directives are carried out.

- *Information and communication* are the identification, capture, and exchange of information in a form and time frame that enable people to carry out their responsibilities.

- *Monitoring* is a process that assesses the quality of internal control performance over time.

The above components of internal control are applicable to the audit of every entity. The components should be considered in the context of the following:

- the entity's size

- the entity's organization and ownership characteristics

- the nature of the entity's business

- the diversity and complexity of the entity's operations

- the entity's methods of transmitting, processing, maintaining, and accessing information

- applicable legal and regulatory requirements

Cash Management

2-31. Another issue frequently faced by not-for-profit entities is the amount of cash and available reserves or net assets (fund balance) that the organization should maintain. This will vary with the organization and depend upon many factors, including the type of organization, future needs or plans, future fund-raising possibilities, and outstanding obligations or commitments. Organizations with large fixed costs such as mortgage payments, employment contracts, long-term leases, etc. will generally need to have a higher level of reserves than those organizations with fewer obligations.

2-32. Because of the importance of cash flow, many organizations prepare internal budgets and reports on a cash basis. Where cash accounting is used for internal purposes and accrual accounting is used for external reports, the internal reports must be reconciled to the external financial statements at fiscal year end. These reconciliations should be reviewed by the external auditors and reported to the board.

2-33. Cash flow projections should forecast monthly cash receipts and expenditures. Planned expenditures must be constrained by the projected availability of cash. However, contingency plans should also be prepared for periods when there may be an unexpected shortage of cash in order to keep payments to employees and creditors on a current basis.

2-34. Some organizations permit external borrowing, such as a bank line-of-credit, to provide cash during seasonally low income months. Such loans are typically short-term and usually require at least annual repayment. Care should be taken during negotiations to ensure the availability of credit even if the organization's liquidity falls below the lending institution's standard eligibility requirements.

2-35. Organizations should be cautious about getting into situations that involve borrowing from restricted funds or offsetting negative and positive net assets or fund balances in a way that obscures the existence of deficits. The board should establish policies determining the circumstances and extent to which borrowing may be permitted. Internal borrowing, such as from temporarily restricted funds, can leave an organization unable to complete the scheduled projects for which the donations are intended. Furthermore, such borrowing may be a violation of legal requirements or result in a failure to maintain proper reserves for trust funds.

Compliance with these policies should be carefully monitored by the board and reviewed by the external auditors. Some boards will permit internal borrowing only to the extent covered by an external line-of-credit. Others create an internal reserve for short-term cash needs by applying operational surpluses to an internal loan fund or by raising money for that purpose. *(Canadian ministries, see 9-25 to 9-26.)*

2-36. Management should differentiate between the normal seasonal fluctuations of cash and changes in revenue or expenditure patterns indicative of longer-term trends. Short-term borrowing (whether internal or external) should not be undertaken if conservative projections cannot provide for repayment by year end, unless as part of a board-approved, long-range plan to eliminate the deficit.

Ratios

2-37. In for-profit entities, certain ratios such as net income, inventory turnover, return on investment, and earnings per share have been developed to help monitor the activities of the organization. Unfortunately, there are not such easily used generic measurements which can be readily applied to organizations in the not-for-profit sector due to its nature and diversity. Management (and the board) should determine appropriate measurements for their organization to help monitor results on a regular basis.

2-38. Actual results should be compared to preplanned goals or standards, such as percent of income or expenditures against budget, donations or number of responses received, fund-raising costs as a percentage of funds received, etc. Monitoring progress during the year also promotes the evaluation of the effectiveness of the organization's activities.

2-39. Since few not-for-profit organizations are exactly alike, often the most useful ratios or other analytical tools will be those based upon comparison with the past experience of the organization itself. Another useful monitoring tool is comparison with other, similar organizations using industry averages where available. This information is often available from denominational headquarters for churches or industry publications for certain types of charitable organizations.

2-40. One of the most commonly watched ratios among not-for-profit organizations is the percentage of funds spent on program, fund-raising, and management and general expenses compared to either total income or total expenses. However, these amounts will vary depending on many factors, such as the type of organization, nature of its programs, age of the organization, the type of fund-raising typically used, and the level of endowment or institutional support. The diversity among organizations defies any clear basis for comparison. Organizations should not compromise effective support for programs in order to have "good ratios."

EJAC believes that rather than merely striving for arbitrary ratios, organizations should make sound decisions on the costs of fund-raising and management and general activities based on evaluating their effectiveness and level of merit to further the most effective programs and program accomplishments. Fund-raising and management and general activities are vital to effective program accomplishments and should be managed for reasonableness and effectiveness rather than avoided to the detriment of mission accomplishment.

Ratios do not measure performance. They are merely indicators. Functional expense ratios are based on allocations that inherently have a measure of imprecision and subjectivity. Performance can only truly be measured by evaluating outcomes and program accomplishments in respect to related costs.

Chapter 3

Net Assets

Contents

NET ASSETS AND FUND ACCOUNTING 33

CLASSES OF NET ASSETS 33

PERMANENTLY RESTRICTED NET ASSETS.............. 37

TEMPORARILY RESTRICTED NET ASSETS 38

UNRESTRICTED NET ASSETS 40

RECLASSIFICATION (TRANSFER) OF NET ASSETS.... 41

OTHER CHANGES IN NET ASSETS 44
    Accounting Changes and Extraordinary Items........ 44
    Prior Period Adjustments 45
    International Currency Translations 46
    Return of Contributions 46

Net Assets

NET ASSETS AND FUND ACCOUNTING

3-1.   The net assets of a not-for-profit organization represent the difference between the entity's assets and its liabilities. It is a residual amount, affected by all events that increase or decrease total assets by different amounts than they increase or decrease total liabilities. Thus, net assets are increased or decreased by the entity's financial operations, other financial events, and circumstances affecting the entity.

One of the differences between previous accounting literature and FASB Statement No. 117 is in the name of the "net worth" section (excess of assets over liabilities) on the balance sheet. The traditional terminology has been "fund balances." FASB Statement No. 117 and this guide use the term "net assets" in lieu of "fund balances." The term "fund balances" may still be used in financial statements for management purposes.   However, the term "net assets" should be used for general purposes for annual statements. See also 3-7. (Compare Appendix C, Exhibits 1 and 4, Sample Large Christian Organization and Sample Camp/Conference Center, respectively.) *(Canadian ministries, see 9-52 and 9-53.)*

CLASSES OF NET ASSETS

3-2.   A donor stipulation may specify a purpose or period of use restriction that is more specific than the overall purposes of the organization. FASB Statement No. 117 stipulates that net assets should be set forth in up to three classes based on the presence or absence of donor-imposed restrictions and their nature. This is generally necessary to gain a proper understanding of the financial position of a not-for-profit organization, including its financial flexibility and ability to continue to render services.

The classes of net assets are:
- permanently restricted
- temporarily restricted
- unrestricted

3-3.   Information about permanent restrictions is useful in determining the extent to which an organization's net assets are unavailable to present or prospective lenders, suppliers, or employees and thus, are unavailable for providing services or paying creditors. Information about the extent of unrestricted net assets and temporarily restricted net assets is useful in assessing an organization's ability or limitations on its ability to allocate resources to provide services or particular kinds of services or to transfer resources to creditors in the future.   (Paragraph 3-6 discusses restrictions on specific assets.) *(Canadian ministries, see 9-13 to 9-43.)*

3-4.   Restrictions are normally placed upon an organization's net assets rather than specific assets.

Paragraphs 101 and 102 of FASB Concepts Statement No. 6 provide the following concerning restrictions that affect net assets rather than particular assets:

101. Restrictions impose responsibilities on management to ensure that the organization uses donated resources in the manner stipulated by resource providers. Sometimes donor-imposed restrictions limit an organization's ability to sell or exchange the particular asset received. For example, a donor may give a painting to a museum stipulating that it must be publicly displayed, properly maintained, and never sold.

102. More commonly, donors' stipulations permit the organization to pool the donated assets with other assets and to sell or exchange the donated assets for other suitable assets as long as the economic benefits of the donated assets are not consumed or used for a purpose that does not comply with the stipulation. For example, a donor may contribute 100 shares of Security A to an organization's endowment, thereby requiring that the amount of the gift be retained permanently but not requiring that the specific shares be held

indefinitely. Thus, permanently restricted net assets and temporarily restricted net assets generally refer to amounts of net assets that are restricted by donor-imposed limits, not to specific assets.

3-5.   Unrestricted net assets may be used for any of the organization's purposes.

Paragraph 94 of FASB Concepts Statement No. 6 provides the following:

> 94.   Unrestricted net assets is the part of net assets of a not-for-profit organization that is neither permanently restricted nor temporarily restricted by donor-imposed stipulations—that is, the part of net assets resulting (a) from all revenues, expenses, gains, and losses that are not changes in permanently or temporarily restricted net assets and (b) from reclassifications from (or to) other classes of net assets as a consequence of donor-imposed stipulations, their expiration by passage of time, or their fulfillment and removal by actions of the organization pursuant to those stipulations. The only limits on unrestricted net assets are broad limits resulting from the nature of the organization and the purposes specified in its articles of incorporation (or comparable document for an unincorporated association) or bylaws and perhaps limits resulting from contractual agreement—for example, loan covenants—entered into by the organization in the course of its operations.

3-6.   If a gift solicitation and other communication with a prospective donor indicates that the recipient organization will use the donation for a particular purpose or during a particular period, the gift is restricted. A contrary statement on the donation receipt or other after-the-fact documents will not affect the restriction; the donor must agree to any lifting or lessening of the gift restriction. *(Canadian ministries, see 9-8.)*

3-7.   Donor stipulations may occur by verbal or written communication from the donor or by the donor's response to an appeal for funds or a need's presentation. Such a response may create an "implied contract" between the donor and the recipient organization which can be legally binding. EJAC recommends that all organizations periodically disclose their financial policies related to contributions and their use, including any assessments for administrative purposes against donor stipulated gifts. This can be presented in a brochure describing financial policies, a newsletter, or the notes to the financial statements.

Paragraph 100 of FASB Statement No. 117 provides the following:

> 100. . . . while definitions are necessary to make the distinctions required by this Statement, stringent requirements to use specific terms are not necessary to faithfully represent those distinctions . . . encourages the use of the terms unrestricted, temporarily restricted, and permanently restricted net assets; however, the Board knows that other labels exist. For example, equity may be used for net assets, and other or not donor-restricted may be used with care to distinguish unrestricted net assets from the temporarily and permanently restricted classes of net assets.

For example, the net asset section might be arranged as follows:

Donor restricted:		
Permanently		$ XXX
Temporarily		XXX
Other:		
Designated by the Board	$ XXX	
for [purpose]		
Undesignated	XXX	XXX
Net assets		$ XXX

At a minimum, the amounts for each of the three classes of net assets and the total of net assets must be reported in a statement of financial position, and the captions used to describe those amounts must correspond with their meanings, as defined by this Statement. . . .

EJAC recommends the use of the term *net assets*; however, other terms such as *equity* or *excess of assets over liabilities* are not precluded.

The term *fund balance* can still be used to refer to the net assets of a specific fund or fund group which does not correspond to a class of net assets. (See Appendix C, Exhibit 4, Sample Camp/Conference Center.)

It is the intention of FASB to allow organizations flexibility in the financial statement format, as long as the minimum reporting and disclosure requirements of Statement No. 117 are met. Organizations are urged to develop formats that are appropriate for their individual circumstances while being understandable to readers and consistent with the accounting and reporting practices discussed in this Guide.

PERMANENTLY RESTRICTED NET ASSETS

3-8.   Permanently restricted net assets are not available for program expenses, payments to creditors, or other organizational needs. For example, organizations may receive endowment gifts that have permanent restrictions placed on them by the donor. Generally, only the investment income (not the principal) from such permanently restricted gifts is available for use in current operations. The gift instrument and relevant law control the availability of any income or gain earned on permanently restricted net assets. *(Canadian ministries, see 9-36.)*

Another example of permanently restricted net assets is a revolving loan fund. Gifts may be donor-restricted for self-perpetuating purposes such as a fund to be loaned for church building purposes or student loans that will be loaned again after repayment. A third example is an annuity gift (normally time restricted), the corpus of which will, upon maturity, become a permanent endowment.

Paragraphs 100 and 92 of FASB Concepts Statement No. 6 provide the following:

> 100. . . . [Some] donors [may] stipulate that resources be maintained permanently—not used up, expended, or otherwise exhausted—but permit the organization to use up or expend the income (or other economic benefits) derived from the donated assets. That type of restricted gift is often called an endowment. The restriction lasts in effect forever. It cannot be removed by actions of the organization or passage of time.

The donations do not increase the organization's unrestricted net assets in any period, and the donated assets are not available for payment to creditors.

92.   Classes of Net Assets
Permanently restricted net assets is the part of the net assets of a not-for-profit organization resulting (a) from contributions and other inflows of assets whose use by the organization is limited by donor-imposed stipulations that neither expire by passage of time nor can be fulfilled or otherwise removed by actions of the organization, (b) from other asset enhancements and diminishments subject to the same kinds of stipulations, and (c) from reclassifications from (or to) other classes of net assets as a consequence of donor-imposed stipulations.

TEMPORARILY RESTRICTED NET ASSETS

3-9.   Temporary restrictions are restrictions which will expire with the passage of time or actions of the organization that fulfill specific stipulations.

Paragraphs 99 and 93 of FASB Concepts Statement No. 6 provide the following:

99.   Some donors stipulate that their contributions be used in a later period or after a specified date rather than be expended immediately; those are often called time restrictions. Other donors stipulate that their contributions be used for a specified purpose, such as sponsoring a particular program or service, acquiring a particular building, or settling a particular liability; those are often called purpose restrictions. Time and purpose restrictions have in common that they can be satisfied, either by passage of time or by actions of the organization, and that the contributed assets can be expended. Those restrictions are temporary. Once the stipulation is satisfied, the restriction is gone.

93.   Temporarily restricted net assets is the part of the net assets of a not-for-profit organization resulting (a) from contributions and other inflows of assets whose use by the

organization is limited by donor-imposed stipulations that either expire by passage of time or can be fulfilled and removed by actions of the organization pursuant to those stipulations, (b) from other asset enhancements and diminishments subject to the same kinds of stipulations, and (c) from reclassifications to (or from) other classes of net assets as a consequence of donor-imposed stipulations, their expiration by passage of time, or their fulfillment and removal by actions of the organization pursuant to those stipulations.

3-10. FASB Statement No. 117 requires disclosure either on the face of the statement of financial position or in the footnotes about the nature and amount of temporarily restricted net assets. In addition, EJAC believes it is important enough for a proper understanding of the financial statements that it recommends the temporarily restricted class of net assets (if material) be divided in the net assets section of the balance sheet into two subclasses:

a. Purpose restricted—these are contributions stipulated for specific purposes, such as staff or program support, or for projects or acquisition of fixed assets. These are often referred to as expendable.

b. Time restricted—these are contributions, often in the form of trusts, annuities, term endowments, or other agreements, which can only be released to the ministry through the passage of a period of time or the occurrence of an event such as death. Also included are gifts stipulated for use in and pledges payable in future periods. These time-restricted contributions may or may not also be purpose restricted. These are often referred to as nonexpendable.

EJAC recommends that this distinction be made to more clearly show that release of time-restricted resources is determined by events outside the control of the organization. (For an example of balance sheet presentation, see Appendix C, Exhibit 2, Sample Small Ministry; for footnote disclosure, see Appendix C, Exhibit 3, Sample Religious Broadcaster, Footnote 6.)

3-11. If the restrictions relating to temporarily restricted contributions are fully satisfied on or before the end of the fiscal year in which the gifts were received, such gifts may be reported as unrestricted support, provided that accounting policy is consistently applied to all temporarily restricted contributions and disclosed in the notes to the financial statements. (Appendix C, Exhibit 1, Sample Large Christian Organization, includes disclosure of this accounting policy.)

UNRESTRICTED NET ASSETS

3-12.   Unrestricted net assets are available to be used currently in carrying on the organization's ministries in accordance with its charter and bylaws or may be carried forward to future periods for any organizational need. The major sources of unrestricted net assets are unrestricted contributions, administrative assessments against and reclassifications from temporarily restricted net assets, unrestricted bequests and legacies, investment income, and revenue from fees and the sale of goods or services. *(Canadian ministries, see 9-39.)*

3-13.   The governing board of an organization is responsible for the appropriate use of net assets. It may designate portions of its unrestricted net assets for general or specific purposes, or for investment. Accounting for these designations should be maintained within the unrestricted net assets class as shown in Appendix C. Such designations do not preclude these net assets from being used (with board approval) for any organizational purpose or being legally accessible to creditors because designations may be removed at the discretion of the organization's board.

3-14.   When unrestricted net assets include amounts invested in land and buildings or amounts designated for specific purposes and not readily available, EJAC recommends that organizations further segregate unrestricted net assets into the following subsections as appropriate:

   a.   Amounts invested in land, buildings, and equipment (net of depreciation and any amounts borrowed for their acquisition or improvement still outstanding) (See Appendix C, Exhibit 4, Sample Camp/Conference Center.)

   b.   Amounts designated by the board for specific purposes such as future acquisition of fixed assets, long-term investments (quasi-endowment), special projects, retirement programs, or self-insurance reserves

c. Undesignated amounts available for general operations

An example of such a presentation is as follows:

Net Assets:
    Temporarily restricted–Note X
    Unrestricted:
        Designated–Note Y
        Undesignated
        Equity in land, buildings, and equipment

3-15. The designation of net assets for specific purposes by the organization itself does not constitute a basis for classifying them as temporarily or permanently restricted. The only basis for classifying net assets as restricted is a limitation placed on the use of net assets by donors. (Note: An organization must reclassify unrestricted net assets as restricted if required by a donor stipulation under the matching provisions of a particular contribution.)

Paragraph 96 of FASB Statement No. 117 provides the following:

. . . information about the effects of donor-imposed restrictions on net assets is relevant to users of financial statements of not-for-profit organizations. . . . Because they also place limits on the use of resources, donors' restrictions may impinge upon an organization's performance and its ability to provide a satisfactory level of services. Information about how managers discharge their stewardship responsibilities for donor-restricted resources also is useful in assessing an organization's performance.

RECLASSIFICATION (TRANSFER) OF NET ASSETS

3-16. FASB Statement No. 117 requires that all expenses be reported as decreases in unrestricted net assets, including expenses that fulfill temporary donor restrictions. Expenses themselves are not restricted. Rather, expenditures that result in fulfilling purpose restrictions and the release of time or event restrictions are events that result in reclassification (transfer) of restricted net assets to unrestricted net assets. The reclassification is simply that; no additional revenue is recorded. Thus, in a single accounting period, unrestricted expenses may often exceed unrestricted revenues with unrestricted net assets being "reimbursed" through reclassifications from restricted net assets.

Paragraphs 114, 115 and 116 of FASB Concepts Statement No. 6 provide the following:

114. Reclassifications between classes of net assets result from donor-imposed stipulations, their expiration by passage of time, or their fulfillment and removal by actions of the organization pursuant to those stipulations. Reclassifications simultaneously increase one class and decrease another class of net assets; they do not involve inflows, outflows, or other changes in assets or liabilities.

115. Reclassifications include events that remove or impose restrictions on an organization's use of its existing resources. Restrictions are removed from temporarily restricted net assets when stipulated conditions expire or are fulfilled by the organization. Time-restricted net assets generally become unrestricted when the stipulated time arrives; for example, net assets that are restricted by contribution of assets during 1985 for use in 1986 become unrestricted on January 1, 1986. Purpose-restricted net assets generally become unrestricted when the organization undertakes activities pursuant to the specified purpose, perhaps over several periods, depending on the nature of donors' stipulations. The resulting reclassifications increase unrestricted net assets, often at the same time that the activities that remove the restrictions result in expenses that decrease unrestricted net assets. . . . Temporarily restricted net assets may become unrestricted when an organization incurs liabilities to vendors or employees as it undertakes the activities required by donor stipulations, rather than at the time those liabilities are paid. Restrictions occasionally may be withdrawn by the donor or removed by judicial action.

116. The nature of a donor's gift may impose restrictions on

otherwise unrestricted net assets. For example, some donors provide endowment gifts on the condition that the organization agree to "match" them by permanently restricting a stated amount of its unrestricted net assets. Accordingly, "matching agreements" that are not reversible without the donors' consent result in a reclassification of unrestricted net assets to permanently restricted net assets or to temporarily restricted net assets.

3-17. EJAC recommends the use of the following categories for showing the reclassification and expenditure of temporarily restricted resources in the statement of activities or notes thereto:

a. Assessments that meet purpose restrictions: Administrative, retirement, medical, or other similar assessments that meet purpose restrictions pertaining to contributions to the ministry in accordance with established organizational policies and procedures should be reported as reclassifications in the period in which the assessment is made.

b. Expenditures that fulfill purpose restrictions: Expenditures that fulfill donor purpose restrictions should be reported as reclassifications in the period the cost is incurred.

c. Expiration of time or event restrictions: Upon expiration of time or event restrictions on net assets such as expendable time-restricted gifts, annuities, trusts, term endowments, or other fiduciary agreements, these amounts should be reported as reclassifications (transfers) to the unrestricted class or to the expendable temporarily restricted class if there also exist purpose restrictions, in which case the provisions of 3-17b would apply.

d. Capital expenditures that fulfill restrictions: Upon the fulfillment of a temporary restriction for the purchase or construction of property or equipment, a reclassification (transfer) to the unrestricted net assets section is required, as discussed in Chapter 6.

3-18. EJAC recommends that reclassifications be reported in the revenue section of the statement of activities or directly following that section. (See Appendix C for illustrations of EJAC's recommendations on financial statement format relating to reclassifications.)

OTHER CHANGES IN NET ASSETS

Accounting Changes and Extraordinary Items

3-19. Changes in net assets that should not be included in the support and revenue or expense sections of the statement of activities are usually the result of an accounting change or an extraordinary item. These items are rarely encountered by Christian ministries. Accounting Principles Board (APB) Opinions No. 9 and No. 20 explain the accounting and reporting requirements for accounting changes; APB Opinions No. 9 and No. 30 explain requirements for extraordinary items.

3-20. Extraordinary items are events or transactions that are distinguished by their unusual nature and by the infrequency of their occurrence. Examples include expropriation of assets and destruction of an organization's assets through a natural disaster. Both of the following criteria must be met in order to classify an event or transaction as an extraordinary item:

    a. Unusual nature—the underlying event or transaction possesses a high degree of abnormality and is of a type clearly unrelated to, or only incidentally related to, the ordinary and typical activities of the organization, taking into account the environment in which it operates.

    b. Infrequency of occurrence—the underlying event or transaction is of a type that would not reasonably be expected to recur in the foreseeable future, taking into account the environment in which the ministry operates.

The effect of an extraordinary event or transaction should be classified separately in the statement of activities if it is material. (Paragraph 1-12 discusses materiality.) Items shall be considered individually and not in the aggregate in determining whether an extraordinary event or transaction is material. However, the effects of a series of related transactions arising from a single specific and

identifiable event or plan of action that otherwise meets the two criteria shall be aggregated in determining materiality.

The following example shows the recommended presentation of an
extraordinary item and the cumulative effect of an accounting change
in the financial statements. (See Appendix C, Exhibit 3, Sample
Religious Broadcaster.)

Excess (deficit) of support and revenue over expenses before extraordinary item and cumulative effect of a change in an accounting principle	$ XXX
Extraordinary item (describe)–Note X	XXX
Cumulative effect on prior years of change in an accounting principle–Note Y	XXX
Change in Net Assets	$ XXX

Prior Period Adjustments

3-21.   Normally, the beginning net assets will agree with ending net
assets of the prior period. Only in certain circumstances should the
beginning net assets be restated. Restatement of the beginning net
assets is required for a material prior period adjustment which
represents the correction of an error in prior periods or for certain
accounting changes.

3-22.   Errors in financial statements result from mathematical mistakes, mistakes in the application of accounting principles, or oversight or misuse of facts that existed at the time the financial
statements were prepared. In contrast, a change in an accounting
estimate results from new information or subsequent developments
and accordingly from better insight or improved judgment. A change
from an accounting principle that is not generally accepted to one
that is generally accepted is a correction of an error.

The nature of an error in previously issued financial statements and
the effect of its correction on the excess (deficit) of support and
revenue over expenses should be disclosed in the period in which

the error is discovered and corrected along with comparative prior periods. Financial statements of subsequent periods need not repeat the disclosures.

The following example shows the suggested presentation of a prior period adjustment:

Net Assets, Beginning of Year:

As previously reported	$ XXX
Adjustment–Note X	XXX
As restated	$ XXX

International Currency Translations

3-23.   Activities of reporting organizations in other countries or translation of the financial statements of affiliated organizations in other countries should be accounted for in conformity with the provisions of FASB Statement No. 52, *Foreign Currency Translation.* (See Appendix C, Exhibit 1, Sample Large Christian Organization, Note 2, Foreign Operations.)

Return of Contributions

3-24.   Another type of change in net assets is the return of part or all of a contribution to the donor. This type of change should be infrequent. For example, this might occur when a contribution is made and a refund is required pursuant to a court order or the organization decides that it cannot or does not wish to use the gift. (This is a sensitive transaction from both a legal and tax standpoint.) Professional counsel should be consulted in these rare occurrences and tax implications considered. (See also paragraphs 4-17 to 4-21.)

Revenue

Contents

CONTRIBUTIONS 49

   Accounting Principles 51

   Distinguishing Contributions from
      Purchases/Sales Transactions 51

   Contributions Made 53

   Contributions Received 53

   Unrestricted Support 54

   Donor-Restricted Support 54

   Permanently Restricted Support 55

   Temporarily Restricted Support 56

   Change in Temporarily Restricted Net Assets 58

   Direct and Other Designated Gifts 60

      Honoraria and Expense Reimbursements 60

      Personal Gifts 61

      Special Fund-Raising Events 61

   "Pass-Through" Gifts: Cash and Gifts-in-Kind 63

   Promises to Give/Pledges 68

      Intentions to Give 69

      Conditional Promises 70

      Unconditional Promises 70

   Discounting of Pledges... 77

   Deferred Gifts 78

   Legacies and Bequests 79

   Endowments... 79

   Donated and Contributed Services 79

   Valuing Contributed Services 82

Donated Materials and Facilities (Gifts-in-Kind)...... 83

Below Market Rate Loans 89

EARNED INCOME 89

Income Earned on Investments 89

Gains and Losses on Investments 89

Revenue from Sales of Goods and Services 91

TAX MATTERS RELATED TO SUPPORT
AND REVENUE 92

Tax Rules Related to Charitable Giving 93

Support-Raising 94

Tax Reporting Related to Remittances
to Personnel 97

Unrelated Business Income 97

Unrelated Business Activity 98

Debt-Financed Income 100

Managing Unrelated Business Income................... 102

Sales Tax Requirements 103

Private Foundation Status 103

Revenue

4-1.   The statement of revenues and expenses should report all types of revenue, including contributions (commonly referred to as *support* or *gifts*) and revenue from exchange transactions (commonly referred to as *earned income*). This guide distinguishes the two for clarity and discusses the different accounting principles for each. It is important, however, to identify what is and is not revenue to an organization. For example, amounts received as an agent or intermediary for another person or organization are not revenue to the agent. This is discussed further in paragraphs 4-31 to 4-36.

CONTRIBUTIONS

4-2.   Cash contributions usually constitute the major source of support for Christian ministries. They are received directly either as unrestricted contributions; contributions temporarily restricted for specified operating purposes; contributions temporarily restricted for the acquisition of land, buildings, and equipment; contributions temporarily restricted until a certain time or event; permanent or term endowments (the income from which may provide operating revenue); or indirectly through an agency which provides fund-raising services for participating organizations. Contributions may be either unconditional (a promise that depends only on the passage of time or demand by the promisee for performance) or conditional (a promise that depends on the occurrence of a specified future and uncertain event to bind the promisor).

4-3.   Since the governing board has the responsibility for seeing that all contributions are spent in accordance with the organization's stated purposes and policies as well as in accordance with any donor restrictions, all contributions must come under the control of the organization. Organizational policies should stipulate how the support may be used, for example, for salary, ministry expenses, home or field administrative expenses, retirement and insurance benefits, etc. Direction in the allocation and usage of resources must be under the control of the organization. These resources must be used to accomplish the organization's exempt purposes in accordance with any donor restrictions.

4-4.   A Christian ministry should only accept contributions for objectives consistent with the organization's stated purposes. Organizations should establish policies that govern the use of all resources and should clearly communicate these policies to donors. Suggested policies include those dealing with:

- the organization's obligation to use gifts only in accordance with donors' stipulations

- assessment of administrative charges against restricted gifts and/or balances

- use of amounts remaining after donors' stipulations have been fulfilled (paragraph 4-21 discusses holding temporarily restricted resources which the organization is unable to use to fulfill donor restrictions.)

- reservation of the right to redirect amounts donated for the support of the ministry of a specified worker to other similar purposes—such as a scholarship, benevolence, or relief fund—in situations where the particular ministry is overfunded

- reservation of the right to determine the specific individual who will benefit from a particular gift (this reservation is necessary to preserve the income tax deductibility of the donor's gift)

- the organization's intention to advise the donor if a gift is redirected to another purpose under either of the two previous policies

- the case where a gift is received for a purpose not previously approved by the organization's governing board, the organization's intention to communicate with the donor before the gift is either used or returned

- how gifts-in-kind are valued for financial reporting purposes and that the organization will not function as an appraiser of such gifts for the donor

- whether unrestricted earnings on unremitted amounts held for specified purposes are allocated to the same purpose as the original gift or are used for general purposes

- the requirement that capital gains attributable to a restricted endowment fund will be used for the same purpose as income from the fund unless the donor has stipulated otherwise (or state law requires a different use; e.g., reinvestment)

(Canadian ministries, see 9-7 to 9-9.)

Accounting Principles

4-5.   GAAP for contributions are now contained in FASB Statement No. 116, *Accounting for Contributions Received and Contributions Made.* It sets forth standards for almost all aspects of accounting for contributions, including:

- unrestricted and donor restricted gifts

- donated services of volunteers

- promises to give (pledges)

- reporting and disclosure of contributions (This topic is also discussed in FASB Statement No. 117, *Financial Statements of Not-for-Profit Organizations,* Chapter 2, and the illustrative financial statements of this Guide in Appendix C.)

A flowchart for distinguishing contributions from agency transactions is presented at Appendix J.

Distinguishing Contributions from Purchases/Sales Transactions

4-6.   FASB Statement No. 116 applies to nonreciprocal transactions, such as contributions (commonly referred to as *support* or *gifts*). Statement No. 116 does not apply to exchange transactions, such as purchases or sales of goods or services. It is not, however, always easy to distinguish the two in practice. Usually a judgment based on all the facts of the situation must be made. Appendix B, Exhibit 1, contains a list of factors EJAC considers relevant in making that judgment. However, if a purchase is made at a bargain rate (i.e., favorable to the charity) and there is evidence that there is a gift element in it, the gift portion should be accounted for separately as a contribution. (Note: In this case, the charity should not issue a receipt to the vendor specifying the amount of the gift since no separate tax deduction is available to the vendor for this kind of gift; the reduction in the vendor's taxable income results from recording the sale at the lower price.)

4-7.   For example, a contractor would normally build a building for $100,000 but charges a religious organization only $70,000; the contractor has probably made a $30,000 gift to the organization. Why "probably"? In some cases, vendors who give discounts are merely engaging in normal trade practices and such a discount would be available to anyone who asks. Examples include quantity discounts, discounts for prompt payment, discounts to build customer loyalty, discounts to reflect the fact that business is otherwise slow at certain times of the year, and discounts to match competition. In these cases, there is no charitable intent on the part of the vendor, and the price recorded by the purchaser would be the actual price paid, not the normal retail price. It should be assumed that discounts are trade, not charitable, discounts unless there is positive evidence of the vendor's charitable intent. (Paragraph 4-67 to 4-76 discuss gifts-in-kind.)

4-8.   For organizations which are the recipient of grants from governmental agencies, the question often arises as to whether such grants are contributions or exchange transactions. Some believe that governments never give away anything without an expectation of receiving value in return and, hence, all government grants represent exchange transactions. While many such grants are in essence exchanges, EJAC believes that this is not always the case, and thus each grant should be evaluated individually to determine which kind of transaction it is.

(See Appendix B, Exhibit 1)

Contributions Made (grants and pledges)

4-9.   Christian ministries which make gifts to other organizations (for example, a church making a gift to a mission organization, a convention of churches contributing to a local parish or to a welfare organization, etc.) are also required to follow the rules of FASB Statement No. 116 in accounting for these gifts made. Further, for-profit entities which contribute to charities are also covered by Statement No. 116. In the case of entities making gifts, however, all journal entries are reversed: expense instead of revenue, liability instead of asset. All of the rules in the statement about timing of recognition of gifts and recording and discounting of pledges apply equally to donors. (Paragraphs 5-36 to 5-40 discuss grants made.)

Organizations that solicit gifts from for-profit businesses should also be aware of how the forms of proposed gifts will affect the donor's accounting. (Donees do not have a responsibility to verify the accounting by the donor, however.) A charity might seek unconditional pledges, but a donor may wish to make its pledge conditional in order to record the expense in a later period.

Contributions Received

4-10.   Contributions, as defined in this paragraph, include pledges. (Paragraphs 4-37 to 4-50 discuss pledges further.)

Paragraph 8 of FASB Statement No. 116, provides the following concerning contributions received:

8.   Except as provided in paragraphs 9 [contributed services of volunteers—see paragraph 4-58 to 4-66] and 11 [museum collections], contributions received shall be recognized as revenues or gains in the period received and as assets, decreases of liabilities, or expenses depending on the form of the benefits received. Contributions received shall be measured at their fair values. . . .

Unrestricted Support

4-11.   Support received without donor restriction is reported as revenue in the unrestricted class of net assets when received or unconditionally promised (i.e., pledged). This rule applies even though such amounts may later be designated by the board for a specific purpose. Pledges are considered implicitly temporarily restricted (time restrictions) and are reported in the temporarily restricted class until due. (Paragraph 4-51 to 4-54 discuss discounting of pledges.)

Donor Restricted Support

4-12.   Donor-restricted support includes all contributions that are either temporarily or permanently restricted as the result of donor stipulations as discussed in paragraph 14 of FASB Statement No. 116 and in Chapter 2.

> 14.   . . . A restriction on an organization's use of the assets contributed results either from a donor's explicit stipulation or from circumstances surrounding the receipt of the contribution that make clear the donor's implicit restriction on use. . . .

Appendix B, Exhibit 2 of this Guide helps organizations determine whether a particular gift is purpose restricted or unrestricted. All contributions which are not explicitly or implicitly donor restricted should be classified as unrestricted. Note that only a donor or other outside party can create a restriction that is binding on an organization. An organization's governing board may vote or otherwise decide to designate, appropriate, or in some other way set aside amounts for some specified or unspecified purpose, but such an internal process does not create a restriction since a board can decide to undesignate it later. (An exception to this rule is that unrestricted amounts used to match a donor-restricted challenge grant take on the restrictions specified by the donor.)

4-13.   Amounts received as permanent or temporary endowments or irrevocable trusts should be reported as either permanently or temporarily restricted support. Gains (and losses) from sales of investments of these restricted assets should be accounted for in accordance with any explicit donor stipulations (or, if the donor is silent as to the gains, then in the same manner as the income from the endowment) and applicable law (usually that of the state in which the organization is headquartered and, in some cases, the place of residence of the donor). (Paragraph 4-78 discusses investment income and Chapter 6 includes further discussion of the reporting of gains and losses.) For split-interest trusts requiring payments to lifetime beneficiaries, investment income should be included in the line item on the Statement of Activities entitled *Change in the Value of Split-Interest Agreements,* shown net of distributions and other amounts. EJAC recommends that the notes to the financial statements include appropriate disclosure of the gross components of change in the value of split-interest agreements. (Chapter 7 discusses split-interest agreements further.)

4-14.   The costs of soliciting these types of gifts are fund-raising expenses as discussed in Chapter 5. Ongoing administrative expenses related to these types of giving programs, such as those discussed in paragraphs 5-14 to 5-15, should be reported as general and administrative expenses. Investment management expenses related to these assets may be netted against the investment income for financial statement purposes as discussed in paragraph 5-44 and paragraph 24 of FASB Statement No. 117.

Permanently Restricted Support

4-15.   Permanent endowments, which may be in the form of permanent irrevocable trusts, are a type of permanently restricted income that Christian ministries typically receive. These contributions from a donor who has stipulated that the principal remain intact in perpetuity are also referred to as "pure" or "true" endowments. Another type of permanently restricted income is a contribution received to establish a revolving loan fund (see paragraph 3-8). Permanently restricted support is recognized as revenue when cash is received or an unconditional promise to give is made.

Contributions from a donor who has stipulated that part or all of the gift be held until a future accounting period and disbursed at that time are referred to as "term" endowments and are temporarily restricted.

The term "quasi-endowment" is used to describe unrestricted net assets that a board has designated for a particular purpose.

Quasi-endowments remain unrestricted net assets *after* the designation. *(Canadian ministries, see 9-36.)*

4-16. The income earned on endowments may be expended for the general purposes of the organization unless otherwise restricted by the donor. (Note that irrevocable trusts that provide for principal restrictions that expire upon termination of lifetime beneficiary interests are temporarily restricted.) (Paragraph 3-8 discusses permanently restricted net assets, paragraph 4-78 discusses investment income, and Chapter 7 includes a more detailed discussion of deferred gifts.)

Temporarily Restricted Support

4-17. Under FASB Statement No. 116, temporarily restricted gifts should be recognized as income when received or unconditionally promised and, if they have not yet been used for the stipulated purpose at the reporting date, should be displayed in the balance sheet as part of the net assets section (temporarily restricted). Contributions subject to explicit donor stipulations that the contribution be refunded if certain conditions are not met should be reported as refundable advances (liabilities) until the conditions are substantially met. Contributions that would otherwise be considered conditional should be considered unconditional if the possibility that the condition will not be met is remote.

4-18. It is a common practice for Christian ministries to raise and receive temporarily restricted gifts to support ministry conducted by particular workers, such as missionaries (also see 4-90). Gifts in support of the organization's ministry conducted by specific workers should be treated as revenues and expenses of the organization only if they represent contributions to the organization; i.e., for the ministry of an individual (rather than for the individual personally). Tax rules use terms such as *preferenced* or *designated* to describe donor stipulations. The IRS takes the position that in order for the gifts to be tax-deductible contributions (rather than nondeductible gifts to individuals), organizations must have complete control and discretion over the funds to use them exclusively for exempt purposes.

EJAC believes the substance of gifts that are intended to support ministry conducted by particular workers, such as missionaries, are temporarily restricted for GAAP purposes while meeting the IRS requirements for charitable contributions. Accordingly, such gifts should be accounted for in accordance with the provisions of paragraph 4-17. Also, because of the unique circumstances surrounding projects and support of missionaries in the field, the organization's reservation of the contingent right to redirect the gift for other purposes of the organization if the project cannot be completed (for example, if the missionary leaves the organization) does not negate the temporarily restricted nature of the gift. (Paragraphs 4-27 and 4-28 discuss personal gifts.)

4-19. When a supported person leaves the organization, any balance in the person's "ministry" account should remain under the control of the organization. Policy statements of the organization normally provide that such balances may be redirected by the organization for a similar use. Many organizations contact donors for input as well, but organizational policy statements to cover such contingencies should be provided to both the supported person and the donor. When a supported person leaves, donors should be notified immediately so that a redirection of future contributions may be accomplished if the donor desires. *(Canadian ministries, see 9-8.)*

4-20. Contributions restricted by donors for specified operating purposes or for acquisition of land, buildings, and equipment should be recorded as temporarily restricted support until such time as the resources are used for the specified purpose. (Paragraph 3-17(d) discusses recording reclassifications resulting from using these resources.)

4-21. Sometimes an organization inadvertently (it should not do this intentionally) finds itself in the position of holding temporarily restricted resources, which it is unable to use to fulfill donor restrictions. *(Canadian ministries, see 9-8.)* This can occur either because it has accomplished the purpose for which the gifts were solicited and some amounts remain unspent, or there is an inability to proceed with a project for some reason (i.e., the need no longer exists, there are political problems in the country, the organization has been unable to attract other resources needed, or the organization's priorities have shifted elsewhere). In this situation, the organization must decide what to do with the remaining amount. Its choices include:

- seeking donor permission to redirect the amounts to other projects

- seeking a court order (under the doctrine of cy pres) to redirect the amounts without donor permission (may be required if the donor cannot be contacted for any reason)

- redirecting the amounts to a project with a similar enough purpose to fulfill the donor's intent (if it is impossible to contact a donor and the amount involved is insignificant)

- refunding unspent amounts to donors (this should rarely be done and must be done with legal counsel considering tax reporting requirements)

In the latter three cases, legal advice should be sought before proceeding. A question that may arise in this situation is just whose gifts remain unspent: a pro rata portion of all gifts which were restricted for the project or all of the most recently received gifts? The assumption of the latter makes it easier to redirect unspent amounts. In all such solicitations, there should be clear disclosure to donors of the organization's policy with respect to unspent amounts.

Change in Temporarily Restricted Net Assets

4-22. Paragraphs 123 and 124 of FASB Concepts Statement No. 6 provide the following:

123. Change in Temporarily Restricted Net Assets

Change in temporarily restricted net assets of a not-for-profit organization during a period is the total of (a) contributions and other inflows during the period of assets whose use by the organization is limited by donor-imposed stipulations that either expire by passage of time or can be fulfilled and removed by actions of the organization pursuant to those stipulations, (b) other asset enhancements and diminishments during the period subject to the same kinds of stipulations, and (c) reclassifications to (or from) other classes of net assets during the period as a consequence of donor-imposed stipulations, their expiration by passage of time, or their fulfillment and removal by actions of the organization pursuant to those stipulations.

124. Characteristics of Change in Temporarily Restricted Net Assets

Most increases in temporarily restricted net assets of a not-for-profit organization are from its accepting contributions of assets that donors limit to use after a specified future time— for example, to be used for next year's operations or to be invested for 10 years before becoming available for operations—or for a specified purpose—for example, sponsoring a particular program activity or acquiring a particular building or piece of equipment. Temporary restrictions pertain to contributions with donor stipulations that expire or can be fulfilled and removed by using assets as specified.

And, in contrast to permanent restrictions, which pertain to assets that can provide economic benefits indefinitely and must be maintained in perpetuity by the receiving organization, temporary restrictions pertain to assets that by their nature are spent or used up in carrying out the receiving organization's activities or, if capable of providing economic benefits indefinitely, need not be retained after a stipulated time (term endowment).

4-23. Reclassifications from temporarily restricted net assets to unrestricted net assets will include the following:

- expenditures that fulfill donor-imposed purpose restrictions

- expiration of time restrictions, including promises to give that are due, expiration of term endowments, and maturity of annuity and life income funds

- assessments that meet purpose restrictions pertaining to contributions in accordance with organizational policy (this should be communicated to donors)

- placing donated long-lived assets in service if the organization has elected to consider the restriction on such gifts to be fulfilled when the assets are placed in service

- use of long-lived assets over the useful life of the donated asset (usually equal to depreciation) if the organization has elected such an accounting policy

4-24. If the organization has both unrestricted and temporarily restricted net assets available for a particular purpose and uses some net assets for that purpose, the temporarily restricted net assets are deemed to have been used first (FASB Statement No. 116, paragraph 17).

Direct and Other Designated Gifts

Honoraria and Expense Reimbursements

4-25. When board or staff members speak on behalf of a ministry, they often receive contributions, honoraria, or expense reimbursements. It is generally helpful for ministries to adopt policies regarding the ownership, control and handling of such funds. Such policies may be helpful in determining if a conflict of interest has occurred. If it is the organization's policy to consider such amounts as contributions to the ministry of the organization, then adequate internal controls and reporting practices should be established. Appropriate internal reporting should include the donor name and address, date and amount of the gift, and any donor restrictions. Expenditures made should come under the regular control, authorization, and reporting procedures of the ministry.

4-26. Payments are occasionally received directly by an individual in the "field," often during a visit to another ministry or when speaking for various groups. Sometimes such payments are intended to be kept by the individual or they may be intended for the individual sponsoring organization. In the latter case, when the payment is by check, if possible the check should be made payable to the organization. If this is not possible (the check has already been filled out before the person learns of it) or if the payment is in cash, the individual should make arrangements to promptly remit the amount to the organization, usually by check.

Personal Gifts

4-27.   This term refers to gifts made to an individual that are not tax deductible. It should be noted that because gifts to individuals are not tax deductible to the donor (even if passed through a tax-exempt organization as a service to the donor and/or the recipient), organizations may not issue tax deduction receipts and should affirmatively advise donors of this fact. Similarly, such gifts are not taxable income to the recipient. Under some circumstances, an organization may agree to process such gifts as a convenience to donors and recipients, such as where communication might otherwise be cumbersome. Such gifts are not considered revenue to the organization since it has no discretion over what to do with them. (Paragraphs 4-31 to 4-36 discuss resources over which the organization has no discretion— FASB Statement No. 136.) When received, they should be recorded as liabilities, and when remitted to the specified recipient, the liability should be reduced. (See Appendix C, Exhibit 1, Sample Large Christian Organization.)

4-28.   Unremitted personal amounts held on behalf of members or employees are custodial (agency) funds which should be reported as assets and liabilities. If the organization presents its balance sheet in disaggregated form showing the three classes of net assets in separate columns, EJAC recommends that these custodial funds be included in the assets and liabilities of the unrestricted class. (There will, of course, be no net asset amount since the liability will equal the asset.) The reason that these assets and liabilities should be reported as unrestricted is that these amounts are not gifts to the organization and thus do not qualify as donor-restricted.

Special Fund-Raising Events

4-29.   Special fund-raising events are generally affairs in which something of value is provided directly to donor participants or designees for a payment which is in part a contribution and in part an exchange transaction (payments for goods or services). Some organizations hold special fund-raising events, such as rallies, banquets, or special entertainment, from which the donor receives a direct benefit (e.g., book, tape, meal, theater ticket) in exchange for a stipulated "gift." Some may also collect offerings to cover costs and to generate support. Others may sell merchandise or ministry-related items as a fund-raising technique.

4-30. FASB Statement No.117 requires that revenues and expenses from special events be reported gross, unless the events are peripheral or incidental activities, in which case organizations are permitted but not required to report the net amounts of those revenues and expenses. To report the revenues of the special event gross, organizations may report the revenue (both the contribution and exchange transaction revenue) as special events support. Alternatively, organizations can consider revenue from special events and other fund-raising activities as part exchange (for the fair value the participant received) and part contribution (for the excess of the payment over that fair value) and report the two parts separately. EJAC recommends that gross revenues from such events be reported as special events support in the statement of activities. The costs of direct donor benefits that are not program related (for example, facilities rental, food, and entertainment at a dinner) and that are provided in exchange transactions should be reported as a separate supporting category, such as cost of sales, and should not be reported as fund-raising. (However, the costs of donor benefits that are not program related and that are provided in transactions that are other than exchange transactions, such as a fund-raising dinner for which there is no charge to attend, should be reported as fund-raising.)

The cost of direct benefits to donors may be reported either (1) as a line item deducted from the special event revenues or (2) in the same section of the statement of activities as are other programs or supporting services and allocated, if necessary, among those various functions. EJAC recommends that the costs of direct benefits to donors be reported on a separate line as a deduction from the gross special event support. Disclosure of the deduction parenthetically or in a footnote is not sufficient. Other expenses such as publicity, travel, salaries, and administration of the event should be reported either as (a) fund-raising expenses, or (b) allocated between fund-raising, program, and management and general, subject to the constraints of SOP 98-2, *Accounting for Costs of Activities of Not-for-Profit Organizations and State and Local Governmental Entities That Include Fund-Raising,* which is discussed in paragraphs 5-28 and 5-29 of this Guide (paragraphs 4-88 and 4-89 discuss related tax considerations and paragraph 5-55 includes further discussion of financial statement presentation.) (See Appendix C, Exhibit 1, Sample Large Christian Organization, Note 10.) *(Canadian ministries, see 9-9.)*

"Pass-through" Gifts: Cash and Gifts-in-Kind

4-31. FASB Statement No. 136, *Transfers of Assets to a Not-for-Profit Organization or Charitable Trust That Raises or Holds Contributions for Others,* provides guidance to help distinguish agency and intermediary transactions from contributions. Specifically, as stated in the Statement's summary:

> [The] Statement establishes standards for transactions in which an entity — the donor — makes a contribution by transferring assets to a not-for-profit organization or charitable trust — the recipient organization — that accepts the assets from the donor and agrees to use those assets on behalf of or transfer those assets, the return on investment of those assets, or both to another entity — the beneficiary — that is specified by the donor. It also establishes standards for transactions that take place in a similar manner but are not contributions because the transfers are revocable, repayable, or reciprocal.

> This Statement requires a recipient organization that accepts cash or other financial assets from a donor and agrees to use those assets on behalf of or transfer those assets, the return on investment of those assets, or both to a specified unaffiliated beneficiary to recognize the fair value of those assets as a liability to the specified beneficiary concurrent with recognition of the assets received from the donor. However, if the donor explicitly grants the recipient organization variance power or if the recipient organization and the specified beneficiary are financially interrelated organizations, the recipient organization is required to recognize the fair value of any assets it receives as a contribution received. Not-for-profit organizations are financially interrelated if (a) one organization has the ability to influence the operating and financial decisions of the other and (b) one organization has an ongoing economic interest in the net assets of the other.

This Statement does not establish standards for a trustee's reporting of assets held on behalf of specified beneficiaries, but it does establish standards for a beneficiary's reporting of its rights to assets held in a charitable trust.

This Statement requires that a specified beneficiary recognize its rights to the assets held by a recipient organization as an asset unless the donor has explicitly granted the recipient organization variance power. Those rights are either an interest in the net assets of the recipient organization, a beneficial interest, or a receivable. If the beneficiary and the recipient organization are financially interrelated organizations, the beneficiary is required to recognize its interest in the net assets of the recipient organization and adjust that interest for its share of the change in net assets of the recipient organization. If the beneficiary has an unconditional right to receive all or a portion of the specified cash flows from a charitable trust or other identifiable pool of assets, the beneficiary is required to recognize that beneficial interest, measuring and subsequently remeasuring it at fair value, using a valuation technique such as the present value of the estimated expected future cash flows. If the recipient organization is explicitly granted variance power, the specified beneficiary does not recognize its potential for future distributions from the assets held by the recipient organization. In all other cases, a beneficiary recognizes its rights as a receivable.

This Statement describes four circumstances in which a transfer of assets to a recipient organization is accounted for as a liability by the recipient organization and as an asset by the resource provider because the transfer is revocable or reciprocal. Those four circumstances are if (a) the transfer is subject to the resource provider's unilateral right to redirect the use of the assets to another beneficiary, (b) the transfer is accompanied by the resource provider's conditional promise to give or is otherwise revocable or repayable, (c) the resource provider controls the recipient organization and specifies an unaffiliated beneficiary, or (d) the resource provider specifies itself or its affiliate as the beneficiary and the transfer is not an equity transaction. If the transfer is an equity transaction and the resource provider specifies itself as beneficiary, it records an interest in the net assets of the recipient organization (or an increase in a previously recognized interest). If the resource provider specifies an affiliate as beneficiary, the resource provider records an equity transaction as a separate line item in its statement of activities, and the affiliate named as beneficiary records an interest in the net assets of the recipient organization. The recipient organization records an equity transaction as a separate line item in its statement of activities.

This Statement requires certain disclosures if a not-for-profit organization transfers assets to a recipient organization and specifies itself or its affiliate as the beneficiary or if it includes in its financial statements a ratio of fund-raising expenses to amounts raised.

4-32. Many gifts (both cash and gifts-in-kind) are passed through one organization to another organization, either because (a) that is the most effective way to place the resources where they are needed or (b) for internal organizational management purposes. The accounting question stemming from this is (a) whether the recipient (pass-through) organization should record the gift as its own revenue and later as a gift made (expense) to the beneficiary (third) organization or individuals, or (b) whether the recipient (pass-through) organization should record the initial receipt of the assets as a liability (amounts held on behalf of others or agency funds) and later as a reduction of this liability. In the first case, the gift will be reported as revenue and program expense of the recipient (pass-through) organization; in the second case, it will never be reported in the recipient (pass-through) organization's statement of revenue and expenses.

4-33. The conceptual issue addressed by Statement No. 136 is how to determine whether the recipient (pass-through) organization is merely acting as an agent or intermediary for either the original donor or for the specified beneficiary, or whether the recipient (pass-through) organization has itself received a contribution. This question can be particularly relevant when the assets involved are "gifts-in-kind," such as food, medicine, and similar items. These types of gifts are frequently transferred from one charitable organization to another before reaching the ultimate beneficiaries.

4-34. Historically, prior to FASB Statements No. 116 and 136, some organizations followed a policy that if donated materials passed through the organization to its charitable beneficiaries, the organization was merely serving as an agent for the donors, and the donations normally were not recorded as a contribution. Under Statement No. 136, whether those materials (as well as cash, promises to give, and other assets) are reported as contributions by the recipient (pass-through) organization depends on the following [Note that for most ministries the circumstances described in items (e) and (f) below are more likely to exist than are the circumstances described in items (a) through (d) below. The circumstances in items (a) through (d) are listed first, however, because, in conformity with the guidance in Statement No. 136, they should be considered before the circumstances in items (e) and (f)]:

a. If the transfer is subject to the resource provider's unilateral right to redirect the use of the assets to another beneficiary, the recipient has not received a contribution.

b. If the transfer is accompanied by the resource provider's conditional promise to give or is otherwise revocable or repayable, the recipient has not received a contribution.

c. If the resource provider controls the recipient organization and specifies an unaffiliated beneficiary, the recipient has not received a contribution.

d. If the resource provider specifies itself or its affiliate as the beneficiary, the recipient has not received a contribution. (The transfer may be an equity transaction under paragraph 18 of Statement No. 136.)

If (a) through (d) above are not applicable, the recipient may have received a contribution, depending on the following:

e. If the recipient organization has variance power (the unilateral power to redirect the use of the assets to another beneficiary), the recipient should report a contribution, measured at fair value.

f.   If the recipient (pass-through) and the beneficiary are financially interrelated, as defined in Statement No. 136, the recipient should report a contribution, measured at fair value.

If the recipient has not reported a contribution based on (a) through (f) above, and the transaction is not an equity transaction, the recipient is acting as an agent or intermediary and should not report a contribution. An organization that receives cash or other financial assets as an agent or intermediary should report those assets and a liability to the specified beneficiary. An organization that receives nonfinancial assets, such as clothing or food, as an agent or intermediary is permitted, but not required, to report those assets and liabilities, provided that the organization reports consistently from period to period and discloses its accounting policy.

4-35.   Similar to the guidance discussed in paragraph 4-33, if an organization is a beneficiary of assets passed through another organization, the beneficiary organization should recognize its interest in those assets unless the recipient (pass-through) organization has variance power (the unilateral right to redirect the use of the assets to another beneficiary); the resource provider retains the right to redirect the assets to another beneficiary; the transfer is accompanied by a conditional promise to give, or is otherwise revocable; or the resource provider controls the recipient and specifies an unaffiliated beneficiary. That interest should be recognized as either a (a) beneficial interest (if the recipient and beneficiary are financially interrelated or if the beneficiary's right is to receive specified cash flows from a pool of assets, such as a charitable trust), or (b) receivable, in all other circumstances. (Paragraph 4-61 discusses circumstances in which contributed services may pass through from one organization to another.)

4-36.   The determination of whether an organization is acting as an agent is based on applying the guidance in FASB Statement No. 136 and necessarily requires judgment in each case. The following summarizes key factors to consider in determining how substantive the involvement of the "intermediary" organization is with respect to the gift:

●   the extent and nature of the relationships between the organizations involved

- the similarity of the uses of the items to the organization's stated purposes

- circumstances surrounding the solicitation and use of the items

- how the items are physically handled

- the extent and nature of the organization's own direct involvement ("value added") with the items

In summary, organizations which: (1) merely pass gifts from donors to recipients, (2) have little substantive decision-making power over or involvement (value added) with the items, (3) never take physical possession of the items, and/or (4) receive items not directly related to the organizations' stated purposes, should consider carefully whether it is appropriate to record the gifts as revenue.

Appendix J is a Flowchart for Distinguishing Contributions from Agency Transactions, as set forth in FASB Statement No. 136.

Promises to Give

4-37. Pledges are promises to transfer cash or other assets to an organization at a future date. FASB Concepts Statement No. 6, paragraph 25, defines assets as items having "probable future economic benefits obtained or controlled by a particular entity as a result of past transactions or events." FASB Statement No. 116, paragraph 6, defines a promise to give as: "A written or oral agreement to contribute cash or other assets to another entity. A promise to give may be either conditional or unconditional." It further defines an unconditional promise to give as one "that depends only on passage of time or demand by the promisee for performance." A conditional promise to give is one "that depends on the occurrence of a specified future and uncertain event to bind the promisor" (FASB Statement No. 116, paragraph 67). Appendix B, Exhibit 3 provides additional information on factors to be considered in assessing whether a donor has made a bona fide pledge to a donee.

As discussed elsewhere in this chapter, unconditional promises to give should be reported as revenue when received (that is, when the promise is made, rather than, for example, when a cash payment fulfilling the promise is received). Conditional promises to give should be reported as revenue when conditions are substantially met. Also, contributions that would otherwise be considered conditional should be considered unconditional if the possibility that the condition will not be met is remote. *(Canadian ministries, see 9-55.)*

4-38. Accounting for some donor communications, particularly those commonly referred to as *faith promises,* may pose special challenges under GAAP. Though GAAP includes provisions to distinguish among unconditional promises, conditional promises, or expressions of intentions to give, such distinctions may require subjective judgments and be difficult to make in practice, particularly for ministries.

Determining whether a communication is an expression of an intention to give, a conditional promise, or an unconditional promise

Intentions to Give

4-39. EJAC believes that including the following (or substantially similar) phrases would result in the communication not being recorded as a contribution because these phrases indicate only an intention to give under GAAP, not an unconditional promise:

- I intend to give

- By faith I intend to give

- Subject to God's provision I intend to give

- I (we) will endeavor to give

- This statement may be revised or canceled at any time should circumstances necessitate

Conditional Promises

4-40. EJAC believes that the inclusion of any of the following (or substantially similar) phrases would result in the communication not being recorded as a contribution, because these phrases lead to the conclusion that the communication is a conditional promise under GAAP (as discussed in paragraph 4-50, organizations should disclose conditional promises received but not recorded):

- Subject to the sale of a specific business or asset

- Conditioned on the organization undertaking a program to help the homeless

- Conditioned on the organization establishing a new church

- Subject to the organization raising matching gifts by December 31, 2xxx

- Conditioned on John Doe continuing to provide ministry services for Organization A

Appendix B, Exhibit 4 provides factors to be considered in deciding whether a gift or pledge subject to donor stipulations is conditional or restricted.

Unconditional Promises

4-41. EJAC believes that the use of the following (or substantially similar) phrases would result in the communication being recorded as a contribution because these phrases lead to the conclusion that the communication is an unconditional promise under GAAP:

- By faith I will give

- Subject to God's provision I will give

- I will give

- Is intended to be over and above my regular gifts

- I will receive monthly updates of the progress of the project

4-42. The above provides EJAC's recommendations regarding the effect of certain phrases in considering whether a communication is an expression of an intention to give, a conditional promise, or an unconditional promise. These conclusions are based on the assumption that these phrases are the main or only ones in the communication that are relevant in determining whether the communication is an expression of an intention to give, a conditional promise, or an unconditional promise.

4-43. In other situations, communications may include more than one phrase that is relevant in making that determination. If a communication includes a phrase that by itself leads to the conclusion that it is an intention, as well as a phrase(s) that by itself leads to the conclusion that it is either a conditional or an unconditional promise to give, the phrase that leads to the conclusion that it is an intention is the preeminent phrase and the communication is therefore an intention. Similarly, if a communication includes a phrase(s) that by itself leads to the conclusion that it is a conditional promise to give, as well as a phrase that by itself leads to the conclusion that it is an unconditional promise to give, the phrase that leads to the conclusion that it is a conditional promise to give is the preeminent phrase and the communication is therefore a conditional promise to give.

4-44. EJAC believes that including the phrases "by faith" and "subject to God's provision" do not create conditions. Rather, they are pervasive and fundamental concepts inherent in all contributions. In other words, all contributions are made by faith and are subject to God's provision.

Examples that Provide Guidance to Help Determine Whether a Communication is an Expression of an Intention to Give, a Conditional Promise, or an Unconditional Promise

Example 1

Communication to Support a Ministry

The following is an example of an unconditional promise to give that should be reported as contribution revenue (temporarily restricted for Worthy Project):

Desiring to be a part of the expanding work of ABC ministries, *by faith,* subject to God's provision, I (we) will give a total of $xxx during the next 36 months to be paid as follows starting _____ in support of the Worthy Project:

_____ monthly
_____ quarterly
_____ semiannually
_____ annually

My commitment and understanding is:

1. that this is intended to be over and above my regular gifts for operations, other projects and missionaries,
2. that I will receive monthly updates of the progress of the project,
3. that funds received will be used for the Worthy Project,

Name and address, no signature requested

Note the following:

- If the document, or any other document, was revised to include the phrase "this statement may be revised or canceled at any time should circumstances necessitate," it would be an intention to give that did not result in reporting contribution revenue because that phrase would remove any obligation (social, moral, legal, or otherwise) that the resource provider would have had to transfer the described amounts.

- If the introductory paragraph was revised to include the phrase "Desiring to be a part of the expanding work of ABC ministries, by faith, subject to God's provision, I (we) will **endeavor to** give a total of $xxx during the next 36 months to be paid as follows..." this would be an intention to give that would not result in reporting contribution revenue because the word *endeavor*, which is commonly understood to mean "an earnest attempt," would remove any obligation (social, moral, legal, or otherwise) that the resource provider would have to transfer the described amounts.

- If the document was revised to include the stipulation "subject to the sale of a specific business or asset"; "conditioned on the organization undertaking a program to help the homeless"; "conditioned on the organization establishing a new church"; or "subject to the organization raising matching gifts by December 31, 2xxx," this would be a conditional promise to give because those phrases would establish specified future and uncertain events whose occurrence is required to bind the promisor.

- Including the words "by faith, subject to God's provision" in the introductory sentence does not in and of itself result in the communication *not* being an unconditional promise. Such phrases are pervasive and fundamental concepts inherent in all contributions, rather than specific and measurable conditions in applying these financial accounting standards.

- Use of the word "intended" in the phrase "this is intended to be over and above my regular gifts for operations, other projects and missionaries" does not in and of itself result in the communication being an intention to give, rather than a promise. The notion of "intent" in that phrase is used in a different context and is merely meant to clarify the amount of the potential contribution.

- Requiring monthly updates on the progress of the project does not create a condition under FASB Statement No. 116.

- The fact that the document is not signed would not in and of itself result in it not being a promise to give.

Example 2

Communication to Support a Missionary

The following is an example of an unconditional promise to give that should be reported as contribution revenue (temporarily restricted for the ministry of John Doe), if it can be reliably measured (paragraph 4-45 discusses measurement of similar contributions):

In expression of my desire to invest in outreach ministry conducted by John Doe, by faith, subject to God's provision, I (we) will give $xxx to Organization A

_____ monthly
_____ quarterly
_____ annually (no stated term)

or $X one time gift.

This contribution will be made with the understanding that Organization A has complete discretion and control over the use of all donated funds.

Example 3

Communication to Support a Missionary

The following is an example of a conditional promise to give that should be disclosed in the notes to the financial statements:

In expression of my desire to invest in outreach ministry conducted by John Doe, by faith, subject to God's provision, I (we) *will* give $xxx to Organization A

_____ monthly
_____ quarterly
_____ annually (no stated term)

or $X one time gift.

This promise is conditioned on John Doe continuing to provide ministry services for Organization A. This contribution will be made with the understanding that Organization A has complete discretion and control over the use of all donated funds.

Example 4

Communication to Support a Missionary

The following is an example of an intention to give that should not be reported as contribution revenue:

In expression of my desire to invest in outreach ministry conducted by John Doe, by faith, subject to God's provision, I (we) *intend* to give $xxx to Organization A

_____ monthly
_____ quarterly
_____ annually (no stated term)

or $X one time gift.

This contribution will be made with the understanding that Organization A has complete discretion and control over the use of all donated funds.

4-45. If a communication should be reported as an unconditional promise to give, organizations should consider at what amount it should be reported. As discussed in paragraph 4-10, FASB Statement No. 116 requires that contributions be reported at fair value. In determining the fair value of an unconditional promise, organizations should consider the present value of expected cash flows, as discussed in paragraph 4-51. In considering measurement of expected cash flows for unconditional promises, organizations should consider the likelihood that the donor may discontinue payments at some point in time due to circumstances such as financial hardship, death of the donor, discontinuance of a program or key individual, or for other reasons.

Donors may facilitate their donations by authorizing an organization to make periodic direct charges against the donor's bank account and/or the donor's credit card. Organizations should consider the nature of such authorizations and whether there is verifiable documentation of donor intent to make an unconditional promise.

Likewise, donors may make promises to give a periodic amount without a stated term, commonly referred to as "open-ended promises." EJAC recommends that organizations consider whether their open-ended promises are unconditional promises to give and, if so, whether they can be reliably measured. If they are unconditional promises that can be reliably measured, they should be reported as contributions. If they are not unconditional promises, or cannot be reliably measured, they should not be reported as contributions but may be disclosed in the notes to the financial statements.

4-46.   EJAC recommends that fund-raisers consult with the organization's accountants and attorneys, as needed, to ensure that the language used in pledge and other contribution-related documents is worded clearly and unambiguously, with consideration of the accounting implications.

4-47.   Oral pledges can be considered unconditional promises to give provided that there is sufficient evidence in the form of verifiable documentation that a promise was made and received. Such evidence may include tape recordings, written contemporaneous registers, follow-up written confirmations, and other means that permit subsequent verification of the oral communication. Organizations and their auditors need to carefully consider what audit evidence can be relied on to justify the recording of such pledges. This requirement may be met after the fact by a confirming communication sent to the pledgor by the pledgee or by the auditor. For example, in activities involving phone pledges, a letter or card is immediately sent asking the potential donor to confirm the pledge in writing or, at a minimum, to notify the organization if there is disagreement.

4-48.   Unconditional promises to give should be reported as support in the same manner as cash contributions, as discussed in paragraph 4-10. Amounts payable in future periods are considered temporarily restricted until due. Organizations should normally record pledges as an asset and as support at their estimated fair value, which can usually be estimated as the present value of expected cash flows, as discussed in paragraph 4-51.

As discussed in paragraphs 87, 88, 97, 98, 99, and 108 of FASB Statement No. 116, a promise need not be legally enforceable to be considered an unconditional promise to give. A social and moral obligation to transfer the resources is sufficient to conclude that a promise to give exists.

4-49.   As previously discussed, certain communications may constitute expressions of intent to give where all discretion to transfer the resources rests with the donor, and the donor has the right to modify the commitment. Appendix B, Exhibits 3 and 4 to this Guide include a list of factors EJAC considers relevant to help organizations determine whether a particular communication from a donor qualifies as an unconditional promise to give.

4-50.   Financial statements should include certain footnote disclosures about pledges, including amounts of unconditional promises due in one year, one to five years, and after five years. In addition, the amount of any allowance for uncollectible pledges and quantifiable information about conditional promises received but not recorded should be disclosed in the notes to the financial statements (FASB Statement No. 116, paragraphs 24 and 25). Concentrations of credit risk in respect to pledges should be disclosed (FASB Statement No. 105, paragraph 12). (See Appendix C, Exhibit 2, Sample Small Ministry.)

Discounting of Pledges

4-51.   Unconditional promises to give that are expected to be collected or paid in more than one year should be discounted to their estimated present value to reflect the time value of money. Thus, a fully collectible pledge of $10,000 payable in five years might be initially recorded at $8,000 depending on the interest rate assumption used. (FASB Concepts Statement No. 7, *Using Cash Flow Information and Present Value in Accounting Measurements,* provides a detailed discussion of present value and its use in accounting measurements.) An organization may report the full $10,000 with the $2,000 offset, or it may present only the $8,000 net amount. [Note that this example assumes a $10,000 pledge that is expected to be fully collected. If the organization expects to collect only $7,000 of the pledge, then it should report the pledge at the present value of $7,000 (which would be approximately $5,600 depending on the interest rate assumption used), rather than the present value of $10,000 (which would be approximately $8,000 depending on the interest rate assumption used). The $3,000 that is expected to be uncollected is not reported as bad debt nor as an allowance for doubtful accounts. Organizations should use a subsidiary ledger to retain information concerning the $10,000 face amount of contributions promised in order to monitor collections of contributions promised.]

4-52. The $2,000 difference is then recognized as income over the period up to maturity. This practice is in conformity with Accounting Principles Board (APB) Opinion No. 21, *Interest on Receivables and Payables,* which should be considered for further guidance. However, unlike APB 21, FASB Statement No. 116 requires the subsequent accretion, or build-up, of the discount to be recorded as contribution income rather than as interest income. This is appropriate since there is no opportunity cost of lost interest associated with not collecting a pledge until a future period.

4-53. APB Opinion No. 21 does not apply to receivables and payables between "parent and subsidiary companies or between subsidiaries of a common parent" (paragraph 3f). SOP 94-3, *Reporting of Related Entities by Not-for-Profit Organizations,* which is discussed further in Chapter 8, provides guidance for determining whether a parent-subsidiary relationship exists.

4-54. Conditional promises to give (for example, a matching pledge or a pledge contingent on the occurrence of a natural disaster) should not be recorded until the conditions are substantially met. Also, conditional contributions that would otherwise be considered conditional should be considered unconditional if the possibility that the condition will not be met is remote. An advance payment against a conditional pledge should be recorded as a refundable advance (a liability) until the condition is substantially met. The amount of conditional pledges received should be disclosed in the footnotes.

Deferred Gifts

4-55. The term deferred gifts refers to a variety of giving arrangements in which ultimate receipt of the benefits of a gift is deferred until some later date or event. A simple example is a bequest. More complicated examples include lead trusts, remainder trusts, gift annuities, and life insurance. Trusts can be revocable or irrevocable. See Chapter 7 for a more extensive discussion of deferred gifts.

Legacies and Bequests

4-56.   Legacies and bequests made through a will or revocable living trust can always be changed prior to death. Therefore, such amounts are conditional and should not be reflected in the accounting records until the transfer has been approved by the probate court and the proceeds are measurable. Sometimes an individual will informally indicate to an organization that it is mentioned in that person's will and may disclose the amount involved. Only if the person has made a formal unconditional promise to include a certain bequest in a will would there possibly be a binding pledge, in which case the gift should be accounted for like any other pledge made while the person is alive.

Endowments

4-57.   Endowments are contributions from a donor who has stipulated that the principal remain intact in perpetuity or until the occurrence of a specified time or event. Endowment funds which are to remain intact in perpetuity (pure or true endowments) should be reported as permanently restricted support; term endowments should be reported as temporarily restricted support.

Income earned on endowment funds should be reported in the class of net assets consistent with any donor restrictions on the income or directly in the unrestricted class if there are no restrictions. Management may wish to initially record the income for internal financial statements in the same class as the endowment, but the income must be shown directly in the appropriate class for external financial reporting purposes. (Paragraphs 4-79 and 4-82 discuss gains and losses.) *(Canadian ministries, see 9-36.)*

Donated and Contributed Services

4-58.   Most organizations will face the issue of recording donated or contributed services at some time. The criteria for doing so are set forth in FASB Statement No. 116 and are fully applicable to all organizations. *(Canadian ministries, see 9-57.)*

Paragraphs 9 and 121 of FASB Statement No. 116 provide the following:

9.   Contributed Services

Contributions of services shall be recognized if the services received (a) create or enhance nonfinancial assets or (b) require specialized skills, are provided by individuals possessing those skills, and would typically need to be purchased if not provided by donation. Services requiring specialized skills are provided by accountants, architects, carpenters, doctors, electricians, lawyers, nurses, plumbers, teachers, and other professionals and craftsmen. Contributed services and promises to give services that do not meet the above criteria shall not be recognized. [Paragraph 10 sets forth certain disclosure requirements regarding contributed services.]

121. . . . [FASB] believes the conditions of paragraph 9 of this Statement limit recognition to only those services that will provide information that is clearly relevant, clearly measurable, and obtainable at a cost that does not exceed the benefits of the information provided. . . .

4-59. Examples of the kinds of contributed services frequently received by Christian ministries which may not meet the recognition criteria in Statement No. 116 and are therefore usually not recorded include Sunday school teachers, ushers, choir members, altar guild, vestry (or similar governing board members, as discussed in paragraphs 201–202 of FASB Statement No. 116), work groups, and workers at fairs, crusades, conferences, and the like. *A tax deduction is never allowed for the value of a volunteer's time.*

4-60. When the criteria for recognizing contributed services are met, organizations should record a value for the services contributed. FASB Statement No. 116, however, provides no guidance for determining an adequate, objective, clearly measurable basis for determining the value of contributed services. In circumstances in which contributed services meet the recognition in Statement No. 116, organizations should develop an objective basis for determining the fair value of those services. However, they should recognize that time and financial costs may be required to meet the complexities of this process. While volunteer labor is at the heart of most Christian ministries, attempts to compute a very precise amount for its value may divert time and resources from the ministry while contributing little to strengthen the ministry. In most cases, amounts which are sufficiently accurate for financial reporting purposes can be computed by using overall estimates of time worked by volunteers and appropriate average rates per hour for valuation of their services.

4-61. A question often encountered by Christian organizations is just which organization is the actual recipient of donated services. In many cases one organization will recruit, train, and deploy volunteers to a project, while the real beneficiaries of the services are other organizations or individuals. Examples include volunteers on work crusades, teachers, preachers, medical personnel, or Bible translators assigned to projects in remote locations. Judgment is required in such cases to determine whether the reporting organization is the true recipient of a contribution or merely an intermediary in facilitating the provision of volunteer services elsewhere by bringing together a willing donor and donee. Appendix B, Exhibit 5 to this Guide includes additional guidance on this matter that EJAC considers relevant. Key to the determination is the degree of ongoing control over the activities of the volunteers exercised by the reporting organization.

4-62.   When considering the application of the guidance in paragraph 4-58 [Statement No. 116, paragraph 9(b)], although the Statement lists some examples of what it means by "specialized skills," it gives no operational definition of such skills. Thus, organizations are on their own when assessing types of services other than those listed as to whether the skills qualify as specialized. Appendix B, Exhibit 6 to this Guide includes a list of factors EJAC believes relevant in making this assessment. As for the question of whether the organization would otherwise typically need to purchase the services if volunteers were not available, this will have to be determined by each ministry on a case-by-case basis for each kind of service. Note that this factor is not whether the organization would purchase the service, but whether it would need to purchase the service if not provided by donation. EJAC suggests that organizations would need to purchase the service when the services are related to support and revenue or if a major program would cease to exist if the services were not provided. Appendix B,

Exhibit 7 to this Guide includes a list of factors which EJAC believes may be helpful in making this judgment.

Valuing Contributed Services

4-63.   For volunteers who create or enhance nonfinancial assets, the basis of valuation would normally be the value (or added value) of the assets involved, less any purchased components, such as materials or paid workers. For other kinds of volunteers, two possible evaluative bases are:

- Recording of actual time worked by each individual. The hours worked should be valued at a reasonable locally available equivalent wage. For example, a surgeon who voluntarily forfeits a $200,000 a year salary in a major U.S. city to work in a mission in a developing nation for $30,000 has not really made a $170,000 contribution if the equivalent wage for similar surgeons in the developing country is $30,000.

  In determining fair value, hours worked or hourly wages may also need to be adjusted downward to reflect inefficiencies encountered due to the inexperience of volunteers.

- Application of a locally acceptable appraisal of the completed project, reduced to the individual cost components. The contributed value would exclude costs paid in cash (materials, contract labor, employee staff labor, or other paid services) and any profit component.

In any case, reasonableness of the value determined must be assured. Where the service has been provided through the auspices of an organization for a local ministry entity, concurrence as to reasonableness of the value assigned should be obtained from the benefited entity. The amount recorded, however, should not exceed the fair value of the asset or the service at the location in question. (See Appendix C, Exhibit 6, Sample Rescue Mission, Note 2.)

4-64.   Where this recognition of value is for construction type projects, the value of the contributed services must also be included in the recorded capitalized value of the constructed asset and subsequently depreciated. (If the project consists of constructing an asset which will later be given to another organization or to a needy individual, such as renovations of deteriorated housing or books recorded on tape for the blind, the value of the contributed services will be included in the recorded expense related to the value of the asset given away.) (See Appendix C, Exhibit 3, Sample Religious Broadcaster, Note 4.)

4-65.   When a ministry recognizes contributed labor, EJAC strongly recommends a conservative valuation of these services. The amount, nature, and extent of such services should be disclosed in the notes to the financial statements, as well as a description of the programs or activities for which the services were used. In addition, EJAC recommends that the method of valuation should be clearly disclosed in the notes to the financial statements. FASB Statement No. 116 encourages organizations to disclose the fair value of contributed services received but not recognized, if practicable. EJAC recommends that organizations disclose those amounts.

4-66.   When a person is provided with an amount which is stated to be (and in fact is) equivalent only to a "living allowance" in the location assigned (usually overseas) or nominal pay which is less than regular pay for comparable work within the organization at that location, the person is still considered a volunteer. For example, a retired hospital administrator who used to be paid $100,000 works as a missionary managing an organization's activities. The organization would otherwise have to pay $30,000 to hire someone. If the missionary receives a living allowance or pay of $5,000, the difference of $25,000 should be recorded as a gift.

Donated Materials and Facilities (Gifts-in-Kind)

4-67.   Donated materials, facilities (including the use of facilities for free or at below market rents, which is discussed further in paragraphs 4-74 and 4-75), and other assets (including intangibles such as patents, copyrights, and royalties) should be recorded at fair value when received or promised. Recording is necessary to properly account for all transactions of the organization, as well as to aid in control over all property received.

Fair values of contributions should be measured according to the criteria in Accounting Principles Board Opinion No. 29, *Accounting for Nonmonetary Transactions.* Paragraph 25 of that Opinion states that fair value "should be determined by referring to estimated realizable values in cash transactions of the same or similar assets, quoted market prices, independent appraisals, . . . and other available evidence." Paragraph 5.08 of the *AICPA NPO Guide* provides that "in determining fair value, organizations should consider the quality and quantity of the gifts, as well as any applicable discounts that would have been received by the organization, including discounts based on that quantity if the assets had been acquired in exchange transactions. If the gifts have no value, as might be the case for certain clothing and furniture that cannot be (a) used internally by the not-for-profit organization or for program purposes or (b) sold by the organization, the item received should not be recognized." *Interagency Gifts-in-Kind Standards* (January 1999), prepared by the Association of Evangelical Relief and Development Agencies (AERDO), also notes that the "fair value of a GIK donation is to be based on the market in which the items are most commonly sold, given the quantities donated; normally this would not be equivalent to retail price paid by an individual consumer." (See Appendix C, Exhibit 6, Sample Rescue Mission, especially Note 4.)

4-68. Gifts-in-kind which are intended to be sold or auctioned in fund-raising events by transferring them to another resource provider should initially be valued at the fair value at the date of receipt of the item. If the ultimate selling (auction) price is higher, the difference is accounted for as additional contribution revenue (reduction in contribution revenue if the price is less).

4-69. If a pledge (promise to give) is denominated in terms of a specified noncash item (e.g., so many shares of a specific common stock, a specific work of art, a specific piece of land, etc.), the fair value of the gift when finally received may differ from the fair value at the date of initial recording of the pledge. This difference may arise from either or both of two reasons: the donor may not give the same quantity of the item as was promised, or the value at the date of transfer may have changed due to changes in the fair value of the item given. How to account for such changes depends on what kind of item is involved, whether the change is an increase or decrease, and whether the change is due to a change in the collectibility of the pledge or a change in the intrinsic value of the item.

Guidance for recording such changes is in paragraph 5.55 to 5.61 of the *AICPA NPO Guide 2000*. *(Canadian ministries, see 9-55.)*

4-70.   It should be noted that the value in the hands of the donor or the amount of tax deduction which the donor is permitted to take is not necessarily the value which should be recorded by the recipient. Similarly, recipients of gifts of property are under no obligation to, and generally should not, provide substantiation of the value of a gift to the donor for purposes of supporting a tax deduction amount. The recipient should, of course, provide a receipt to the donor, but the receipt should merely acknowledge receipt of the described items. It is the responsibility of the donor to obtain independent substantiation of the value if needed for tax purposes. *(Canadian ministries, see 9-56.)*

4-71.   The basis for whether or not nonfinancial assets received (such as water, food, clothing, medical supplies, and building supplies received as part of disaster relief efforts) should be recorded as either (a) contribution revenue and program expense or (b) transfers of assets that are not contributions pursuant to the provisions of FASB Statement No. 136 depends on the nature of the arrangement and the control over those resources. (Paragraphs 4-31 to 4-36 discuss FASB Statement No. 136.) For example, Organization A solicits goods for disaster relief (or other such projects) in a particular country. The resource providers give to Organization A and do not know or specify exactly how the goods will or should be distributed or to whom. Organization A determines when the goods will be transferred, how they will be transferred, and to whom they will be given. The goods are under the control of Organization A and constitute gifts that should be objectively measured and reported as revenue and expense in Organization A's statement of activities.

In contrast, Organization A (or others) may make arrangements with Organization B to handle the transport and distribution of goods in a particular area in which Organization B has workers, identified needs, and the ability to carry out the distribution in a more efficient and effective manner than Organization A. Organization B should consider the guidance in FASB Statement No. 136 to determine whether it should report either (a) contribution revenue and program expense or (b) transfers of assets that are not contributions pursuant to the provisions of FASB Statement No. 136. If Organization B acts as an agent or intermediary and merely distributes the resources according to specific instructions provided by Organization A, Organization B should not report contribution revenue or program expense. Organization B is permitted, but not required, to report assets and liabilities for nonfinancial assets that it holds as an agent or intermediary at the balance sheet date, provided that it reports consistently from period to period and discloses its accounting policy.

4-72. Contributions of inventory should be reported in the period received and should be measured at fair value. If items are held for sale, the estimated selling price may be used as an estimate of fair value. While that amount is not known exactly until the items are sold (since some items never sell and others are marked down from the initial selling price), overall estimates will usually produce acceptable values to use for financial reporting purposes. EJAC believes that for most organizations following this Guide, there is no expectation that detailed inventory procedures, such as used by commercial entities, will be used, as the time and costs involved would often exceed the benefits of such efforts.

One method of estimating inventory is to base year-end inventory amounts on sales subsequent to year end, using the average inventory turnover to compute the correct amount; another is to use overall average values per pound, box, pallet, rack, truckload, or some similar unit of measure times the estimated quantity on hand. Either method should produce, at little cost, a value that is acceptably close to the precise amount if it were known. As discussed in paragraph 4-67, if the gifts have no value, as might be the case for certain clothing and furniture that cannot be (a) used internally by the not-for-profit organization or for program purposes or (b) sold by the organization, the item received should not be recognized.

A related issue is reporting of revenue related to donated items. For example, if items worth $1,000 are donated and later sold for $1,000 cash, it would be possible to either (1) report $1,000 of revenue or (2) report $1,000 of contributions, $1,000 of sales, and $1,000 cost of sales. The net result is the same: $1,000 increase in net assets. EJAC believes that the second method is preferable, since it more closely resembles the reporting used by commercial entities.

4-73. Organizations should be aware that there are significant governmental regulations regarding appraisal of and reporting the subsequent sale of certain gifts-in-kind. (Paragraphs 4-88 and 4-89 discuss tax rules related to charitable giving.)

4-74.   If an organization is the recipient of a long-term lease of property at no (or nominal) cost, this arrangement amounts to an unconditional promise—a pledge over the term of the lease. The fair value of the contribution is the present value of the rent that would otherwise have been payable less the stated amount of the lease payments (similar to the calculation of a capital lease under FASB Statement No. 13). However, the amount reported as contributions should not exceed the fair value of the property. An asset should be recorded at the time the initial contribution is recorded. That asset is a contribution receivable, but may be described in the financial statements based on the item whose use is being contributed, such as "building," rather than "contribution receivable." The revenue should be reported in the temporarily restricted class (the first year's amount is unrestricted) when the lease is entered into and a portion of the net assets reclassified to unrestricted each year as the property is used. An amount should be charged to rent expense and the contribution receivable reduced each year as the property is used. Because the initial contribution revenue is reported at the present value of the rent that would otherwise be payable less the stated amount of the lease payments, additional contribution revenue should be reported each year representing amortization of the discount on the contribution receivable and a corresponding amount reported as a reduction in the discount. (Paragraph 4-52 discusses accretion of discounts on contributions receivable.)

4-75.   A special case involving the donated use of facilities is sometimes encountered by missionary organizations: provision by an individual or organization of free use of living or working facilities to a missionary in the field or while on home leave. How to account for this use depends on the intent of the provider of the facilities. If the provider's intent is to support the organization which sponsors the missionary, then the use of the facilities should be recorded by the organization as described above. (If the facilities are contributed to the organization, the organization should consider whether taxable compensation to the employee for the use of the facilities is properly reported.) If, however, the provider's intent is primarily to support the missionary personally, then no amount should be recorded by the organization. In determining the appropriate reporting, the organization should consider (a) whether it would otherwise pay for comparable facilities for use by the individual and (b) evidence about the provider's intent. If the organization would otherwise pay for comparable facilities for use by the individual, it should report a contribution unless persuasive evidence exists that the provider intends to support the individual rather than the organization. (See paragraph 4-27 for discussion of tax issues related to such gifts.)

4-76. If expenses which benefit the reporting organization are paid directly on its behalf by another organization (whether affiliated or not) and not reimbursed, the other organization may have made a contribution to the reporting organization which should be recorded by both. (Note: The other organization, if taxable, may deduct the amount of expenses paid on behalf of an organization from its taxable income, which is eligible to receive tax-deductible gifts, but may not deduct the value of donated services of its personnel or use of its facilities. It may deduct the salaries or wages of the personnel and the costs of operating the facilities.)

Not every action by every person everywhere that somehow serves to further the purposes of an organization should be considered as a contribution to the organization. To determine whether a contribution has been made, organizations should consider who controls the provision of the service, the type of service provided, its relationship to the programs of the recipient, as well as the nature of the relationship between the provider of the services and the organization benefited. For example, an organization whose purpose is to preach the Gospel overseas does not have a basis to record a contribution to it for the value of every effort made by unrelated persons who just happen to be working for the same cause. Exhibit 5 in Appendix B may be helpful in making these judgments.

For there to be a basis for an organization to record a contribution, there must be some evidence that the provider of the services intended to further the programs of the specific organization and that the organization has some control over the provision of the service. Also, for a contribution to be recognized, there generally would be some formal or informal relationship between the organization and the provider.

Below-Market Rate Loans

4-77. Some organizations receive loans of cash that are interest free or that have below-market interest rates. Interest expense and contribution revenue should be reported in connection with loans of cash to organizations that are interest free or that have below-market interest rates (regardless of whether the loan is between related parties). Those contributions should be measured at fair value, which is the difference between the fair value of the loan at market rates and the fair value of the loan at its stated rate. The corresponding entry would be to interest income for the donor and to interest expense for the donee. (This issue is addressed in AICPA Technical Practice Aid No. 6140.05.) *(Canadian ministries, see 9-57.)*

EARNED INCOME

Income Earned on Investments

4-78. In general, accounting for investment income is governed by provisions of FASB Statement Nos. 117 and 124. Unrestricted investment income (interest, dividends, and the like) from investments of all classes of net assets should be reported as revenue (when it is earned) in the unrestricted net asset class of the statement of activities.

Income earned on investments of one of the restricted classes of net assets should only be included as revenue in a restricted net asset class if the earnings are expressly donor restricted. If the earnings are legally available for unrestricted purposes, they should be reported as unrestricted revenue. (See Appendix C, Exhibit 1, Sample Large Christian Organization.)

Gains and Losses on Investments

4-79. Gains and losses include both realized gains/losses on investments sold, as well as unrealized gains/losses resulting from changes in fair value of investments held. Prior to adoption of FASB Statement No. 124, there were two issues to consider in recording gains and losses on investments: when and how much to record, and how to record—that is, in which class of net assets. When and how much to record depends on the organization's accounting policy with respect to the carrying value of investments. This is discussed in Chapter 6. After adoption of FASB Statement No. 124, the timing question is largely moot as all marketable securities will be adjusted to market each period.

Paragraphs 8 and 9 of FASB Statement No. 124 provide the following:

8.   . . . gains and losses on investments shall be reported in the statement of activities as increases or decreases in unrestricted net assets unless their use is temporarily or permanently restricted by explicit donor stipulation or by law.

9.   . . . investment income shall be reported in the period earned as increases in unrestricted net assets unless the use of the assets received is limited by donor-imposed restrictions. Donor-restricted investment income is reported as an increase in temporarily restricted net assets or permanently restricted net assets, depending on the type of restriction.

Accounting for sales or exchanges of investments between classes of net assets, one of which is restricted, will result in a realized gain or loss in the selling class if sold at a price other than the carrying amount.

4-80.   Under paragraph 22 of FASB Statement No. 117, capital gains and losses are considered to be unrestricted revenue unless explicitly restricted:

- by a donor, or

- under the laws of the jurisdiction of domicile of the organization. Usually the law in question is the Uniform Management of Institutional Funds Act.

(See further discussion in Chapter 6.)

4-81.   Gains and losses on investments of endowment and trust funds (including realized and, if investments are carried at fair value, unrealized gains and losses) should be reported as changes in unrestricted net assets, unless gains and losses are temporarily or permanently restricted by explicit donor stipulations or by law that extends a donor's restriction to them. In applying that guidance, donor restrictions on the use of income of an endowment fund also extend to the net appreciation on the endowment fund. Applicable laws should be considered when determining the proper recording of these amounts.

4-82.   The notes to the financial statements should set forth a summary of the total realized and unrealized gains and losses and income derived during the fiscal period from investments held by all funds exclusive of life income and custodial funds.

Revenue from Sales of Goods and Services

4-83.   Many Christian organizations sell goods or services as part of their activities. Examples include sales of publications, air time on broadcasting stations, use of meeting facilities, educational conferences, special religious services such as weddings and funerals, and tuition and fees at educational institutions. Revenue from the sale of goods or services should be recorded when earned. If payment is received in advance, such as for an educational conference, the payment should be recorded as deferred revenue until the services are rendered. If payment is to be made at a later date, a receivable should be recorded when the services are rendered. This method should also be used for payments of bona fide membership dues. (See Appendix C, Exhibit 4, Sample Camp/Conference Center.)

It should be emphasized that all revenue which is not a contribution or donor-restricted investment income or gains is reported in the unrestricted class of net assets; only donated revenue can be reported in a restricted class. This is true even for some types of revenue which are subject to legal limitations resulting from sources other than a restriction imposed on a gift (or investment income on a gift) by the donor. For example, if a college needs to build a new dormitory but does not have the cash to pay for it, it may choose to finance construction by issuing revenue bonds. One provision in the bond indenture is likely to require the college to deposit all dormitory fees into an escrow account to be used to retire the bonds. Despite the legal limitation on the use of the fees, they are reported in the unrestricted class because the limitations are not the result of a donor-imposed restriction on a gift—dormitory fees are not gifts. EJAC recommends that there be clear disclosure of such legal limitations, either on the face of the balance sheet or in a note to the financial statements.

4-84.   Certain financial transactions between an organization and its personnel, such as expense reimbursements from individuals, should be recorded on a net basis; i.e., revenues netted against expenses. For example, if a missionary buys a book at the organization's bookstore or rents organization housing using mission funds, the amounts should be eliminated when the missionary's individual financial activity is combined with that of the organization for financial statement purposes. Other transactions should be recorded gross.

4-85.   Some organizations collect amounts which are called dues but for which "members" receive little or no benefits in return. Such payments are essentially contributions and should normally be accounted for as such. True membership dues (exchange transactions) should be amortized into income over the period covered by the amount paid. If a payment is genuinely part dues (exchange transaction) and part gift, as is often the case with certain "categories" of members (often referred to as "contributing," "sustaining," "benefactor," etc. members), then each part of the payment should be accounted for (that is, the earned portion computed) separately, in accordance with the normal rules for that type of revenue. Both parts may (but do not have to) be reported on a single line in the revenue section. (Paragraphs 5.15 and 5.16 of the *NPO Guide 2000* discuss membership dues.)

TAX MATTERS RELATED TO SUPPORT AND REVENUE

The following paragraphs discuss laws applicable in the United States. Readers should consult applicable laws of other countries as appropriate.

4-86.   There are several aspects of support and revenue of not-for-profit organizations which may give rise to tax concerns. These include:

- state and local charitable solicitation laws and registration requirements

- tax rules related to deduction of gifts by donors

- payroll tax reporting by the organization

- possible unrelated business income reporting and taxation

- possible state sales tax collection requirements

- the distinction between private foundations and public charities

4-87. It is not the purpose of this Guide to discuss these rules in detail; such information is available from sources listed in the bibliography. Organizations should also be aware of relevant national and local tax rules of all jurisdictions in which they operate (including other countries) and comply with them.

Tax Rules Related to Charitable Giving

4-88. There are two broad categories of such rules: those applicable to donors and those applicable to donees. Organizations which receive gifts do not, of course, have to comply with rules applicable to donors, but it is wise for them to be aware of such rules and be prepared to assist donors with their compliance. This is a matter of self-interest for the recipient; a donor who loses a tax deduction or has to pay a penalty for failure to comply with a tax law will be less likely to contribute to that recipient in the future. Some of these tax rules were discussed earlier at paragraphs 4-27 and 4-70. Additional information about deductibility of charitable gifts is set forth in Internal Revenue Service Publication 1391, *Deductibility of Payments Made to Charities Conducting Fund-Raising Events* and Publication 1771, *Charitable Contributions—Substantiation and Disclosure Requirements.*

4-89. The value of direct benefits or merchandise received by the donor (quid pro quo transactions) and the net deductible gift must be disclosed to a person making a gift in excess of $75 who receives a direct benefit. Participants in events providing a benefit to the donor should also be advised that the amount of the tax deduction which they can take must be reduced by the value (to the participant, not the cost to the event sponsor) of the benefit received. Note, however, that if a participant makes only a free-will offering (rather than paying admission or a mandatory fee), the full amount of the donation is deductible. *(Canadian ministries, see 9-9.)*

Tax law requires donors to obtain a receipt indicating the amount of the contribution for all separate gifts of $250 or more from the donee; otherwise a tax deduction for the gift will be disallowed. EJAC recommends that all tax-deductible gifts be properly acknowledged. Note that no deduction is available for gifts of services or for the use of property. However, out-of-pocket expenses incurred in connection with such gifts may be deducted when the services or use of property is given to a qualified charitable organization—not an individual.

Support-Raising

4-90. Under the support-raising concept, also called deputational fund-raising, the ministry generally determines an amount each staff member and/or volunteer is responsible to raise. Funds raised are often recorded in a support account identified for each worker. Charges are made against the support account to fund the worker's particular sphere of the charity's ministry. Charges for the ministry's overhead are often made against the support accounts.

This practice has occasionally been controversial because of the tendency on the part of some fund-raisers to represent that contributions will only be used to support the work of the individual doing the fund-raising. Although giving through an organization to earmarked individuals is not tax deductible, and conduit organizations operated to facilitate such are not tax exempt, unearmarked contributions to a qualified organization for use in its exempt programs are tax deductible.

Deputized fund-raising was recognized, and in at least some forms approved by the IRS in the 1950s and 60s. After decades of little attention, in the 1990s the IRS issued an adverse private letter ruling, challenged organizations' exemptions, and denied contribution deductions. The IRS appeared to believe that gifts in support of deputized fund-raising (traditional missionary ministry support) might represent nondeductible gifts to individuals rather than charitable gifts to an exempt organization. It consistently favored a "pooled" approach or system. (Under a pooled fund-raising concept, the amount of compensation does not bear a direct relationship to the amount raised by an individual worker. The ministry raises money to support a group of workers instead of worker-by-worker. There might just be one group—all the self-supported workers. Or, the group might be a team of workers, or all of the workers in a country, or all of the workers in a group of foreign fields, and so on.)

Following recent challenges and concerns, a group of Christian professionals initiated a series of contacts with the IRS in the late 1990s seeking definitive guidelines on what is necessary to protect the donor's deduction, and the organization's tax-exempt status.

The IRS initially addressed these issues informally in its *Technical Instruction Program for Fiscal Year 1999.* In a February 2000 letter, the IRS acknowledged that deputized fund-raising was compatible with tax exemption of the organization, and tax deduction of the donor's contributions.

The IRS has identified two essential principles:

1. The donor must intend to make a gift to the organization, not to the individual.

2. The organization must fully control the funds to accomplish its exempt purposes.

If either of these principles is missing, the donor's gift does not qualify for tax deduction. If the organization receives substantial support from deputized fund-raising of contributions that do not qualify, it may lose its tax-exempt status.

The IRS acknowledged that although tracking by an organization of funds raised by an individual missionary, staff member, or volunteer may show that contributions are earmarked, the organization may demonstrate that it has full control by the totality of the facts and circumstances.

The IRS suggested language to be included in solicitations that would help show that the organization has the necessary control: assuming that there is no conflicting language in other materials or understandings between the parties: "Contributions are solicited with the understanding that the donee organization has complete discretion and control over the use of all donated funds."

EJAC believes the suggested language (noted above) is in keeping with duties of control inherent for tax-exempt organizations and that it does not conflict with what may, from an accounting standpoint, be considered donor restricted for particular exempt purposes. The IRS concern is that funds are fully under organizational control for exempt purposes, rather than being controlled by or directed to particular individuals.

EJAC recommends organizations take the following action:

1. Adopt the recommended language (noted above) for all solicitations and donor receipts.

2. Develop training and supervision for workers to set forth communications that reinforce ministry control of resources.

3. Review communications with donors (including prayer letters, newsletters, solicitation literature and donor receipts) to remove statements or assurances inconsistent with the recommended language and control elements.

4. Utilize a budgetary approval process that includes supported worker funds.

5. Periodically review all programs and policies of the organization, including those relating to supported workers.

6. Conduct thorough screening of potential workers based on qualifications established by the ministry. The qualifications should principally be related to the ministry's exempt purposes and not primarily related to the amount of funds that may be raised by a worker.

7. Assign supported workers to programs and project locations by the ministry, based upon its assessment of an individual's skills and training and the specific needs of the ministry.

8. Set annual compensation levels for all workers to establish maximum compensation, based on reasonable compensation assessments for similar organizations.

9. Review financial policies and control practices to assure that control elements exist and are well documented. Among these controls should be the approval of work-related expenses, approval of general and overhead allocations, and the ability to redirect funds within the ministry's operation in the event a worker is terminated or the worker's ministry must be changed.

Tax Reporting Related to Remittances to Personnel

4-91. In addition to the normal withholding and reporting requirements relating to payroll, ministries may receive gifts for support of personnel at home or in the field. Tax authorities in other countries may consider the remittance of these gifts to ministry personnel as a payment of salaries or wages and, thus, subject them to local payroll tax withholding and reporting requirements.

Unrelated Business Income

4-92. Christian ministries may own or control activities or entities that generate income from activities beyond those described in the organization's mission statement. These are considered "unrelated business income" under provisions of governmental taxation laws. Unrelated business income (UBI), generally, is income resulting from activities that taxing authorities do not consider to be directly related to the organization's tax-exempt purposes. UBI should be reported to the appropriate federal and state governmental taxing authorities, if required. For additional information on this subject, see Internal Revenue Service Publication No. 598, *Tax on Unrelated Business Income of Exempt Organizations* and *The Law of Tax-Exempt Organizations,* Seventh Edition, Bruce R. Hopkins, John Wiley & Sons, Inc., 1998.

Unrelated business income should be reported in the financial statements as gross revenue, with related direct costs shown as either a deduction from the gross revenue or as an expense. Related income taxes should be recorded and disclosed, including deferred taxes (in accordance with Statement of Financial Accounting Standards No. 109) if applicable. EJAC encourages Christian ministries to disclose the nature of any unrelated business activity and the existence of debt-financed income.

There are two broad categories of UBI. One is, as the name implies, income from an unrelated business activity. The other is debt-financed income.

Unrelated Business Activity

4-93.   The activities which result in unrelated business income have three characteristics: (1) there is a trade or business, (2) it is regularly carried on, and (3) it is not related to the exempt purposes of the organization.

- Trade or business

  The "trade or business" characteristic provides that the activity be carried on similarly to, or in the manner and style which is typically associated with a trade or business. An important element of a customary business enterprise is the expectation of income or profit. When the organization is engaged in the selling of goods or services which are comparable to goods and services provided by commercial (for-profit) businesses, the activity could be considered a "trade or business."

- Regularly carried on

  An activity is "regularly carried on" if it is performed with the frequency and continuity of similar activities performed by commercial businesses. If a particular activity is performed by a commercial business on a year-round basis, it is not "regularly carried on" by an exempt organization doing it only two or three time a year. However, if an activity is commercially performed one month out of the year, it would be "regularly carried on" by an exempt organization doing it for that month. The critical comparison is with commercial (for-profit) businesses which also conduct the activity.

- Not related to exempt purposes

  An activity which is substantially related to the performance of a charity's tax-exempt purposes is not an unrelated business activity. Thus, the sale of religious magazine subscriptions is typically considered to further the tax-exempt purpose of a religious organization. However, a subcomponent may not be related. For example, the selling of advertising in a magazine may not be related to the exempt purposes, though the selling of subscriptions to the magazine would be.

4-94.   There are some specific exceptions to the UBI rules. Tax law provides two major areas where business activity will not result in unrelated business income. These are: (1) traditionally "charitable businesses" and (2) passive income items.

- Charitable business

  Three specific exemptions from UBI are provided for traditionally charitable businesses:

  - a business selling merchandise which has been received through gifts or contributions (example: a thrift shop)

  - a business existing primarily for the convenience of the members, students, patients, officers, and employees of the organization (example: a church or college book-store, noting items which are not convenience items may be taxable)

  - a business in which most of the work is performed by volunteers (example: some thrift shops)

- Passive income

  Charitable organizations have traditionally held temporary investments as well as long-term investments for endowment and other funds. The Internal Revenue Code specifically recognizes exemptions for many passive investment items including:

- dividends and interest

- royalties (from licenses of literary or other artistic efforts, patents, trademarks, and some kinds of mineral rights), but not royalties from debt-financed property or from a controlled organization

- rents from real property unless the property rented is debt-financed (but not rents from personal property such as equipment and vehicles, and not rents from real property where there are significant services provided with the real property, such as the rental of a hotel room)

- income from the sale of property (includes both real property and personal property), but the exemption does not include property considered inventory or otherwise held for sale in an unrelated business activity or for debt-financed property

4-95. Controlled organizations are the exception to the exceptions. The specific exemption of interest, royalties, and rents as previously discussed does not apply when an exempt organization receives them from a controlled entity. When a tax-exempt organization controls another entity (normally a taxable subsidiary, over 80% control), the interest, royalties, and rents received from the controlled entity are subject to tax in most situations. Dividends from a controlled corporation are still exempt.

Debt-Financed Income

4-96. Congress imposed a tax on debt-financed income for tax-exempt organizations that borrow money to purchase passive income items (similar to for-profit entities). Debt-financed income may exist if:

- an organization incurs debt because of the purchase of, or in order to purchase, an income-producing asset, whether or not the asset secures a debt and even if the debt was incurred before or after the actual purchase

- some of that debt remains within the twelve months prior to the income being received from the asset, whether through a sale, rent, dividend, interest, etc.

Debt-financed income may also exist if an organization accepts gifts or bequests of "mortgaged" property. The two most common circumstances are:

- the organization accepts responsibility to pay off the debt or mortgage

- the mortgage was put on the property within five years of being given to the organization, or the donor owned the property for less than five years

A charitable remainder trust that runs any business or farm or incurs debt to purchase or improve property or other income-producing assets loses its tax-exempt status and is deemed to have UBI.

4-97.   Exceptions to the debt-financed income rule include:

- Substantially all (85% or more) of any property is used for an organization's exempt purposes. Thus, if an organization leases out more than 15% of any property on which it has debt, it may be subject to tax unless another exception applies.

- The rented property is used by a related exempt organization to further its tax-exempt purposes.

- The lease of property is to a medical clinic entered into primarily for exempt purposes of the lessor.

- Life income contracts—if the remainder is payable to an exempt charitable organization.

- Neighborhood land rule—if an organization acquires real property in its "neighborhood" to use it primarily for tax-exempt purposes within ten years. Rental income may not be treated as debt-financed income. For churches, the land does not have to be in the immediate neighborhood of the primary structure. In addition, a church has up to fifteen years to use the property for its exempt purposes.

Managing Unrelated Business Income

4-98. If a Christian ministry has unrelated business income, wise planning includes:

- Keeping the records of income and expenses for the unrelated business activities separate from those of the other activities of the organization. Alternately, you may be able to separate such business expenses by use of consistent formula. Employee expenses, allocation of rental income, and expense for space utilized (including depreciation) for the unrelated business activity and appropriate allocation of overhead (including management time) all need particular attention and careful documentation.

- Having records and accounting systems that regularly identify and allocate all allowable UBI expenses. Doing this requires three things:

  1. A written method for identifying and allocating all expenses directly connected with generating unrelated business income

  2. A comprehensive chart of accounts that segregates specific related and unrelated income and expenses

  3. Recordkeeping forms and accounting procedures that capture the necessary data

- Paying estimated federal and state tax on anticipated unrelated business income quarterly.

- Filing Form 990-T, Exempt Organization Business Income Tax Return, reporting the UBI if the gross UBI is $1,000 or greater in a tax year. Net UBI in excess of $1,000 is taxed at the normal corporate rates. For charitable remainder trusts, Form 1041 is filed, and net UBI is taxed at taxable trust rates.

- Filing appropriate state tax returns.

- Evaluating if the organization's involvement in producing the unrelated business income is not substantial and therefore will not endanger an organization's tax exemption. No precise measure of "substantial" exists. The involvement of personnel, assets, finances, and time would all be considered.

Sales Tax Requirements

4-99. Organizations which receive revenue from the sales of some types of goods or services (e.g., books, tapes, seminars, etc.) may be required by the laws of the jurisdictions in which the sales occur to collect and remit sales taxes on taxable sales. Rules vary among jurisdictions as to what types of sales are taxable and when and how taxes are to be remitted to the government. Organizations contemplating such sales—even at temporary locations, such as conferences or crusades—should determine in advance the applicable requirements. Note that religious organizations are usually not exempt from such requirements merely by virtue of the nature of their activities, or if the payment is categorized as a "donation." For example, a $15 book provided or distributed in exchange for a $15 payment called a "suggested contribution" may be considered a sale, depending upon the substance of the transaction and state law, whereas a $15 book provided or distributed in exchange for a $500 gift would generally be considered a premium and thus not subject to sales tax. See also paragraph 4-89 regarding the receipting of gifts where benefits are received.

Private Foundation Status

4-100. The Internal Revenue Code classifies organizations exempt under Sec. 501(c)(3) (the section covering most religious organizations) as either "private foundations" or "public charities." Public charity status is by far the more desirable one to have, but organizations which receive much of their income in the form of (any or all of):

- investment income

- gifts totaling a large amount from any one donor

- gifts from "insiders" (members of the governing board, management, and their families)

- grants from private foundations

run the risk of being classified as a private foundation. This is not to say that organizations should refuse to accept these forms of revenue, but they should be aware of the possible consequences of having too much (usually over two-thirds) of their revenue come from these sources unless they are classified as a supporting organization (supporting a public charity or a church).

Chapter 5

Expenses

Contents

FUNCTIONAL CLASSIFICATION OF EXPENSES.......... 109

PROGRAM SERVICES 110

SUPPORTING ACTIVITIES 111
    Management and General Activities....................... 112
    Fund-Raising Activities 114
    Membership Development Activities 116

ALLOCATION OF EXPENSES....................................... 117
    Accounting for Costs Involving Fund-Raising 119
        Accounting for Joint Activities 119
        Purpose 119
        Audience 126
        Content 127
        Allocation Methods 128
        Incidental Activities 128
        Disclosures 129
    Furloughs, Sabbaticals, and Study Leaves 131

NATURAL CLASSIFICATION OF EXPENSES............... 132

GRANTS (INCLUDING SUPPORT TO AFFILIATED
    ORGANIZATIONS) 133

COSTS RELATED TO SALES OF GOODS AND SERVICES 137

Reductions in Amounts Charged for Goods and Services 137

ADVERTISING COSTS 138

INVESTMENT EXPENSES 139

POSTEMPLOYMENT EXPENSES 139

START-UP ACTIVITIES 141

NTERNAL USE SOFTWARE 141

LOSSES 143

Expenses

5-1.   Expenses of a Christian ministry are normally incurred in carrying out its program services and supporting activities. All expenses should be reported in the statement of activities as "decreases in unrestricted net assets" (FASB Statement No. 117, paragraph 20). No expenses should be reported in the restricted sections of the statement of activities. [When restrictions on temporarily restricted net assets have expired or been met, those amounts should be reclassified to unrestricted net assets. (Paragraphs 3-16 to 3-18 discuss reclassification of net assets.) The expenditure of these amounts (sometimes in an accounting period later than the period in which the restriction is met) is reported on the statement of activities as a reduction of unrestricted net assets.]

5-2.   Revenues and expenses result from an organization's ongoing major or central operations. Gains and losses result from an organization's peripheral or incidental activities and from events and circumstances that are largely beyond the control of the organization. Transactions that result in revenue or expenses for one organization may result in gains or losses for another organization. The reporting requirements for gains and losses are different from the requirements for reporting revenue and expense. (Paragraphs 5-52 through 5-55 discuss losses.)

5-3.   Expenses should be recognized on the accrual basis of accounting. (Paragraphs 1-8 to 1-11 discuss accrual accounting.)

Paragraph 13.05 of the *AICPA NPO Guide 2000* provides the following:

> 13.05. Expenses are recognized when an organization's economic benefits are used up in delivering or producing goods, rendering services, or other activities or when previously recognized assets are expected to provide reduced or no future benefits. Some expenses, such as cost of goods sold, are recognized simultaneously with revenues that result directly and jointly from the same transactions or other events as the expenses. Some expenses, such as

salaries, are recognized when cash is spent or liabilities are incurred for goods and services that are used up simultaneously with acquisition or soon after. Some expenses, such as depreciation, are allocated by systematic and rational procedures to the periods during which the related assets are expected to provide services. An expense or loss is also recognized if it becomes evident that the previously recognized future economic benefits of an asset have been reduced or eliminated, or that a liability has been incurred or increased, without associated economic benefits.

5-4.   There are two commonly accepted methods of reporting expenses—either by function or by natural (object) classification. *(Canadian ministries, see 9-6.)* These methods are described as follows:

- *Functional classification* reports expenses according to the purpose for which the costs are incurred. Examples of functional classifications are program services (goods or services being distributed to beneficiaries, customers, or members that fulfill the purposes or mission for which the organization exists) and supporting activities (all activities other than program activities—sometimes thought of as those indirectly related to the purposes for which the organization exists but necessary for its conduct; e.g., management and general, fund-raising, and membership development).

- *Natural classification* reports expenses according to the nature of the items acquired; e.g., salaries, benefits, travel, utilities, insurance, depreciation, interest expense, grants, professional fees, etc.

5-5.   Christian ministries are required by paragraph 26 of FASB Statement No. 117 to classify expenses so that the functional use of resources is shown in the financial statements or notes thereto. (Paragraphs 5-6 to 5-32 discuss the functional classification of expenses.) FASB Statement No. 117 requires Christian ministries that meet the definition of a *voluntary health and welfare organization* (and encourages all others) to also display expenses by their natural classification in a matrix format. (Paragraphs 5-33 to 5-35 discuss the natural classification of expenses.) EJAC recommends that not-for-profit organizations, other than voluntary health and welfare organizations, also provide information about expenses by their natural classification. (See Appendix C for illustrations.)

FUNCTIONAL CLASSIFICATION OF EXPENSES

5-6.   Users of financial statements are interested in information about the cost of major program services and the cost of supporting activities in carrying out those programs. This information becomes available only when expenses are summarized in the statement of activities or notes on a functional basis.

Paragraph 26 of the FASB Statement No. 117 states the following:

26.   Information about an Organization's Service Efforts

To help donors, creditors, and others in assessing an organization's service efforts, including the costs of its services and how it uses resources, a statement of activities or notes to financial statements shall provide information about expenses reported by their functional classification such as major classes of program services and supporting activities. . . .

5-7.   Functional reporting of program services and supporting activities requires that the ministry combine the expenses of particular activities according to their essential purpose. For example, if an organization recognizes the operation of Bible schools and seminaries as one of its major programs, it should include in the gross expenses of that program the expenses of instructional activities, direct supervision of the program, and auxiliary activities (such as the dining hall, the infirmary, and the bookshop), which are integral parts of that program. Some expenses may need to be allocated among several functions. (Paragraphs 5-24 to 5-32 discuss the allocation of expenses.)

5-8.   Expenses for program services should be separated from expenses for supporting activities of the organization. Each should be clearly disclosed in the financial statements or notes thereto (see Appendix C for examples). EJAC recommends that a brief description of each category of functional expenses (program services and supporting activities) also be included in the notes to the financial statements. *(Canadian ministries, see 9-6.)*

PROGRAM SERVICES

Paragraph 27 of the FASB Statement No. 117 provides the following:

27.   Program services are the activities that result in goods and services being provided to beneficiaries, customers, or members that fulfill the purposes or mission for which the organization exists. Those services are the major purpose for and the major output of the organization and often represent several major programs. For example, a large university may have programs for student instruction, research, and patient care, among others. Similarly, a health and welfare organization may have programs for health or family services, research, disaster relief, and public education, among others.

5-9.   Expenses of an organization should be to further its stated purposes as articulated in its charter, bylaws and, if applicable, its representations to tax authorities. The organization should report its major program services and the applicable expenses for each. Typical expenses of program services include salaries and benefits, travel, supplies, printing, noncapitalized equipment, depreciation, and all other direct or indirect expenses applicable to the activity.

5-10.   The functional reporting classifications for program services will vary from one organization to another, depending upon the nature of ministries in which each organization is involved. A single functional reporting classification may be adequate to portray the program services of some organizations. However, most organizations provide more than one identifiable program and should report separately for each major program or group of programs. In addition, some organizations may want to present their program expenses by location; e.g., region, country, or continent.

Appendix F of this Guide provides examples of program services for various types of Christian ministries. Use of these categories (where applicable) will help promote more uniformity and understanding in reporting by not-for-profit organizations in general. EJAC recommends that adaptations be made only if these categories do not properly reflect the activities of a particular organization.

5-11. In order to maximize the amount reported as program expenses, ministries sometimes seek to charge as much as possible of their expenses to program services. However, unless a reasonable, practical, and verifiable reason exists for charging an expense to a specific program, it should be charged to the appropriate supporting activity.

5-12. If the components of total program expense are not evident on the face of the statement of activities, the notes to the financial statements should disclose total program expense and should provide information about why total program expense disclosed in the notes does not directly tie into the statement of activities.

SUPPORTING ACTIVITIES

5-13. Supporting activities make it possible to perform the program services of the organization. These activities include management and general, fund-raising, and membership development. *(Canadian ministries, see 9-6.)*

Paragraph 28 of the FASB Statement No. 117 provides the following:

> 28. Supporting activities are all activities of a not-for-profit organization other than program services. Generally, they include management and general, fund-raising, and membership-development activities. Management and general activities include oversight, business management, general record keeping, budgeting, financing, and related administrative activities, and all management and administration except for direct conduct of program services or fund-raising activities. . . .

Paragraph 13.34 of the *AICPA NPO Guide 2000* provides the following:

> 13.34. Management and general activities are those that are not identifiable with a single program, fund-raising activity, or membership-development activity but that are indispensable to the conduct of those activities and to an organization's existence.

They include oversight, business management, general record keeping, budgeting, financing, soliciting revenue from exchange transactions, such as government contracts and related administrative activities, and all management and administration except for direct conduct of program services or fund-raising activities. The costs of oversight and management usually include the salaries and expenses of the governing board, the chief executive officer of the organization, and the supporting staff. (If such staff spend a portion of their time directly supervising program services or categories of other supporting services, however, their salaries and expenses should be allocated among those functions.) The costs of disseminating information to inform the public of the organization's "stewardship" of contributed funds, announcements concerning appointments, and the annual report, among other costs, should similarly be classified as management and general expenses. The costs of soliciting funds other than contributions, including exchange transactions (whether program related or not), should be classified as management and general expenses.

Management and General Activities

5-14. General purpose financial statements should show management and general expenses as a separate functional category. The following is a representative (but not comprehensive) list of typical management and general expenses:

- general board and committee meetings

- executive direction and corporate planning

- office management

- corporate legal services

- procuring personnel, except volunteers (as discussed in paragraph 5-19, soliciting volunteers is a fund-raising activity)

- purchasing and distributing materials (other than materials that are used for program or fund-raising purposes)

- receptionist, switchboard, mail distribution, filing, and other office services

- organization and procedure studies

- accounting, auditing, budgeting, and external financial reporting

- internal financial and management reporting

- interest and other financing expenses to the extent not allocated to other functions (paragraph 5-25 discusses allocating interest and other financing expenses)

- management information systems

- a portion of occupancy costs

- advertising (paragraph 5-43 discusses reporting advertising activities)

- other activities indispensable to the organization's existence but not identifiable with any program, fund-raising, or membership development activity

5-15. Supervision and employee training should be reported as management and general, fund-raising, or program if they apply directly to one of those functions: direct supervision of specific individual programs should be charged to the specific program; the costs of domestic and overseas administrative personnel not chargeable to a specific program are to be reported as management and general; administrative costs directly related to fund-raising activities should be charged to fund-raising. Some activities in the above list may be reported as a function other than management and general; for example, legal services related to acquiring land for a camping program, or committees gathered to coordinate a specific program or fund-raising project.

Routine acknowledgment of contributions or dues is management and general if the acknowledgment includes a further appeal for funds or if donor records beyond those required for adequate accountability are maintained; however, those activities should be accounted for in conformity with SOP 98-2, *Accounting for Costs of Activities of Not-for-Profit Organizations and State and Local Governmental Entities That Include Fund-Raising,* which is discussed in paragraphs 5-28 and 5-29 of this chapter.

Expenses incurred in keeping a ministry's name before the public (ministry awareness) may be management and general rather than fund-raising. The cost of disseminating information to inform the public of the ministry's stewardship of contributed funds (the annual report, etc.) should likewise be classified as management and general. However, if the activity is done in conjunction with a fund-raising appeal, it should be accounted for in conformity with SOP 98-2, which is discussed in paragraphs 5-28 and 5-29 of this chapter.

Fund-Raising Activities

5-16.   Fund-raising activities involve encouraging regular and potential donors to contribute money, securities, materials, facilities, other assets, services or time to the organization. Activities that are undertaken with the hope of receiving contributions are considered fund-raising activities, even if the activities do not explicitly ask for contributions. For example, an organization or individual making support needs or investment opportunities known is undertaking fund-raising activities. The financial statements should disclose total fund-raising expenses.

The *AICPA NPO Guide 2000* Glossary provides the following:

> Fund-raising activities are activities undertaken to induce potential donors to contribute money, securities, services, materials, facilities, other assets, or time. They include publicizing and conducting fund-raising campaigns; maintaining donor mailing lists; conducting special fund-raising events; preparing and distributing fund-raising manuals, instructions, and other materials; and conducting other activities involved with soliciting contributions from individuals, foundations, governments, and others.

5-17.   God provides for all our needs, but as Elijah was required to ask the widow of Zarephath for food (I Kings 17: 8-16), Christian ministries generally receive God's provision when, by faith, they contact those through whom God will provide. Thus, ethical fund-raising is a proper part of an organization's activities. In Christian ministries, this is generally referred to as securing support, deputation, extension, mission challenge, donor relations, public relations, constituency development, promotion, stewardship, planned giving, or similar terms.

5-18.   Expenditures that generally should be charged to this function include costs of developing, producing, and transmitting appeals for contributions (including the appropriate portion of radio and TV programs, printing, postage, consultants, addressing, and maintenance of mailing lists and other records), preparation and distribution of fund-raising manuals, and the salaries of personnel connected with the fund-raising activity. Salaries and other expenses of any staff members who support fund-raising activities should be proportionately allocated to fund-raising. Fund-raising expenses of affiliates should also be charged to this function.

5-19.   Fund-raising includes encouraging potential donors to contribute their services and time, so costs related to recruiting volunteers (unpaid workers) should be included in fund-raising expenses, regardless of whether the services contributed by those volunteers meet the recognition criteria for contributed services. (Paragraphs 4-58 to 4-66 of Chapter 4 discuss accounting for contributed services.) (Paragraph 5-24 discusses reporting the costs of recruiting personnel for compensated positions.)

5-20.   In some cases, fund-raising activities are carried out jointly with other activities. When this occurs, allocation of joint costs may be required. If certain activities (e.g., furlough activity such as discussed in 5-30 to 5-32) include a significant element of encouraging contributions to the organization, a portion of the expenses of that activity may also be required to be allocated to fund-raising. (Paragraphs 5-28 and 5-29 discuss SOP 98-2.)

5-21.   Even if fund-raising activities result in donor-restricted income, the fund-raising expenses must be reported as a reduction of unrestricted net assets. Fund-raising costs should be expensed as incurred even if the activity is expected to produce benefits in future periods. Costs are incurred when an item or service has been rendered. Accordingly, a supply of brochures or production costs of broadcasts not yet aired should be expensed even though the brochures have not yet been distributed or the broadcast has not aired.

Membership Development Activities

5-22.   Organizations which derive revenue from members' dues generally incur expenses related to that revenue. Such expenses, if material, should be reported in a membership development category within supporting activities. (Expenses incurred to solicit dues which are in fact contributions should be reported as fund-raising activities. Paragraph 4-85 of Chapter 4 discusses accounting for membership dues. If membership dues are in part contributions and in part exchange transactions, soliciting membership dues is a joint activity and should be accounted for in conformity with SOP 98-2, which is discussed in paragraphs 5-28 and 5-29 of this chapter. Under SOP 98-2, some or all of the costs of soliciting those dues should be reported as fund-raising in circumstances in which membership dues are a joint activity.) The focus is upon the form of revenue rather than governance. This category of functional expenses does not apply to most churches, colleges, or missionary organizations; however, associations of such organizations frequently collect dues from their member organizations.

Paragraph 28 of the FASB Statement No. 117 provides the following:

. . . Membership-development activities include soliciting for prospective members and membership dues, membership relations, and similar activities.

5-23.   Membership organizations should report, in a separate category of supporting expenses, the cost of soliciting prospective members, sending membership renewal notices, and similar expenses, subject to the constraints of SOP 98-2, which is discussed in paragraphs 5-28 and 5-29 of this chapter.

ALLOCATION OF EXPENSES

5-24. Most not-for-profit organizations have multiple functions; therefore, one expense may apply to more than one function. In those cases, expenses should be allocated to the program services and supporting activities benefited, including the possible allocation of salary and related expenses of an individual among two or more activities. For example, (1) the salary of a Bible school teacher might be allocated to the Bible school ministry for eight months and to church growth and evangelism for the rest of the year (where he/she is involved during the four "nonschool" months), (2) the automobile expenses of an administrator who, in addition to the otherwise 400-mile route to a management seminar, drives 100 miles in order to solicit a prospective donor could be allocated 20% to fund-raising and 80% to management and general, and (3) the expenses of a home telephone used occasionally for employment-related calls should be treated as a personal expense except for long-distance or other specific charges which can be attributed directly to employment.

GAAP is not explicit about costs of activities that may be commonly considered general and administrative activities, but which in fact can be identifiable with a particular function other than general and administrative, such as the costs of a human resource department, including recruiting costs. EJAC recommends that to the extent those costs can be identified with a particular function and it is practicable to allocate them, the costs should be allocated. For example, costs of a human resource department that are identifiable with particular functions, such as orientation of new field personnel of a mission-sending agency and related training on cross-cultural issues, should be reported as costs of the functions to which those persons will be assigned. Costs of core human resource activities that are not identifiable with a particular function should be reported as general and administrative costs. Additionally, EJAC recommends that the costs of recruiting personnel for compensated positions be reported as a cost of the function served by the position. Similarly, EJAC recommends that the costs of training and managing either volunteer or compensated personnel be reported as a cost of the function for which they are being trained and managed.

5-25. Building expenses, such as depreciation, utilities, and directly related interest, should be allocated to functions based on use of the building.

Paragraph 13.40 of the *AICPA NPO Guide 2000* provides the following:

> 13.40 . . . the expenses associated with occupying and maintaining a building, such as depreciation, utilities, maintenance, and insurance, may be allocated based on the square footage of space occupied by each program and supporting service. If floor plans are not available and the measurement of the occupied space is impractical, an estimate of the relative portion of the building occupied by each function may be made. Occupying and maintaining a building is not a separate supporting service.
>
> Interest costs, including interest on a building's mortgage, should be allocated to specific programs or supporting services to the extent possible; interest costs that cannot be allocated should be reported as part of the management and general function.

If capitalized interest costs are allocated to more than one function (or for other reasons are not reported as a single amount in the statement of activities), total interest cost should be disclosed in the notes to the financial statements.

5-26. Extensive detailed records maintained for the purpose of allocating expenses are not required; reasonable estimates based on objective criteria may be used. However, the basis for allocating expenses should be consistent from period to period and any changes in the basis for allocating expenses should be disclosed.

5-27. For further examples of expense allocation methods, see Appendix F. A not-for-profit organization seeking more detailed expense allocation methods may find the following useful:

- National Health Council's *Standards of Accounting and Financial Reporting for Voluntary Health and Welfare Organizations* (1998), Chapter V and Appendix 1

- *Financial and Accounting Guide for Not-for-Profit Organizations*

(Sixth Edition, 2000) by Malvern J. Gross, Jr., Richard F. Larkin, and John H. McCarthy

Accounting for Costs Involving Fund-Raising

5-28. In 1998, the AICPA issued SOP 98-2, *Accounting for Costs of Activities of Not-for-Profit Organizations and State and Local Governmental Entities That Include Fund-Raising,* which supersedes SOP 87-2, *Accounting for Joint Costs of Informational Materials and Activities of Not-for-Profit Organizations That Include a Fund-Raising Appeal* (as incorporated in the *NPO Guide*).

The SOP defines a joint activity as an "activity that is part of the fund-raising function and has elements of one or more other functions, such as program, management and general, membership development, or any other functional category used by the entity," and provides as follows:

Accounting for Joint Activities

7. If the criteria of purpose, audience, and content are met, the costs of a joint activity that are identifiable with a particular function should be charged to that function and joint costs should be allocated between fund-raising and the appropriate program or management and general function. If any of the criteria are not met, all costs of the joint activity should be reported as fund-raising costs, including costs that otherwise might be considered program or management and general costs if they had been incurred in a different activity, subject to the exception in the following sentence. Costs of goods or services provided in exchange transactions that are part of joint activities, such as costs of direct donor benefits of a special event (for example, a meal), should not be reported as fund-raising.

Purpose

8. The purpose criterion is met if the purpose of the joint activity includes accomplishing program or management and general

functions. (Paragraphs 9 and 10 provide guidance that should be considered in determining whether the purpose criterion is met. Paragraph 9 provides guidance pertaining to program functions only. Paragraph 10 provides guidance pertaining to both program and management and general functions.)

9. Program functions. To qualify as program functions, the activity should call for some specific action by the audience that will help accomplish the entity's mission. For purposes of applying the guidance in this SOP, the following are examples of activities that do and do not call for specific action by the audience that will help accomplish the entity's mission:

- An entity's mission includes improving individuals' physical health. For that entity, motivating the audience to take specific action that will improve their physical health is a call for specific action by the audience that will help accomplish the entity's mission. An example of an activity that motivates the audience to take specific action that will improve their physical health is sending the audience a brochure that urges them to stop smoking and suggests specific methods, instructions, references, and resources that may be used to stop smoking.

- An entity's mission includes educating individuals in areas other than the causes, conditions, needs, or concerns that the entity's programs are designed to address (referred to hereafter in this SOP as "causes"). For that entity, educating the audience in areas other than causes or motivating the audience to otherwise engage in specific activities that will educate them in areas other than causes is a call for specific action by the audience that will help accomplish the entity's mission. Examples of entities whose mission includes educating individuals in areas other than causes are universities and possibly other entities. An example of an activity motivating individuals to engage in education in areas other than causes is a university inviting individuals to attend a lecture or class in which the individuals will learn about the solar system.

- Educating the audience about causes or motivating the audience to otherwise engage in specific activities that will educate them about causes is not a call for specific action by the audience that will help accomplish the entity's mission. Such activities are considered in support of fund-raising. (However, some educational activities that might otherwise be considered as educating the audience about causes may implicitly call for specific action by the audience that will help accomplish the entity's mission. For example, activities that educate the audience about environmental problems caused by not recycling implicitly call for that audience to increase recycling. If the need for and benefits of the specific action are clearly evident from the educational message, the message is considered to include an implicit call for specific action by the audience that will help accomplish the entity's mission.)

- Asking the audience to make contributions is not a call for specific action by the audience that will help accomplish the entity's mission.

  If the activity calls for specific action by the audience that will help accomplish the entity's mission, the guidance in paragraph 10 should also be considered in determining whether the purpose criterion is met.

10. Program, management and general functions. The following factors should be considered, in the order in which they are listed, [FN5 In considering the guidance in paragraph 10, the factor in paragraph 10a (the compensation or fees test) is the preeminent guidance. If the factor in paragraph 10a is not determinative, the factor in paragraph 10b (whether a similar program or management and general activity is conducted separately and on a similar or greater scale) should be considered. If the factor in paragraph 10b is not determinative, the factor in paragraph 10c (other evidence) should be considered.] to determine whether the purpose criterion is met:

a. Whether compensation or fees for performing the activity are based on contributions raised. The purpose criterion is not met if a majority of compensation or fees for any party's performance of any component of the discrete joint activity varies based on contributions raised for that discrete joint activity. [FN6 Some compensation contracts provide that compensation for performing the activity is based on a factor other than contributions raised, but not to exceed a specified portion of contributions raised. For example, a contract may provide that compensation for performing the activity is $10 per contact hour, but not to exceed 60 percent of contributions raised. In such circumstances, compensation is not considered based on amounts raised, unless the stated maximum percentage is met. In circumstances in which it is not yet known whether the stated maximum percentage is met, compensation is not considered based on amounts raised, unless it is probable that the stated maximum percentage will be met.] [FN7 The compensation or fees test is a negative test in that it either (a) results in failing the purpose criterion or (b) is not determinative of whether the purpose criterion is met. Therefore, if the activity fails the purpose criterion based on this factor (the compensation or fees test), the activity fails the purpose criterion and the factor in paragraph 10b should not be considered. If the purpose criterion is not failed based on this factor, this factor is not determinative of whether the purpose criterion is met and the factor in paragraph 10b should be considered.]

b. Whether a similar program or management and general activity is conducted separately and on a similar or greater scale. The purpose criterion is met if either of the following two conditions is met:

    (1) Condition 1:

        The program component of the joint activity calls

for specific action by the recipient that will help accomplish the entity's mission and

A similar program component is conducted without the fund-raising component using the same medium and on a scale that is similar to or greater than the scale on which it is conducted with the fund-raising. [FN8 Determining the scale on which an activity is conducted may be a subjective determination. Factors to consider in determining the scale on which an activity is conducted may include dollars spent, the size of the audience reached, and the degree to which the characteristics of the audience are similar to the characteristics of the audience of the activity being evaluated.]

(2) Condition 2:

A management and general activity that is similar to the management and general component of the joint activity being accounted for is conducted without the fund-raising component, using the same medium and on a scale that is similar to or greater than the scale on which it is conducted with the fund-raising.

If the purpose criterion is met based on the factor in paragraph 10b, the factor in paragraph 10c should not be considered.

c. Other evidence. If the factors in paragraph 10a or 10b do not determine whether the purpose criterion is met, other evidence may determine whether the criterion is met. All available evidence, both positive and negative, should be considered to determine whether, based on the weight of that evidence, the purpose criterion is met.

11. The following are examples of indicators that provide evidence for determining whether the purpose criterion is met:

a. Evidence that the purpose criterion may be met includes:

- Measuring program results and accomplishments of the activity. The facts may indicate that the purpose criterion is met if the entity measures program results and accomplishments of the activity (other than measuring the extent to which the public was educated about causes).

- Medium. The facts may indicate that the purpose criterion is met if the program component of the joint activity calls for specific action by the recipient that will help accomplish the entity's mission and if the entity conducts the program component without a significant fund-raising component in a different medium. Also, the facts may indicate that the purpose criterion is met if the entity conducts the management and general component of the joint activity without a significant fund-raising component in a different medium.

b. Evidence that the purpose criterion may not be met includes:

- Evaluation or compensation. The facts may indicate that the purpose criterion is not met if (a) the evaluation of any party's performance of any component of the discrete joint activity varies based on contributions raised for that discrete joint activity or (b) some, but less than a majority, of compensation or fees for any party's performance of any component of the discrete joint activity varies based on contributions raised for that discrete joint activity.

c. Evidence that the purpose criterion may be either met or not met includes:

- Evaluation of measured results of the activity. The entity may have a process to evaluate measured program results and accomplishments of the activity (other than measuring the extent to which the public was educated about causes). If the entity has such a process, in evaluating the effectiveness of the joint activity, the entity may place significantly greater weight on the activity's effectiveness in accomplishing program goals or may place significantly greater weight on the activity's effectiveness in raising contributions. The former may indicate that the purpose criterion is met. The latter may indicate that the purpose criterion is not met.

- Qualifications. The qualifications and duties of those performing the joint activity should be considered.

  - If a third party, such as a consultant or contractor, performs part or all of the joint activity, such as producing brochures or making telephone calls, the third party's experience and the range of services provided to the entity should be considered in determining whether the third party is performing fund-raising, program (other than educating the public about causes), or management and general activities on behalf of the entity.

  - If the entity's employees perform part or all of the joint activity, the full range of their job duties should be considered in determining whether those employees are performing fund-raising, program (other than educating the public about causes), or management and general activities on behalf of the entity. For example, (a) employees who are not members of the fund-raising department and (b) employees who are members of the fund-raising department but who perform non-fund-raising activities are more likely to perform activities that include program or management and general functions than are employees who otherwise devote significant time to fund-raising.

- Tangible evidence of intent. Tangible evidence indicating the intended purpose of the joint activity should be considered. Examples of such tangible evidence include:

  - The entity's written mission statement, as stated in its fund-raising activities, bylaws, or annual report

  - Minutes of board of directors', committees', or other meetings

  - Restrictions imposed by donors (who are not related parties) on gifts intended to fund the joint activity

  - Long-range plans or operating policies

  - Written instructions to other entities, such as script writers, consultants, or list brokers, concerning the purpose of the joint activity, audience to be targeted, or method of conducting the joint activity

  - Internal management memoranda

Audience

12. A rebuttable presumption exists that the audience criterion is not met if the audience includes prior donors or is otherwise selected based on its ability or likelihood to contribute to the entity. That presumption can be overcome if the audience is also selected for one or more of the reasons in paragraph 13a, 13b, or 13c. In determining whether that presumption is overcome, entities should consider the extent to which the audience is selected based on its ability or likelihood to contribute to the entity and contrast that with the extent to which

it is selected for one or more of the reasons in paragraph 13a, 13b, or 13c. For example, if the audience's ability or likelihood to contribute is a significant factor in its selection and it has a need for the action related to the program component of the joint activity, but having that need is an insignificant factor in its selection, the presumption would not be overcome.

13. In circumstances in which the audience includes no prior donors and is not otherwise selected based on its ability or likelihood to contribute to the entity, the audience criterion is met if the audience is selected for one or more of the following reasons:

   a. The audience has a need to use or a reasonable potential to use the specific action called for by the program component of the joint activity.

   b. The audience has the ability to take specific action to assist the entity in meeting the goals of the program component of the joint activity.

   c. The entity is required to direct the management and general component of the joint activity to the particular audience, or the audience has reasonable potential for use of the management and general component.

Content

14. The content criterion is met if the joint activity supports program or management and general functions, as follows:

   a. Program. The joint activity calls for specific action by the recipient that will help accomplish the entity's mission. If the need for and benefits of the action are not clearly evident, information describing the action and explaining the need for and benefits of the action is provided.

   b. Management and general. The joint activity fulfills

one or more of the entity's management and general responsibilities through a component of the joint activity. [FN9 Some states or other regulatory bodies require that certain disclosures be included when soliciting contributions. For purposes of applying the guidance in this SOP, communications that include such required disclosures are considered fund-raising activities and are not considered management and general activities.]

15. Information identifying and describing the entity, causes, or how the contributions provided will be used is considered in support of fund-raising.

Allocation Methods

16. The cost allocation methodology used should be rational and systematic; it should result in a reasonable allocation of joint costs; and it should be applied consistently given similar facts and circumstances.

Incidental Activities

17. Some fund-raising activities conducted in conjunction with program or management and general activities are incidental to such program or management and general activities. For example, an entity may conduct a fund-raising activity by including a generic message, "Contributions to Organization X may be sent to [address]" on a small area of a message that would otherwise be considered a program or management and general activity based on its purpose, audience, and content. That fund-raising activity likely would be considered incidental to the program or management and general activity being conducted. Similarly, entities may conduct program or management and general activities in conjunction with fund-raising activities that are incidental to such fund-raising activities. For example, an entity may conduct a program activity by including a generic program message such as "Continue to pray for [a particular

cause]" on a small area of a message that would otherwise be considered fund-raising based on its purpose, audience, and content. That program activity would likely be considered incidental to the fund-raising activity being conducted. Similarly, an entity may conduct a management and general activity by including a brief management and general message—"We recently changed our phone number. Our new number is 123-4567"—on a small area of a message that would otherwise be considered a program or fund-raising activity based on its purpose, audience, and content. That management and general activity would likely be considered incidental to the program or fund-raising activity being conducted. In circumstances in which a fund-raising, program, or management and general activity is conducted in conjunction with another activity and is incidental to that other activity, and the conditions in this SOP for allocation are met, joint costs are permitted but not required to be allocated and may, therefore, be charged to the functional classification related to the activity that is not the incidental activity. However, in circumstances in which the program or management and general activities are incidental to the fund-raising activities, it is unlikely that the conditions required by this SOP to permit allocation of joint costs would be met.

Disclosures

18. Entities that allocate joint costs should disclose the following in the notes to their financial statements:

   a. The types of activities for which joint costs have been incurred

   b. A statement that such costs have been allocated

   c. The total amount allocated during the period and the portion allocated to each functional expense category

5-29. In other words, to report any portion of an activity that includes fund-raising as anything but fund-raising requires:

- *Purpose.* The purpose of the activity includes a non-fund-raising component, such as program, management and general, or membership development and a majority of fees for any individual or entity performing the activity do not vary with (are not based on) contributions raised.

- *Audience.* A rebuttable presumption exists that the audience criterion is not met if the audience includes prior donors or is otherwise selected based on its ability or likelihood to contribute to the entity. That presumption can be overcome if the audience is also selected for program or management and general purposes. The extent to which the audience is selected for fund-raising purposes should be weighed against the extent to which the audience is selected for program or management and general purposes.

- *Content.* The content criterion is met if the activity supports program or management and general functions, as follows:

  Program. The activity calls for specific action by the recipient that will help accomplish the entity's mission. If the need for and benefits of the action are not clearly evident, information explaining the need for and benefits of the action, as well as sufficient detail describing the action, is provided.

  Management and General. The activity fulfills one or more of the entity's management and general responsibilities through a component of the activity. (For example, including a request for contributions along with a receipt that is required for IRS purposes.)

  (Information identifying and describing the entity or stating the needs or concerns to be met or how the contributions provided will be used is considered in support of fund-raising.)

For membership development activities that include fund-raising, to the extent that member benefits are received, membership is an exchange transaction. In circumstances in which membership development is in part soliciting revenues from exchange transactions and in part soliciting contributions and the purpose, audience, and content of the activity are appropriate for achieving membership development, joint costs should be allocated between fund-raising and the exchange transaction.

If all three criteria are met (purpose, audience, and content), costs that are specifically identifiable with a particular function should be charged to that function and joint costs should be allocated. If any of the three criteria are not met, all costs of the activity should be charged to fund-raising, including costs that would otherwise be identifiable as program, management and general, or membership development if they had been incurred in a different activity. The exception is that the costs of exchange transactions, such as costs of donor benefits, should not be reported as fund-raising.

The basis for conclusions of the SOP discusses whether general calls to prayer are considered calls to action (and meet the content criterion) for purposes of applying the SOP. (Paragraph C21). AcSEC, the body issuing the SOP, believes that determining whether general calls to prayer meet the content criterion requires judgments based on the particular facts and circumstances. (See Appendix C, Exhibit 6, Sample Rescue Mission, Note 2.)

Furloughs, Sabbaticals, and Study Leaves

5-30. A significant activity of most missionary organizations is furlough, also referred to by some organizations as home service or home assignment. Other organizations have similar activities, such as sabbaticals or study leaves. The nature of these activities does not lend itself to usual allocation techniques; e.g., time summarization would involve too many subjective determinations. A missionary on furlough may be involved simultaneously in many activities.

5-31. In order to properly allocate furlough and other leave expenses, EJAC recommends that the organization periodically conduct a survey of these personnel, listing types of typical activities anticipated. Estimates should be made of the amount of time (in hours) spent on each activity during a test period. Activities should not be grouped or labeled, to avoid influencing the outcome of the survey. If the survey is objective, survey results can then be extended to achieve a reasonable allocation of these costs. For example, the cost of the activities should be appropriately allocated among:

- continuing education—to the program(s) to which the individual will return

- rest and recuperation—to the program(s) in which the individual was previously involved

- maintenance or development of support—to fund-raising

- ministry and program-related reporting activities—to the program(s) affected or to the home ministries program

- recruitment and guidance of new paid workers—to the program(s) benefited

- recruitment of volunteers—to fund-raising

- administrative reporting—to management and general

5-32. All related expenses (e.g., salary, benefits, travel, etc.) should be allocated among the activities described above unless the person's assignment can be clearly identified as fitting one specific activity. For example, a missionary whose sole task is to raise funds for a particular program or project would have all expenses charged to fund-raising. A teacher who is pursuing further education on a full-time basis during leave to enhance his or her qualifications for an assignment should have expenses charged to that particular program.

NATURAL CLASSIFICATION OF EXPENSES

5-33. In addition to the functional classification (program services and supporting activities) of expenses described in the preceding portion of this chapter, many users of financial statements are interested in the natural classification of expenses (salaries, rent, depreciation, etc.) as well.

Paragraph 26 of the FASB Statement No. 117 provides the following:

. . . Voluntary health and welfare organizations shall report [functional classification of expenses] that information as well as information about expenses by their natural classification, such as salaries, rent, electricity, interest expenses, depreciation, awards and grants to others, and professional fees, in a matrix format in a separate financial statement. Other not-for-profit organizations are encouraged, but not required, to provide information about expenses by their natural classification.

5-34. Some Christian ministries would be considered voluntary health and welfare organizations as defined in Appendix D of FASB Statement No. 117: "organizations formed for the purpose of performing voluntary services for various segments of society . . . [They] expend their resources in an attempt to solve health and welfare problems of our society and, in many cases, those of specific individuals . . . [They] include those not-for-profit organizations that derive their revenue primarily from the general public to be used for general or specific purposes connected with health, welfare, or community services." Voluntary health and welfare organizations are required by FASB Statement No. 117, paragraph 26, to prepare a separate financial statement which is a matrix of functional and natural expenses like the statement illustrated in Appendix C, Exhibit 6, Sample Rescue Mission.

5-35. EJAC recommends that functional expenses be displayed in the statement of activities of all Christian ministries. While a matrix of functional and natural expenses is required for voluntary health and welfare organizations, EJAC recommends that all Christian ministries provide such a matrix in a separate statement of functional expenses between the statement of activities and the statement of cash flows.

GRANTS (INCLUDING SUPPORT TO AFFILIATED ORGANIZATIONS)

5-36. Foundations, trusts, and other organizations sometimes make contributions in the form of grants to individuals and to domestic or foreign entities, including local, national, and international affiliates. (Grants may be either contributions or exchange transaction.

For purposes of the discussion of grants in this chapter, grants are considered contributions.) *(Canadian ministries, see 9-2.)*

5-37. Grants awarded to individuals or noncontrolled organizations should be recorded as expenses at the time recipients become entitled to them. A grant which is payable in future periods is an unconditional promise to give (FASB Statement No. 116, paragraphs 5 and 6) if the payments in future periods are legally enforceable (subject only to routine performance requirements by the grantee and not contingent on subsequent review and approval). (As discussed in paragraphs 87, 88, 97, 98, 99, and 108 of FASB Statement No. 116, a promise need not be legally enforceable to be considered an unconditional promise to give. A social and moral obligation to transfer the resources is sufficient to conclude that a promise to give exists.) The grantor should record an expense at the same time and under the same circumstances that the grantee records income. The expense and liability recorded for such a grant must be discounted to their estimated present value and the discount amortized in the manner described in paragraphs 4-52 to 4-53. (FASB Concepts Statement No. 7, *Using Cash Flow Information and Present Value in Accounting Measurements,* provides a detailed discussion of present value and its use in accounting measurements.) However, if the grant instrument specifically allows the grantor to revoke the grant regardless of the performance of the grantee, unpaid grants should not be recorded.

EJAC recommends that the amount of such grants be disclosed separately in the financial statement or footnotes.

5-38. If grants or dues are paid or payable to a related organization, the proper treatment is determined by the nature of the relationship and the terms of the agreement. If the payer and the recipient are part of a single reporting entity (i.e., their financial statements are consolidated or combined), the grants or dues would be eliminated in the consolidation process. If the "grantor" is, in effect, a collecting agent, the obligation would be reported as a liability when the assets are collected and as a reduction of that liability when the funds are remitted. Otherwise, the grant would be reported as an expense and, in the case of grants payable in future periods, a liability with amounts discounted (if a parent-subsidiary relationship does not exist) or at face value (if a parent-subsidiary relationship exists) under the guidance provided in paragraph 4-53 of this Guide. (SOP 94-3, *Reporting of Related Entities by Not-for-Profit Organizations,* which is discussed further in Chapter 8, provides guidance for determining whether a parent-subsidiary relationship exists.)

If the specific purposes of payments to affiliates are determinable (for example, to carry out a specific program or to raise funds), the expenses should be recorded by their functional classification. If portions of payments to affiliates cannot be allocated to specific functions, those portions should be reported on the statement of activities as a separate supporting activity on a line labeled "unallocated payments to affiliated organizations." See Chapter 8 for further discussion of related entities.

5-39. The IRS, regulators, and others look carefully at situations where a contribution is given to a domestic tax-exempt organization, is receipted by that organization, and is then passed on as a grant to an organization in another country. Grants by a not-for-profit organization to organizations in other countries should be planned in view of relevant government regulations. As a general rule, contributions are deductible as charitable contributions only if they are made to domestic tax-exempt organizations. Contributions by a U.S. taxpayer to a foreign organization are not deductible on the taxpayer's domestic tax return.

IRS regulations prohibit U.S. domestic charities from acting as a conduit of funds for foreign recipients, giving a tax-deductible receipt for amounts which would not have been deductible if given directly to the foreign entity. However, if the domestic charity makes a foreign grant in furtherance of its tax-exempt purposes and retains control and discretion of the grant money, then regulators are not likely to challenge the deductibility of contributions which funded the grant. For additional information on this subject, see Internal Revenue Service Publication No. 526, *Charitable Contributions.*

5-40.   Indications of such control and discretion include the following:

1. The domestic organization, through its board or officers, approves a foreign grant only after reviewing the grant request in some detail (and perhaps even after a field investigation of the activities of the requesting foreign organization).

2. Periodic accounting of grant funds is given to the domestic organization by the foreign organization recipient, or the domestic organization exercises oversight by (a) periodic reviews or audits of the financial statements of the foreign organization, or (b) continuous field investigations.

3. The domestic organization can refuse grants that are requested by a foreign organization.

4. The domestic organization retains the right to withdraw approval of a grant and perhaps even to receive a refund of any unexpended grant funds.

5. Funds granted include amounts from the general fund of the domestic organization and are not exclusively from funds that have been earmarked by donors for a particular foreign project or foreign recipient.

6. If a donor has made a request regarding the use of his or her donation, a disclaimer is given by the domestic organization in the solicitation or receipting of that donation regarding the responsibility and authority of the domestic organization to (a) exercise control over the funds, (b) withdraw approval of a grant if it is in the best interests of the domestic organization to do so, and (c) redirect the funds in furtherance of its exempt purposes as it deems appropriate.

7. The domestic organization has a variety of charitable or religious activities underway in the foreign country to which the grant is being directed.

8. A written agreement is in place between the domestic organization and the foreign organization recipient as to the use of the funds.

9. Grant monies are used for specific projects in furtherance of the domestic organization's exempt purposes.

10. The domestic organization only releases grant funds for specific projects on an "as needed" basis.

11. If grant funds are received by a foreign organization recipient, which in turn makes disbursements to other organizations or individuals, the domestic organization making the grant determines the eligibility of the ultimate recipients of the funds.

Not all of the above indications are likely to be present in every situation, but regulators are more likely to consider the grant as being under the control and discretion of the domestic charity if more of the characteristics are present. The first five indications are especially important.

COSTS RELATED TO SALES OF GOODS AND SERVICES

5-41.   The display of costs related to the sales of goods and services depends on whether the sales are (a) a peripheral or incidental activity of the ministry or (b) a major and central activity of the ministry.

If the sales are a peripheral or incidental activity, the related receipts and costs may be netted, and only the net gains or losses are reported. (Paragraph 5-55 discusses reporting peripheral and incidental activities.)

If the sales are a central or major activity, the statement of activities should separately display the gross revenues from sales and the gross related costs. The costs of sales may be displayed immediately after the revenues and before a descriptive subtotal, or the cost of sales may be reported with other expenses. If the cost of sales is reported with other expenses, the cost should be reported as program service (if the sale results in delivering program) or as a separate supporting activity (if the sale does not result in delivering program), whichever is appropriate.

Reductions in Amounts Charged for Goods and Services

5-42.   Christian ministries often provide goods and services at less than market value or even less than cost. If the sale of those goods and services is peripheral or incidental to the ministry's purpose, the costs should be netted against the corresponding receipts, and only the net gains or losses are reported. If the sales are a central or major activity, such reductions in amounts charged for goods and services should be reported as follows:

- If the ministry receives goods or services in exchange for the reduction in the amount it charges for goods or services, the reduction should be reported as an expense. Such an expense should be reported in the same functional classification as the cost of the goods or services provided to the ministry. For example, if a ministry provides a reduction in tuition for a school employee as part of that employee's compensation package, that reduction should be reported as an expense of the function(s) to which the employee is assigned.

- If the ministry does not receive goods or services in exchange for the reduction in the amount it charges for goods or services, the reduction should be reported as:

  - an expense to the extent that the ministry incurs incremental expenses in providing such goods or services. (Such expenses should be reported as described in the previous paragraph.)

  - discounts if the ministry incurs no incremental expense in providing such goods or services. (Such discounts should offset or be netted against the revenue from such goods and services.)

ADVERTISING COSTS

5-43. SOP 93-7, *Reporting on Advertising Costs,* defines advertising as "the promotion of an industry, an entity, a brand, a product name, or specific products or services so as to create or stimulate a positive entity image or to create or stimulate a desire to buy the entity's products or services." Advertising is distinguished from fund-raising (paragraph 5-21 and following) which is not within the scope of SOP 93-7. However, SOP 93-7 does apply to advertising by Christian ministries, including activities that create or stimulate a desire to use the ministry's products or services that are provided without a charge.

Paragraph 13.10 of the *AICPA NPO Guide 2000* provides the following:

13.10. Advertising costs should be expensed either as incurred or the first time the advertising takes place, except for direct-response advertising that results in probable future benefits. Direct-response advertising should be capitalized if it is expected to result in future benefits, as in sales resulting from direct-response advertising of merchandise in excess of future costs to be incurred in realizing those revenues. If no future revenues are anticipated, however, because the products or services advertised are being provided by the organization without charge, there is no basis for capitalizing the costs of direct-response advertising after the first time the advertising takes place.

INVESTMENT EXPENSES

5-44. Expenses related to the production of investment income may be netted against the investment income if the amount of those expenses, such as custodial fees and investment advisory fees, is disclosed either on the face of the statement of activities or in the notes to the financial statements. Even though investment expenses are netted against investment revenue on the statement of activities, such expenses should be reported by their functional classification in the statement (matrix) of functional and natural expenses. Realized and unrealized losses may also be netted against investment revenue, but (because they are losses rather than expenses) they need not be included in the matrix of functional and natural expenses.

POSTEMPLOYMENT EXPENSES

5-45. Pension and other postretirement and postemployment expenses include defined benefit pensions, retirement allowances, severance pay, health care, life insurance, and other benefits provided to former, inactive, or retired personnel. The following Statements of Financial Accounting Standards deal with these issues:

- FASB Statement No. 87, *Employers' Accounting for Pensions*

  This statement applies not only to formal pension plans but also to any arrangement similar in substance to a defined benefit pension plan, even if the arrangement is unwritten, unfunded, and/or not IRS-qualified. The cost of defined benefits must be reported when they are earned by the participant. A liability must be reported for the accrued cost of unfunded or underfunded benefits. (FASB Statement No. 132, *Employer's Disclosures about Pensions and Other Postretirement Benefits,* amends Statement No. 87, and provides reduced disclosure requirements for nonpublic entities.)

- FASB Statement No. 106, *Employers' Accounting for Postretirement Benefits Other Than Pensions*

  This statement prescribes reporting standards for nonpension postretirement benefits, such as health care and life insurance. Its provisions are similar to those of FASB Statement No. 87. (FASB Statement No. 132, *Employer's Disclosures about Pensions and Other Postretirement Benefits,* amends Statement No. 106, and provides reduced disclosure requirements for nonpublic entities.)

- FASB Statement No. 112, *Employers' Accounting for Postemployment Benefits*

  This statement prescribes reporting standards for benefits accrued during an employee's working years, but payable upon termination before the employee's retirement. Such benefits include salary continuation, supplemental unemployment benefits, severance benefits, disability-related benefits, job training and counseling, health care, and life insurance.

5-46.   These standards apply to all not-for-profit organizations which have a material obligation for benefits of the types described above. A Christian ministry should obtain competent counsel to determine the information necessary to comply with these standards. An illustration of an appropriate disclosure is presented in Appendix C, Exhibit 1, Sample Large Christian Organization, Note 13.

5-47. Organizations operating in other countries should understand and comply with any applicable health benefits, severance, retirement, or similar laws of other countries which create legal liabilities upon separation. Expenses and liabilities for such payments must be recorded in accordance with FASB Statement Nos. 87, 106, and 112 when benefits are earned by covered personnel.

START-UP ACTIVITIES

5-48. SOP 98-5, *Reporting on the Costs of Start-Up Activities,* provides guidance on the financial reporting of start-up costs and organization costs. It requires costs of start-up activities and organization costs to be expensed as incurred.

5-49. SOP 98-5 broadly defines start-up activities as those one-time activities related to opening a new facility, introducing a new product or service, conducting business in a new territory, conducting business with a new class of customer or beneficiary, initiating a new process in an existing facility, or commencing some new operations. Start-up activities include activities related to organizing a new entity (commonly referred to as organization costs).

5-50. SOP 98-5 provides that certain costs that may be incurred in conjunction with start-up activities are not subject to the provisions of the SOP and should be accounted for in accordance with other existing authoritative literature. SOP 98-5 provides examples to help entities determine what costs are and are not within its scope. It also includes illustrations in the appendix; one illustration provides a scenario in which a not-for-profit organization that has provided meals to the homeless is opening a shelter to house the homeless. The illustration shows the costs that are and are not subject to the SOP.

INTERNAL USE SOFTWARE

5-51. SOP 98-1, *Accounting for the Costs of Computer Software Developed or Obtained for Internal Use,* provides guidance on accounting for the costs of computer software developed or obtained for internal use. SOP 98-1 identifies the characteristics of internal-use software and provides examples to assist in determining when computer software is for internal use. The SOP provides as follows:

- Computer software meeting the characteristics specified in the SOP is internal-use software.

- In many cases, organizations develop their own software programs to meet specific needs of the organization. Computer software costs that are incurred in the preliminary project stage of such development should be expensed as incurred once the capitalization criteria of the SOP have been met. External direct costs of materials and services consumed in developing or obtaining internal-use computer software; payroll and payroll-related costs for employees who are directly associated with and who devote time to the internal-use computer software project (to the extent of the time spent directly on the project); and interest costs incurred when developing computer software for internal use should be capitalized. Training costs and data conversion costs, except as noted in paragraph .21, should be expensed as incurred.

- Internal costs incurred for upgrades and enhancements should be expensed or capitalized in accordance with paragraphs .20–.23. Internal costs incurred for maintenance should be expensed as incurred. Entities that cannot separate internal costs on a reasonably cost-effective basis between maintenance and relatively minor upgrades and enhancements should expense such costs as incurred.

- External costs incurred under agreements related to specified upgrades and enhancements should be expensed or capitalized in accordance with paragraphs .20–.23. However, external costs related to maintenance, unspecified upgrades and enhancements, and costs under agreements that combine the costs of maintenance and unspecified upgrades and enhancements should be recognized in expense over the contract period on a straight-line basis, unless another systematic and rational basis is more representative of the services received.

- Impairment of capitalized computer software should be recognized and measured in accordance with the provisions of FASB Statement No. 121, *Accounting for the Impairment of Long-Lived Assets and for Long-Lived Assets to Be Disposed Of.*

- The capitalized costs of computer software developed or obtained for internal use should be amortized on a straight-line basis, unless another systematic and rational basis is more representative of the software's use.

- If, after the development of internal-use software is completed, an entity decides to market the software, proceeds received from licensing of the computer software, net of direct incremental costs of marketing, should be applied against the carrying amount of that software.

The SOP identifies the characteristics of internal-use software and provides examples to assist in determining when computer software is for internal use.

EITF (Emerging Issues Task Force) Issue 00-2, *Accounting for Web Site Development Costs,* proposes expensing hosting costs in the period covered, with initial graphics the same as software, and operating costs as incurred.

LOSSES

5-52.   Losses must be distinguished from expenses. Expenses are incurred in carrying out activities that constitute the entity's ongoing major or central operations (FASB Concepts Statement No. 6, paragraph 80). Losses are decreases in net assets resulting from transactions which are only peripheral or incidental to the entity's operations (FASB Concepts Statement No. 6, paragraph 83). Activities are major and central activities if (a) they are normally part of an organization's strategy and it normally carries on such activities, or (b) the activity's gross receipts or costs are significant in relation to the organization's annual budget. Examples of transactions which could result in losses are the sale of investments, changes in market prices of investments accounted for at market values, disposition of fixed assets, changes in actuarial valuations, changes in foreign exchange rates, bad debts from receivables that are represented as restricted net assets, lawsuits, thefts, and natural catastrophes.

5-53. Losses (in contrast to expenses):

- may be recorded in restricted classes of net assets depending on the nature of the transaction which gave rise to the loss

- may be netted against the corresponding source of income

- need not be reported by their functional classification

- need not be included in the matrix that presents expenses according to both their functional and natural classifications

5-54. The sale of land or buildings which are no longer needed for the organization's ongoing activities is a peripheral transaction. The organization's statement of activities should report the net gain or loss rather than report revenue equal to the gross sales proceeds less selling expenses and expense equal to the carrying value. The gross proceeds should be reported in the investing section of the statement of cash flows.

5-55. If special fund-raising events are a peripheral or incidental activity of an organization, the resulting receipts may be reported net of direct expenses. In any case, expenses that do not directly benefit the donor must be reported as fund-raising expenses. However, so-called special events are often ongoing and represent major activities such as an annual banquet; if so, the organization should report the gross revenues and expenses of those events as described in paragraphs 4-29 and 4-30.

Chapter 6

Accounting for Investments and Property and Equipment

Contents

■ INVESTMENTS 147

    Basis of Recording at Acquisition 148

    Carrying Value of Investments 148

    Unrealized and Realized Gains and Losses 149

    Investment Pools 153

■ PROPERTY AND EQUIPMENT 154

    Reporting of Property and Equipment 155

    Capitalization Policy 156

    Depreciation 157

    Classification of Property, Equipment,
        and Depreciation 159

    Property Held in Other Countries 159

Accounting for Investments and Property and Equipment

6-1.   Generally accepted accounting principles apply to accounting for all of an organization's assets. However, the practices and implications for the areas of investments, as well as fixed assets and depreciation, deserve particular attention because these are often the major assets on a Christian organization's balance sheet.

INVESTMENTS

6-2.   Investments frequently present special accounting complexities for not-for-profit organizations due to their substantial size, diversity of types, and the multiplicity of accounting practices currently in use. Investment pools are commonly used to commingle assets of various classes and subclasses which have been internally designated or externally restricted. This chapter discusses these matters and provides amplification and clarification of the recommended accounting practices for these items.

6-3.   Christian ministries often have investment portfolios of the following types:

- investment of assets related to unrestricted and temporarily restricted net assets to earn additional income until such time as the net assets are used for program or other purposes
- investment of endowment assets
- investment of assets which are held in trust or as custodians for others
- investments held at foreign locations owned and controlled by the entity

Assets and liabilities recognized under split-interest agreements, including investments, should be disclosed separately from other assets and liabilities in the balance sheet or in the related notes.

Investments are broadly categorized as:

- equity securities with readily determinable fair (market) value

- debt securities

- other investments

Other investments include, for example, works of art, precious metals and stones, investments in real estate, mortgage notes, venture capital funds, partnership interests, and equity securities that do not have a readily determinable fair value. The glossary of FASB Statement No. 133, *Accounting for Derivative Instruments and Hedging Activities,* includes the definition of fair value.

Basis of Recording at Acquisition

6-4.   Investments purchased by an organization should be recorded at cost, which includes brokerage fees, taxes, and other charges directly applicable to the purchase. Donated investments should be recorded at fair value at the date of donation.

Carrying Value of Investments

6-5.   Investments in equity securities with readily determinable fair value, and all debt securities, should be reported at their fair value at the date of the balance sheet.

Other investments for most Christian ministry organizations (other than those classified as colleges or universities, or voluntary health and welfare organizations) should be reported at either fair value or the lower of cost or fair value. The same method should be used for all assets considered to be other investments. Declines in investments carried at the lower of cost or fair value should be recognized when their aggregate fair value is less than their aggregate carrying amount; recoveries in subsequent periods should be recognized but are limited to the original cost.

Organizations should disclose the methods and significant assumptions used to estimate the fair values of investments other than financial instruments if those other investments are reported at fair value. (FASB Statement No. 107, *Disclosures About Fair Value of Financial Instruments,* includes a definition of financial instruments. The disclosures required by Statement No. 107, however, are optional for ministries with (a) total assets of less than $100 million on the date of the financial statements and (b) no instruments that, in whole or in part, are accounted for as derivative instruments under FASB Statement No. 133, *Accounting for Derivative Instruments and Hedging Activities.*)

Colleges, universities, and voluntary health and welfare organizations should refer to the *AICPA NPO Guide 2000,* Chapter 8, Appendix A for guidance on accounting for other investments.

The guidance on accounting for other investments is intended to maintain the status quo until there are changes by the FASB or by the AICPA.

6-6.   The basis of carrying other investments should be the same for all other investments for all net asset classes and should be clearly disclosed in the financial statements or notes to the financial statements. EJAC recommends that if investments are carried at other than fair value, the total fair value of investments at the date of the statements be disclosed for each type of investment, such as real estate.

6-7.   If investments include *property that would otherwise be considered* depreciable property, they should reflect the net realizable fair value (net of selling costs) on a basis consistent with other investments (fair value or lower of cost or fair value). (See paragraph 6-18.) Periodic appraisals are useful in determining net realizable fair value.

Unrealized and Realized Gains and Losses

6-8.   Changes in the value of investments are commonly recorded in a separate valuation allowance account. EJAC recommends that changes for the period in the valuation allowance account should be separately identified as unrealized gains/losses in the revenue section of the statement of activities or in the notes to the financial statements.

Paragraph 8.10 of the *AICPA NPO Guide 2000* provides the following:

> Unrealized gains and losses arise from changes in the fair value of investments, exclusive of dividend and interest income recognized but not yet received and exclusive of any write-down of the carrying amount of investments for impairment. Unrealized gains and losses are recognized in some circumstances (for example, when the investments are carried at fair value), but not in others (for example, when the investments are carried at cost). To the extent that unrealized gains and losses are recognized, they should be reported in the statement of activities as increases or decreases in unrestricted net assets unless their use is temporarily or permanently restricted by donors to a specified purpose or future period.

Realized gains and losses (net of any previously recognized unrealized gains or losses) should be appropriately reported in the statement of activities or notes thereto.

Paragraphs 8.11, 8.14, 8.15, and 8.16 of the *AICPA NPO Guide 2000* provide the following:

> 8.11.   Realized gains and losses arise from selling or otherwise disposing of investments. Realized gains and losses should be reported in the statement of activities as changes in unrestricted net assets unless their use is temporarily or permanently restricted by explicit donor-imposed stipulations or by law. (Paragraph 8.10 discusses unrealized gains and losses. If realized gains and losses arise from selling or otherwise disposing of investments for which unrealized gains and losses have been recognized in the statement of activities of prior reporting periods, the amount reported in the statement of activities as gains or losses upon the sale or other disposition of the investments should exclude the amount that has previously been recognized in the statement of activities. However, the components of that gain or loss may be reported as the realized amount [the difference between amortized cost and the sales proceeds] and the unrealized amount recognized in prior reporting periods.)

8.14. Donor-Restricted Endowment Funds

A donor's stipulation that requires a gift to be invested in perpetuity or for a specified term creates a donor-restricted endowment fund. Donors or relevant law may require a not-for-profit organization to retain permanently some portion of gains and losses (net appreciation) of donor-restricted endowment funds. Unless net appreciation on donor-restricted endowment funds is temporarily or permanently restricted by a donor's explicit stipulation or by a law that extends a donor's restriction to them, net appreciation on donor-restricted endowment funds should be reported as a change in unrestricted net assets.

Paragraph 11 of FASB Statement No. 124 notes that ". . . if a donor allows the organization to choose suitable investments, the gains are not permanently restricted unless the donor or the law requires that an amount be retained permanently. Instead, those gains are unrestricted if the investment income is unrestricted or are temporarily restricted if the investment income is temporarily restricted by the donor." Accordingly, in the absence of donor stipulations or law to the contrary, donor restrictions on the use of income of an endowment fund also extend to any net appreciation on the fund.

8.15. Classification of recognized gains and losses should be based on the underlying facts and circumstances. If limitations exist that preclude the use of net gains on permanently restricted net assets, either as a result of explicit or clear implicit donor stipulations or by the law of the relevant jurisdiction, the net gains are permanently restricted. Paragraph 125 of FASB Statement No. 117 notes that "because donor stipulations and laws vary, not-for-profit organizations must assess the relevant facts and circumstances for their endowment gifts and their relevant laws to determine if net appreciation on endowments is available for spending or is permanently restricted."

8.16. Paragraphs 12 and 13 of FASB Statement No. 124 provide the following:

12.   In the absence of donor stipulations or law to the contrary, losses on the investments of a donor-restricted endowment fund shall reduce temporarily restricted net assets to the extent that donor-imposed temporary restrictions on net appreciation of the fund have not been met before a loss occurs. Any remaining loss shall reduce unrestricted net assets.

13.   If losses reduce the assets of a donor-restricted endowment fund below the level required by the donor stipulations or law, [footnote omitted] gains that restore the fair value of the assets of the endowment fund to the required level shall be classified as increases in unrestricted net assets.

(After the fair value of the assets of the endowment fund equals the required level, gains that are restricted by the donor should be classified as increases in temporarily restricted net assets or permanently restricted net assets, depending on the donor's restrictions on the endowment fund.)

Realized and unrealized gains and losses from investments may be reported net or separately on the statement of activities. Paragraph 8.23 of the *AICPA NPO Guide 2000* provides that disclosure should minimally include:

a.   The composition of investment return, including, at a minimum, investment income, net realized gains or losses on investments reported at other than fair value, and net gains or losses on investments reported at fair value.

b.   A reconciliation of investment return to amounts reported in the statement of activities if investment return is separated into operating and nonoperating amounts, together with a description of the policy used to determine the amount that is included in the measure of operations and a discussion of circumstances leading to a change, if any, in that policy.

Investment Pools

6-9.   Christian ministries that have a significant amount of investments in more than one fund may find pooling of investments easier to manage. It may also result in a higher rate of return because of the ability to better manage a larger portfolio. However, donor or legal restrictions may prohibit commingling certain assets. For example, assets held in trust should normally not be commingled with general assets of the organization, depending on state law. Furthermore, commingling of the assets of individual trusts may be prohibited by state law or by the trust documents themselves.

6-10.   The principles outlined in the *AICPA NPO Guide 2000* relating to the operation of an investment pool are appropriate here and should be followed. For purposes of computing additions to and withdrawals from the pool, gains/losses (both realized and unrealized) should be allocated proportionately to the funds involved. Before implementing an investment pool, an organization should be sure that it understands the complexities involved in potential inter-organization and intra-organization transactions. Two illustrations of an investment pool are provided in Appendix D of this guide.

Paragraphs 8.12 and 8.13 of the *AICPA NPO Guide 2000* provide the following:

8.12. A not-for-profit organization may pool part or all of its investments (including investments arising from contributions with different kinds of restrictions) for portfolio management purposes. The number and the nature of the pools may vary from organization to organization.

8.13. When a pool is established, ownership interests are initially assigned (typically through unitization) to the various pool categories (sometimes referred to as participants) based on the market value of the cash and securities placed in the pool by each participant. Current market value is used to determine the number of units allocated to additional assets placed in the pool and to value withdrawals from the pool. Investment income and realized gains and losses (and any recognized unrealized gains and losses) are allocated equitably based on the number of units assigned to each participant.

PROPERTY AND EQUIPMENT

6-11. The reporting of property and equipment and recognition of related depreciation expense for long-lived tangible assets is required for all nonprofit organizations in general purpose external financial statements in conformity with GAAP (FASB Statement No. 93, *Recognition of Depreciation by Not-for-Profit Organizations*). This provides the most consistent and reasonable presentation of these transactions for financial reporting purposes. FASB Statement No. 93 requires depreciation (except for land) and provides an exception only for individual works and collections of art or historic treasures whose economic benefit or service potential is used up so slowly that their estimated useful lives are extraordinarily long. Property owned by Christian ministries would not normally be considered works of art or historical treasures.

Paragraphs 5 and 6 of the FASB Statement No. 93 require the following:

5.   Recognition and Disclosure

Not-for-profit organizations shall recognize the cost of using up the future economic benefits or service potentials of their long-lived tangible assets—depreciation—and shall disclose the following:

a. Depreciation expense for the period

b. Balances of major classes of depreciable assets, by nature or function, at the balance sheet date

c. Accumulated depreciation, either by major classes of depreciable assets or in total, at the balance sheet date

d. A general description of the method or methods used in computing depreciation for major classes of depreciable assets

6.   Consistent with the accepted practice for land used as a building site, depreciation need not be recognized on individual works of art or historical treasures whose economic benefit

or service potential is used up so slowly that their estimated useful lives are extraordinarily long. A work of art or historical treasure shall be deemed to have that characteristic only if verifiable evidence exists demonstrating that (a) the asset individually has cultural, aesthetic, or historical value that is worth preserving perpetually and (b) the holder has the technological and financial ability to protect and preserve essentially undiminished the service potential of the asset and is doing that.

Reporting of Property and Equipment

6-12. Purchased fixed assets should be reported at actual cost and donated assets at their fair value on the date of the gift. Fixed assets not used in the organization's program services or supporting activities should be recorded as investments or assets held for sale, not fixed assets. (See paragraph 6-18.)

Paragraph 9.05 of the *AICPA NPO Guide 2000* provides the following:

> 9.05. Contributions of property and equipment (including unconditional promises to give property and equipment) should be recognized at fair value at the date of contribution and, depending on donor restrictions and the organization's accounting policy, should be included in permanently restricted, temporarily restricted, or unrestricted net assets. If the donors stipulate how or how long contributed property and equipment must be used by the organization, the contribution should be reported as restricted support. If the donors do not specify such restrictions, the contribution should be reported as restricted support if the organization has adopted an accounting policy of implying a time restriction on the use of such assets that expires over the assets' useful lives. In the absence of donor restrictions or an organization's policy of implying time restrictions, contributions of long-lived assets should be reported as unrestricted support. . . .

Actual cost may include agent fees, acquisition costs, interest on construction period financing, shipping, installation costs, licensing or zoning fees, sales taxes, and other costs incurred in the purchase or during the period of construction or renovation of the asset, in addition to direct asset costs.

6-13.   If donated services are utilized which meet the criteria of FASB Statement No. 116, paragraph 9:

> [They] ". . . (a) create or enhance nonfinancial assets or (b) require specialized skills . . . ," [then] the depreciable asset cost should include the value of the donated services.

Paragraphs 4-58 to 4-66 provide more detailed information about recording contributed services.

Capitalization Policy

6-14.   In the absence of historical cost records (and only then and in the adoption of these standards), EJAC recommends that another reasonable basis be used to estimate the historical cost of the assets. Other bases might be cost-based appraisals, insurance appraisals, replacement costs, or property tax appraisals adjusted to reflect estimated historical cost at the date of acquisition. In addition, any reported amounts should reflect accumulated depreciation that would have been reported had the asset been reported initially at its acquisition date. If such amounts are material to the financial statements, the basis or method used should be disclosed along with the related amounts.

6-15.   An organization's foreign, depreciable operating property, plant, and equipment should be reflected in its financial statements and depreciation recorded in accordance with the principles outlined above. Entities with assets or operations in foreign countries should follow the provisions of FASB Statement No. 52, *Foreign Currency Translation,* including related disclosure requirements. (See Appendix C, Exhibit 1, Note 2, Foreign Operations, and Note 5, paragraph 3.)

6-16.   For administrative efficiency, organizations ordinarily establish a policy setting an amount below which individual or group purchases of property and equipment are expensed rather than capitalized. Small items of office equipment, minor furnishings, hand tools, and the like are generally too numerous and of too little value to warrant the effort to inventory and value them. This minimum value will vary based on the size of the organization.

Depreciation

6-17.   Because Christian ministries are normally not concerned with tax deductions, use of the straight-line method of depreciation over the estimated useful life of an asset is generally used. However, accelerated methods are not precluded if the nature and/or use of specific items justifies an alternative method.

Paragraphs 9.07 and 9.08 of the *AICPA NPO Guide 2000* provide the following:

> 9.07.   Paragraph 149 of FASB Concepts Statement No. 6, *Elements of Financial Statements,* describes depreciation as a "systematic and rational" process for allocating the cost of using up assets' service potential or economic benefit over the assets' useful economic lives. FASB Statement No. 93, *Recognition of Depreciation by Not-for-Profit Organizations,* requires all not-for-profit organizations to recognize depreciation for all property and equipment except land used as a building site and similar assets and collections. Depreciation should be recognized for contributed property and equipment as well as for plant and equipment acquired in exchange transactions.

> 9.08.   Depreciation expense should be reported in a statement of activities as a decrease in unrestricted net assets. If the property and equipment being depreciated have been contributed to the organization with donor-imposed restrictions on the item's use, temporarily restricted net assets should, over time, be reclassified as unrestricted net assets in a statement of activities as those restrictions expire. The amount reclassified may or may not be equal to the amount of the related depreciation. The amount to be reclassified should be based on the length of time indicated by the donor-imposed restrictions while the amount of depreciation should be based on the useful economic life of the asset. For example, a computer with an estimated useful economic life of five years may be contributed by a donor and restricted for

a specific use by the organization for three years. Reclassification is also necessary if the not-for-profit organization has adopted an accounting policy that implies a time restriction on contributions of property and equipment that expires over the useful life of the contributed assets. Reclassification should be included as "Net Assets Released from Restrictions" in a statement of activities.

6-18.   Property used in the ministry or held for the production of income, such as property used in an unrelated business or rental property, should be depreciated over its estimated useful life. Property specifically held for sale (investment) should not be depreciated. Property held for investment should be revalued for GAAP reporting purposes (generally annually) in accordance with the policy for other investments. (This does not necessarily require a formal appraisal.)

6-19.   Note that permanent impairments of value should also be considered (lower of book value or fair value). (See Appendix C, Exhibit 3, Sample Religious Broadcaster, Note 4.)

Paragraph 9.09 of the *AICPA NPO Guide 2000* provides the following:

9.09.   In conformity with FASB Statement No. 121, *Accounting for the Impairment of Long-Lived Assets and for Long-Lived Assets to Be Disposed Of,* not-for-profit organizations should review long-lived assets to be held and used whenever events or changes in circumstances indicate that the carrying amount of the assets may not be recoverable. In performing the review of recoverability, organizations should estimate the future cash flows expected to result for (a) the use of the asset, such as fees or contributions, and (b) the asset's eventual disposition. If the sum of the expected future cash flows (undiscounted and without interest charges) is less than the carrying amount of the assets, an impairment loss should be recognized. Otherwise an impairment loss should not be recognized. Measurement of the impairment loss should be based on the fair value of the assets. The Statement also prescribes reporting and disclosure requirements for such losses.

Classification of Property, Equipment, and Depreciation

6-20.   The recording of fixed assets in the unrestricted net assets class is discussed in Chapters 2 and 3. However, situations can occur when an asset is acquired with both restricted and unrestricted net assets. In these cases, it is possible that the asset may be split and recorded between two net asset classes, if the organization elects to present a disaggregated balance sheet, and its policy is to release restrictions over the life of the asset, as discussed in paragraph 16 of FASB Statement No. 116. Depreciation expense should be allocated among program services and supporting activities based on the use of the property, and reported as a decrease in the unrestricted net assets class.

Property Held in Other Countries

6-21.   Property held in other countries is often in substance owned by the reporting organization, although held in legal form in the name of a separate foreign corporation. Care should be taken to consider the substantive nature of the relationship and whether or not such assets should be reported as owned by the reporting organization. Consideration should be given to the nature of relationships with related entities as discussed in Chapter 8. Paragraph 8-16 discusses contingencies resulting from legal restrictions by other countries on repatriation of property or proceeds from its sale. (See Appendix C, Exhibit 1, Sample Large Christian Organization, Note 5.)

Annuities, Trusts, and Similar Gifts

Contents

◆ ACCOUNTING FOR SPLIT-INTEREST GIFTS 164

    Lead Interests 165

    Accounting for Lead Interests 166

    Perpetual Trusts Held by a Third Party 169

    Accounting for Perpetual Trusts Held by a
       Third Party 170

    Remainder Interests 171

    Accounting for Remainder Interests........................ 174

    Charitable Gift Annuities.. 176

    Accounting for Charitable Gift Annuities 176

    Pooled Income Funds and Net Income Unitrusts .. 177

    Accounting for Pooled Income Funds and
       Net Income Unitrusts 178

◆ CUSTODIAN (AGENCY) FUNDS 180

◆ REVOCABLE TRUSTS AND OTHER AGREEMENTS.... 180

◆ LIFE INSURANCE... 181

◆ LIFE ESTATES.. 181

Annuities, Trusts, and Similar Gifts

7-1.   Many Christian ministries conduct deferred giving programs under which the ultimate receipt of all the benefits of a gift is deferred until some later date or event. These are often referred to as planned giving, estate planning, or stewardship programs. Such programs are designed to encourage giving through various arrangements which normally provide certain reciprocal benefits to the donor or other beneficiaries (life tenants) for a stated term or lifetime. Deferred giving programs include annuities, trusts, and similar gifts such as charitable current and deferred gift annuities, revocable trusts, irrevocable trusts (including charitable lead trusts, charitable remainder annuity trusts, and unitrusts), pooled income funds, life estates, revocable gift or deposit agreements, life insurance, or similar instruments. The following discussion presents the accounting and reporting practices for these types of agreements.

7-2.   Because of complex legal implications involved in properly administering and accounting for these agreements, due care must be taken to understand and comply with federal and state laws, as well as with the specific provisions of the documents governing such transactions. For example, annuity programs are normally subject to approval and regulation by the insurance commissioner of the state in which the annuitant resides. Also, certain revocable loan (debt) instruments are subject to state securities regulations. Trusts provide binding legal and fiduciary obligations and, if specific requirements are met, may qualify the grantor for a more advantageous charitable contribution deduction. State laws also govern investment practices and the ability to commingle assets of several trusts or the prohibition of commingling trust assets with those of the trustee.

7-3.   EJAC recommends that a committee be established by the board (or an existing committee designated) to assume the responsibility of establishing a policy and monitoring compliance with the aforementioned requirements in the administration of such giving programs. Management must also take the responsibility to establish and monitor internal controls over this area.

7-4.   Care should be taken to ensure that all costs, as well as benefits, are considered in planning such programs, and that the programs meet the objectives of the board before they are implemented and before any such gifts are accepted. It is often difficult to measure the economic benefits of a deferred giving program because of its long-range nature; and the ultimate benefit to the ministry may not be known until many years in the future.

ACCOUNTING FOR SPLIT-INTEREST GIFTS

7-5.   Irrevocable trusts and similar arrangements (generally referred to by the terms split-interest or deferred gifts) can be divided into two fundamentally different types: lead interests and remainder interests.

Lead interests, as traditionally conceived, are those in which the benefit to the organization "leads" or precedes the benefit to the donor (or other person designated by the donor). To put this into the terminology commonly used by trust lawyers, the organization is the "life tenant," and someone else is the "remainderman." The reverse situation is that of the "remainder" interest, where the donor (or the donor's designee) is the life tenant and the organization is the remainderman; that is, the entity to which the assets become available upon termination (often called the maturity) of the trust or other arrangement. There may or may not be further restrictions on the organization's use of the assets and/or the income therefrom after this termination.

7-6.   Under both types of agreements, the donor makes an initial lump-sum payment into a fund. The amount is invested, and the income during the term of the arrangement is paid to the life tenant. In some cases, the arrangement is established as a trust under the trust laws of the applicable state.

In other cases, no separate trust is involved; rather, the assets are simply held by the organization as part of its general assets. In some cases involving trusts, the organization is the trustee; in other cases, a third party is the trustee. Typical third-party trustees include banks and trust companies or other charities, such as community foundations. Some arrangements are perpetual; that is, the organization never gains access to the corpus of the gift. Others have a defined term of existence which will end either upon the occurrence of a specified event such as the death of the donor (or other specified person) or after the passage of a specified amount of time. In addition, with some remainder interests, upon maturity a portion may become the property of another organization (referred to as "amount due other remaindermen").

7-7. Thus, the organization should consider the following criteria applicable to these arrangements:

- Is the organization's interest a lead interest or a remainder interest?

- Is the arrangement in the form of a trust?

- Are the assets held by the organization or by a third party?

- Is the arrangement perpetual or does it have a defined term?

In the case of remainder interests, upon termination of the interest of the life tenant, consider:

- Does the entire amount belong to the organization (or does some part belong to another organization)?

- As to the portion which belongs to the organization, is the corpus unrestricted or restricted?

A flowchart illustrating some of these concepts is in Appendix K. Chapter 6 of the *AICPA NPO Guide 2000* provides additional information on accounting for split-interest agreements.

Lead Interests

7-8. Such arrangements include:

- charitable lead trust

- perpetual trust held by a third party

- permanent endowment fund of the organization

In all of these cases, the organization receives periodic payments representing distributions of income, but it does not ever gain unrestricted use of the assets which produce the income. In the first case, the payment stream is for a limited time; in cases two and three, the payment stream is perpetual.

7-9.   There are four events related to lead interests which require accounting entries by the charitable beneficiary:

- initial creation of the arrangement

- earning of the periodic income

- accretion of the discount by the life tenant

- termination of the arrangement, if it is not perpetual

7-10.   A charitable lead trust is always for a defined term and the assets are usually held by the organization. At the termination of the trust, the corpus (principal of the gift) reverts to the donor or to another person or organization specified by the donor (may be the donor's estate). Income during the term of the trust is paid to the organization; the income may be unrestricted or restricted. In effect, this arrangement amounts to an unconditional pledge of the income from certain assets for a specified period.

The fair value of the pledge is the present value of the estimated stream of income over the term of the trust. (FASB Concepts Statement No. 7, *Using Cash Flow Information and Present Value in Accounting Measurements,* provides a detailed discussion of present value and its use in accounting measurements.) Although the organization manages the assets during the term of the trust (assuming that the organization holds the assets), it has no remainder interest in the assets.

Accounting for Lead Interests

7-11.   If the organization is the trustee (or, if not the trustee, exercises enough control over the trust that consolidation of the trust financial statements into those of the organization is required), the following accounting entries should be used to record these items:

Debit: Assets held in charitable lead trust

Credit: Liability for amounts held for others
Credit: Contribution revenue—temporarily restricted

To record assets held in trust at fair value and revenue at present value of cash flows to be received over the expected life of the donor

- Periodic income:
  Debit: Assets held in charitable lead trust

  Credit: Liability for amounts held for others

  To record collection (accrual) of income of lead trust

Note that the credit side of this entry is not made to an income account because the contribution income was recorded when the trust was initially established.

- Distribution to not-for-profit organization:
  Debit: Cash

  Credit: Assets held in charitable lead trust

  To record the distribution of income to the not-for-profit organization

- Reclassification of net assets:
  Debit: Temporarily restricted net assets—reclassifications out

  Credit: Unrestricted net assets—reclassifications in

  To reclassify amounts equal to the periodic distributions received by the NPO

- Amortization of discount and revaluation of the liability:

  Debit: Liability for amounts held for others

        Credit: Change in value of split-interest agreements—temporarily restricted

  To amortize discount and revalue the liability based on change in life expectancy and other factors (per FASB Statement No. 116, paragraph 20). (Note that under APB 21, the discount rate is not adjusted to reflect changes in interest rates.) Note that the debit and credit could be reversed.

- Termination of trust:

  Debit: Liability for amounts held for others
  Debit/Credit: Change in value of split-interest agreements—temporarily restricted

        Credit: Assets held in charitable lead trust

  To record return of assets to donor (or other remainderman) if the assets were recorded initially by the organization

Or, if the organization does not hold the assets:

- Initial creation: (if the organization is not the trustee and does not consolidate the trust)

  Debit: Contributions receivable from lead trust

        Credit: Contribution—temporarily restricted (per FASB Statement No. 116, paragraph 15)

  To record present value of income to be received over term of trust

  In this and subsequent entries where a "pledge" payable over several years is initially recorded as a contribution, the amount is recorded in the temporarily restricted class. An exception would be if donor stipulations require that the corpus of the gift be retained permanently, in which case the amount would be recorded in the permanently restricted class per FASB Statement No. 116, paragraph 14.

The next type of lead interest, although not usually thought of as conceptually similar to a lead trust, is in fact similar.

Perpetual Trusts Held by a Third Party

7-12.   A perpetual trust held by a third party is the same as a lead trust, except that the organization does not manage the assets and the term of the trust is perpetual. Again the organization receives the income earned by the trust's assets but never gains the use of the corpus. In effect, there is no remainderman. The fair value is the present value of a perpetual stream of income from the assets.

Assuming a perfect market for investment securities, that amount will equal the current quoted market value of the assets of the trust, or if there is no quoted market value, then the "fair value," which is normally determined based on discounted future cash flows from the assets. For example, assume that bonds with a quoted market value of $1 million are put into such a trust. The trust will receive two types of cash flows: semiannual interest payments until maturity and cash representing the face amount of the bonds at maturity. The fair value is $1 million because that is the present value of the total cash flows to be received by the trust.

7-13.   Some may argue that since the organization does not, and never will, have day-to-day control over the corpus of this type of trust, it should only record assets and income as the periodic income distributions are received from the trustee (that is the way the income from this type of gift has traditionally been recorded). This is overcome by the requirement in FASB Statement No. 116, however, that unconditional pledges be recorded in full (discounted) when the pledge is initially received by the pledgee. *(Canadian ministries, see 9-55.)*

This arrangement amounts to a pledge of income. Since FASB Statement No. 116 requires that the organization immediately record the full (discounted) amount of an ordinary pledge, where all the organization has is a promise of future gifts, with the pledger retaining control over the means to generate the gifts, then the organization surely must immediately record the entire amount (discounted) of a "pledge" where the assets which will generate the periodic payments are held in trust by a third party and receipt of the payments by the organization is virtually assured. Under this situation, the accounting entries will be as follows:

Accounting for Perpetual Trusts Held by a Third Party

- Initial creation:

    Debit: Beneficial interest in perpetual trust

    Credit: Contribution income—permanently restricted

    To record the present value of income to be received from trust (generally measured by the fair value of the trust assets)

- Periodic distributions:

    Debit: Cash or investment income receivable

    Credit: Investment income—unrestricted, unless restricted by the donor

    To record periodic distributions (usually from income earned by the trust)

- Periodic Revaluation of asset:

    Debit/Credit: Beneficial interest in perpetual trust

    Credit/Debit: Gain or loss—permanently restricted

    To adjust for changes in present value of expected cash flows (the amount of this entry is based on an annual review using the same basis as used to measure the asset initially)

    The value of the asset may generally be measured by the fair value of the trust assets, unless facts and circumstances indicate that the fair value differs from the present value of expected future cash flows.

- Termination of the trust:
    N/A

7-14.   A variation of this type of arrangement is a trust held by a third party in which the third party has discretion as to when and/or to whom to pay the periodic income. Since in this case the organization is not assured in advance of receiving any determinable amount, no amounts should be recorded by the organization until distributions are received from the trustee. These amounts are then recorded as contributions.

7-15.   A permanent endowment fund is essentially similar to a perpetual trust, except that the organization is the "trustee" of the assets. In effect, the life tenant and the remainderman are the same entity but, as before, the corpus of the remainder interest is never available for use by the organization. In most cases, there is not a formal separate trust; however, many state laws governing charities consider all assets of a charitable organization to be held in a constructive trust for the benefit of the people of the state. As before, the organization has the use of the income from the assets but cannot invade the corpus (except through a very cumbersome legal process known as cy pres). Again, the value is the present value of a perpetual stream of income from the assets involved. This amount is normally equal to the current fair value of the assets.

7-16.   One could argue that the organization's ability, in this case to influence the investment management policies governing the assets (which it usually does not possess when the trustee is a third party), makes the third party trust less valuable than the endowment fund. However, there would appear to be no way to objectively measure such a difference, if indeed one is considered to exist.

Remainder Interests

7-17.   Such arrangements include:

- charitable remainder annuity trust

- charitable remainder unitrust

- charitable gift annuity

- pooled income fund (also referred to as a life income fund)

7-18.   These arrangements are always for a limited term, usually the life of the donor and/or another person or persons specified by the donor—often the donor's spouse. The donor or the donor's designee is the life tenant; the organization is the remainderman. Again, in the case of a trust, the organization may or may not be the trustee; in the case of a charitable gift annuity, the organization is usually the holder of the assets. Upon termination of the arrangement, the corpus usually devolves to the organization (and, possibly in part to other organizations); the donor may or may not have placed further temporary or permanent restrictions on the corpus and/or the future income earned by the corpus.

If the donor has stipulated that the corpus become a permanent endowment, then it converts to the lead interest arrangement (either permanent endowment fund or perpetual trust held by a third party, depending on who will hold the assets) described earlier. In the case of the corpus becoming permanent endowment, the initial recording of the income from the annuity gift would be in the permanently restricted class, as discussed above.

7-19.   In many states, the acceptance of these types of gifts is regulated by the state government of the residence of the donor, often the department of insurance, since, from the perspective of the donor, these arrangements are partly insurance contracts and are essentially similar to a commercial annuity.

7-20.   There are five events related to remainder interests which require accounting entries by the charitable beneficiary:

- initial creation of the arrangement

- earning of the periodic investment income and, if applicable, accretion of discount

- payments to the life tenant

- any required actuarial revaluation of the annuity liability (to reflect changes in the life tenant's life expectancy and the earnings from the assets)

- termination of the arrangement

The illustrated entries are those which are required if the organization is the trustee (or in the case of a gift annuity, the holder) of the assets or, if not the trustee (holder), exercises enough control over the assets that consolidation of the financial statements of the trust (annuity arrangement) into those of the organization would be required. If the organization is not the trustee (holder) and consolidation is not required, entries recording the corpus of the trust (annuity) would not be made by the organization until termination of the life interest.

7-21. The illustrated entries assume that the entire remainder interest will belong to the organization. If an organization is the holder of assets, some of which will belong to one or more other organizations upon termination of the life interest, then each entry to record the creation of the arrangement will have an additional credit component titled "Amount due other remaindermen." The organization's credits to contribution income will be reduced accordingly. Entries to reflect termination of the arrangement will also show the payments to the other remaindermen.

7-22. The illustrated accounting entries do not consider capital gains or losses on the assets held. These should be accounted for in accordance with the terms of the agreement or, if the agreement is silent, in accordance with applicable state law.

7-23. A charitable remainder annuity trust (CRAT) and charitable remainder unitrust (CRUT) differ only in the stipulated method of calculating the payments to the life tenant. An annuity trust pays a stated dollar amount which remains fixed over the life of the trust; a unitrust pays a stated percentage of the then current value of the trust assets. Therefore, the dollar amount of the payments will vary with changes in market value of the corpus. (A variation, the net income unitrust, limits payments to the actual income earned.)

Accounting for the two types is the same except for the method of calculating the amount of the present value of the life interest payable to the life tenant(s). In both cases, if current investment income is insufficient to cover the stipulated payments, corpus may have to be invaded to do so (except in the case of a net income unitrust); however, the total liability to the life tenant is limited to the assets of the trust.

Accounting for Remainder Interests

(For net income unitrust accounting, see below under Pooled Income Fund.)

- Initial creation:
    Debit: Assets held in trust—at current market value

        Credit: Liability under trust agreement
        Credit: Contribution income (the difference)—in the class of net assets appropriate to any donor restrictions on the gift

    To record receipt of assets to establish annuity or unitrust arrangement

- Periodic income and changes in fair value:
    Debit: Assets held in trust

        Credit: Liability under trust agreement

    To record collection (accrual) of income earned by trust assets and changes in fair value

- Payments to life tenant:
    Debit: Liability under trust agreement

        Credit: Assets held in trust

    To record payments to life tenant

- Actuarial revaluation:
    Debit: Change in value of split-interest agreements
        (**See Appendix C, Exhibit 1.)

        Credit: Liability under trust agreement
        (or the reverse, depending on whether the liability increases or decreases)

To record periodic revaluation of the liability to reflect: (1) the life tenant's revised life expectancy, (2) amortization of discount, and (3) variations in actual investment income from that assumed in the initial calculation

(**) The sample income statements in FASB Statement No. 117, Appendix C, show this adjustment in the temporarily restricted class below the expense section, but the text of the Statement does not discuss the subject.

- Termination of arrangement:

  Debit: Liability under trust agreement (if any balance remains)

  Credit: Change in value of split-interest agreements

  To write off any remaining actuarial liability and reserves

  Debit: General assets of organization

  Credit: Assets held in trust

  To record transfer of legal ownership of assets from trust to organization

  Debit: Net assets—temporarily restricted

  Credit: Net assets—unrestricted

  To reclassify remaining temporarily restricted net assets to reflect expiration of time restriction

  This entry is not made if the donor's stipulation was that upon expiration of the life interest the gift would be: (1) permanently restricted—the gift was initially recorded in that class; or (2) temporarily restricted—the gift will remain in that class. In either of these cases, no reclassification is necessary.

Charitable Gift Annuities

7-24.   A charitable gift annuity (CGA) differs from a CRAT only in that there is no trust; the assets are usually held among the general assets of the organization (some choose to set aside a pool of assets in a separate fund to cover annuity liabilities), and the annuity liability is a general liability of the organization limited only by the organization's total assets.

Accounting for Charitable Gift Annuities

- Initial creation:

    Debit: Assets—at current market value

    Credit: Present value of annuity liability
    Credit: Contribution income (the difference)—in
               the class of net assets appropriate to any
               donor restrictions on the gift

    To record receipt of assets to establish charitable gift annuity

In a balance sheet which is disaggregated by class, the assets held to fund the annuity and the annuity liability will be shown in the temporarily restricted class and will exactly offset. Assets received which are in excess of the amount needed to fund the annuity liability are unrestricted (unless the donor has stipulated otherwise) and will be shown in that class.

As an added protection for the donor, additional annuity reserves may be required by the laws of the state where the organization is located or by the state in which the annuitant resides. Also, some organization boards voluntarily set aside an additional amount as a cushion against unexpected actuarial losses. Any legally required reserves should be disclosed in the notes to the financial statements. Additional voluntary reserves are permitted, but not required, to be disclosed.

EJAC recommends that if the balance sheet is disaggregated, net assets pertaining to legally required reserves be reported as temporarily restricted (or permanently restricted if the remainder interest will be permanently restricted), and that voluntary reserves be reported as unrestricted (unless the corpus of the gift will, upon termination, become temporarily or permanently restricted, in which case the reserve should be recorded in the class appropriate to the restriction).

- Periodic income, payments to life tenants, and actuarial revaluation:

  Same as for charitable remainder annuity trust, except that, to the extent that the corpus will be unrestricted upon maturity, the adjustment will be unrestricted

- Termination of arrangement:
  Debit: Annuity payable (if any balance remains)

  Credit: Change in value of split-interest agreements

  To write off any actuarial liability and reserves

Pooled Income Funds and Net Income Unitrusts

7-25. A pooled income fund, also called a life income fund, is actually a creation of the Internal Revenue Code Section 642(c)(5) which, together with Sec. 170, allows an income tax deduction to donors of such funds. (The amount of the deduction depends on the age(s) of the life tenant(s) and the value of the life interest, and is less than that allowed for a simple charitable deduction directly to an organization—to reflect the value which the life tenant will be receiving in return for the gift.) The fund is usually managed by the organization. Many donors contribute to such a fund, which pools the gifts and invests the assets.

During the period of each life tenant's interest in the fund, the life tenant is paid the actual income earned by that person's share of the corpus; in the case of a net income unitrust, that is the lesser of the stipulated percentage or the actual income. (To this extent, these funds function essentially as mutual funds.) Upon termination of a life interest, the share of the corpus attributable to that life tenant becomes available to the organization.

Accounting for Pooled Income Funds and Net Income Unitrusts

- Initial creation:

  Debit: Assets of pooled income fund—at fair market value at date of gift

  > Credit: Liability—discount for future interests (deferred revenue)
  >
  > Credit: Contribution—temporarily restricted (unless the donor has placed a permanent restriction on the gift), at present value of remainder interest

  To record receipt of assets by pooled income fund

  This discount for future interests is not an actuarially determined liability since the payments to the life tenant are limited to the actual income earned by the trust. It is simply the present value of the amounts to be paid out of income.

- Periodic income and payments to life tenant:

  Debit: Assets of pooled income fund

  > Credit: Liability to life beneficiary

  Debit: Liability to life beneficiary

  > Credit: Assets of pooled income fund

  To record income and payments to life tenant (in a pooled income fund, the two parts of this entry will always exactly offset in the long run; any short-term differences are only the result of timing differences in making the payments to the life tenant)

- Accretion of discount:

  Debit: Discount for future interests

  > Credit: Change in value of split-interest agreements—temporarily restricted

  To accrete present value of future interest in pooled income fund/unitrust

- Actuarial revaluation:
  N/A—no actuarial liability

- Termination of trust:

  Debit: General assets of organization

  Credit: Assets of pooled income fund

  To recognize assets available for use upon death of the life beneficiary

  Debit: Discount for future interests

  Credit: Change in value of split-interest agreements—temporarily restricted

  To write off discount and changes in the life expectancy of the beneficiary

  Debit: Net assets—temporarily restricted

  Credit: Net assets—unrestricted

  To record release of time restriction

  The third part of this entry is not made if the donor's stipulation was that upon expiration of the life interest the gift would be: (1) permanently restricted—the gift was initially recorded in that class; or (2) temporarily restricted—the gift will remain in that class. In either case, no reclassification is necessary.

7-26. FASB Statement No. 136, *Transfers of Assets to a Not-for-Profit Organization or Charitable Trust That Raises or Holds Contributions for Others,* provides guidance to help distinguish agency and intermediary transactions from contributions.

This is of significant interest to all entities that solicit and receive funds that are held in trust or passed through to another entity such as federated fund-raising organizations, community foundations, or other charities. It provides more guidance in distinguishing between contributions and agency type transactions. Paragraphs 4-31 to 4-36 of Chapter 4 discuss FASB Statement No. 136 further.

CUSTODIAN (AGENCY) FUNDS

7-27. A custodian fund is used to account for nongift assets received which are not owned or controlled by the organization, but are to be handled or disbursed only on the directions of the person or entity from whom they were received. Examples include bank accounts of auxiliaries, alumni association funds, funds deposited by missionaries for safekeeping, and camp funds. Since custodian funds are not assets of the organization, their activity should not be shown in the statement of activities. These amounts should be segregated from other assets and liabilities in the balance sheet (if the balance sheet is disaggregated by class, in the unrestricted class).

REVOCABLE TRUSTS AND OTHER AGREEMENTS

7-28. Assets may be received through revocable agreements such as revocable gifts, deposit agreements, or loans which, if not revoked, become contributions to the organization at a future date or event. Revocable trusts are similar to custodian funds, except that there is some expectation that the creator of the trust may choose, at a later date, to donate the assets to the organization. Since the organization does not yet have assurance that the assets will ever become its property, such agreements should be reported as liabilities. Unless agreements stipulate that specific assets be held in a balance sheet disaggregated by class, the assets and liabilities are reported in the unrestricted class. Because some such agreements may be considered securities, state banking and securities registration laws should also be considered.

7-29. If a trust agreement is revocable, the resources received are not support to the organization until a future event makes the agreement irrevocable or specific amounts are contributed. The gifts provided by these agreements are recorded as support and net assets only when they become irrevocable (to the extent they will accrue to the organization) or when they are released to the organization. Until such time, the trust assets should be segregated from organizational assets because they are owned by a separate legal entity.

LIFE INSURANCE

7-30. Donors may use whole-life insurance policies in various ways to make gifts to a ministry. Donors may name the organization beneficiary of a policy, while ownership of the policy is retained by the donor. In such cases, the beneficial interest of the charity is changeable and should not be recorded. If the donor pledges to continue the premium payments, the present value of this pledge should be recorded in the usual way. The present value is the face value of the policy discounted from the actuarially expected payment date, less any allowance for uncollectible pledges that is considered appropriate.

7-31. Other forms of life insurance gifts involve transferring ownership of a policy to the organization. If the policy is fully paid up, the value is equivalent to the cash surrender value (CSV). *(Canadian ministries, see 9-58.)*

If the policy requires premiums still to be paid, either the donor may pledge to pay them, or the donor may indicate that any future premiums are the responsibility of the organization. If the donor promises to pay the premiums, the value of the pledge is the same discounted value as above. If the organization is to pay the premiums, the initial value is the CSV at the date of gift. As future premiums are paid, the CSV increases.

LIFE ESTATES

7-32. A special case of a split-interest gift is a life estate, where a donor contributes an asset but retains an irrevocable life interest in the asset (conceptually similar to a contribution to an irrevocable trust). This contribution is often a personal residence. The donor is entitled to use the residence until his/her death, at which time the organization takes possession of the asset. Absent further restrictions by the donor, the organization may then dispose of the residence if it wishes to do so. The donor is considered to have a life estate in the asset.

7-33. Although title is transferred at the time of contribution, the organization does not yet have use of the gift so it would be recorded in the temporarily restricted net asset class. The amount of the gift is the fair value of the asset (which would be titled "future interest in house"), discounted to present value from the date at which the organization is actuarially expected to take possession of the residence, less any related liabilities (such as a mortgage or possibly projected maintenance costs).

Noncash gifts are normally recorded at the market value of the assets received at the date of the gift, which in this case is the current, undiscounted value of the house. However, since the organization cannot sell or otherwise use the asset until the termination of the life interest, the fair value to the *organization* is the discounted amount. If the agreement provides that the organization pay maintenance and other costs, those costs should be recorded as unrestricted expenses when incurred.

Chapter 8

Related Organizations

Contents

◆ CRITERIA TO DETERMINE IF CONSOLIDATION IS
REQUIRED OR PERMITTED 190

◆ AFFILIATION OR JOINT MINISTRIES AGREEMENTS .. 192

◆ DEVELOPING ORGANIZATIONS 193

◆ REVENUE-PRODUCING OPERATIONS 193

◆ OPERATIONS IN OTHER LOCATIONS AND
COUNTRIES 194

◆ FOR-PROFIT ENTITIES 195

◆ CONSOLIDATED FINANCIAL STATEMENTS AND
DISCLOSURES 195

◆ MERGERS OF NOT-FOR-PROFIT ORGANIZATIONS .. 196

Related Organizations

(This Chapter focuses on separate legal entities, rather than divisions, operating units, or other parts of a single entity.)

8-1.   Meaningful financial reporting requires that financial statement users be informed not only about the reporting organization but also about any related organizations. Information should include:

Required by GAAP

- nature of the related entities and relationship with the reporting organization

- financial transactions with related organizations

- amounts due to or from related entities

- which organizations are included in the reporting entity

Recommended by EJAC

- resources held by others on behalf of the reporting organization

- other resources under the control of the reporting organization

8-2.   Unlike for-profit entities with stockholder or other ownership interests, not-for-profit organizations generally have no specifically defined ownership. However, effective control of one organization by another may exist through the organization's articles, bylaws, policies, practices, affiliation agreements, and other legal arrangements. Also, organizations may have control through appointment of board members, historical financial support, by contract, or through other means.

It is important to consider whether such organizations should be consolidated or combined. (Consolidation usually refers to majority ownership or control by the reporting organization, while combination may apply to entities under common control or joint ministry.) Furthermore, organizations should consider the extent of any detailed disclosures about the other organizations in the financial statements, including the notes to the financial statements, and any supplemental schedules.

8-3.   A Christian ministry may be related to other organizations having varying degrees of autonomy. Sometimes these organizations are separate corporate entities, loose associations, or divisions/departments of the organization. These vary from location to location and from time to time. For example:

- an association and its regional or local chapters

- a church and its related church school or other separate ministry

- a church denomination and its related agencies, districts, and publishing house

- a ministry and its related supporting organization or foundation

- affiliated missionary organizations or a missionary organization and its foreign operations or national churches or schools

8-4.   The following is an excerpt from AICPA Statement of Position 94-3.

§8.   Financially Interrelated Not-for-Profit Organizations

Not-for-profit organizations may be related to one or more other not-for-profit organizations in numerous ways, including ownership, control, and economic interest.

§9.   As discussed in paragraphs 10-13, the various kinds and combinations of control and economic interest result in various financial reporting. Certain kinds of control result in consolidation (paragraph 10). Other kinds of control result in consolidation only if coupled with an economic interest (paragraph 11). Still other kinds of control result in consolidation being permitted but not required if coupled with an economic interest (paragraph 12). The existence of control or an economic interest, but not both, is discussed in paragraph 13.

§10. Not-for-profit organizations with a controlling financial interest in another not-for-profit organization through direct or indirect ownership of a majority voting interest in that other not-for-profit organization should consolidate that other organization, unless control is likely to be temporary or does not rest with the majority owner, in which case consolidation is prohibited, as discussed in paragraph 13 of FASB Statement No. 94.

§11. In the case of (a) control through a majority ownership interest by other than ownership of a majority voting interest, as discussed in paragraph 10, or control through a majority voting interest in the board of the other entity and (b) an economic interest in other such organizations, consolidation is required, unless control is likely to be temporary or does not rest with the majority owner, in which case consolidation is prohibited, as discussed in paragraph 13 of FASB Statement No.94.

§12. Control of a separate not-for-profit organization in which the reporting organization has an economic interest may take forms other than majority ownership or voting interest; for example, control may be through contract or affiliation agreement. In circumstances such as these, consolidation is permitted but not required, unless control is likely to be temporary, in which case consolidation is prohibited, as discussed in paragraph 13 of FASB Statement No. 94. If the reporting organization controls a separate not-for-profit organization through a form other than majority ownership or voting interest and has an economic interest in that other organization, and consolidated financial statements are not present, the notes to the financial statements should include the following disclosures:

- Identification of the other organization and the nature of its relationship with the reporting organization that results in control

- Summarized financial data of the other organization including:

  - Total assets, liabilities, net assets, revenue, and expenses

  - Resources that are held for the benefit of the reporting organization or that are under its control

- The disclosures set forth in FASB Statement No. 57, *Related Party Disclosures*

§13. In the case of control and an economic interest, the presentation of consolidated financial statements, as discussed in paragraph 11, or the disclosures, as discussed in paragraph 12, are required. The existence of control or an economic interest, but not both, precludes consolidation, except as stated in the next sentence, but requires the disclosures set forth in FASB Statement No. 57. Entities that otherwise would be prohibited from presenting consolidated financial statements under the provisions of this SOP, but that currently present consolidated financial statements in conformity with the guidance in SOP 78-10, may continue to do so.

§14. If consolidated financial statements are presented, they should disclose any restrictions made by entities outside of the reporting entity on distributions from the controlled not-for-profit organization to the reporting organization, and any resulting unavailability of the net assets of the controlled not-for-profit organization for use by the reporting organization.

8-5.   In determining which entities should be consolidated for financial reporting purposes, the focus is first on whether the organization has control and, if so, what kind of control:

- Controlling financial interest through ownership of a majority voting interest—uncommon for control of one NPO by another because NPOs generally don't have ownership interests;

- Control though a majority ownership interest by other than ownership of a majority voting interest — uncommon for control of one NPO by another, except for membership corporations;

- Control through a majority voting interest in the board of the other entity — the most common form of clear control of one NPO by another; and

- Other kinds of control, such as force of moral persuasion, contract, affiliation agreements, and other means.

After determining whether one NPO controls another, the focus is then on whether an economic interest exists. In most circumstances in which one NPO controls another, an economic interest, as defined in SOP 94-3, will exist.

SOP 94-3 (Glossary)

Control. The direct or indirect ability to determine the direction of management and policies through ownership, contract, or otherwise.

Economic interest. An interest in another entity that exists if (a) the other entity holds or utilizes significant resources that must be used for the unrestricted or restricted purposes of the not-for-profit organization, either directly or indirectly by producing income or providing services, or (b) the reporting organization is responsible for the liabilities of the other entity. The following are examples of economic interests:

- Other entities solicit funds in the name of and with the expressed or implied approval of the reporting organization, and substantially all of the funds solicited are intended by the contributor or are otherwise required to be transferred to the reporting organization or used at its discretion or direction.

- A reporting organization transfers significant resources to another entity whose resources are held for the benefit of the reporting organization.

- A reporting organization assigns certain significant functions to another entity.

- A reporting organization provides or is committed to provide funds for another entity or guarantees significant debt of another entity.

Majority voting interest in the board of another entity. For the purposes of this SOP, a majority voting interest in the board of another entity is illustrated by the following example. Entity B has a five-member board, and a simple voting majority is required to approve board actions. Entity A will have a majority voting interest in the board of Entity B if three or more Entity A board members, officers, or employees serve on or may be appointed at Entity A's discretion to the board of Entity B. However, if three of Entity A's board members serve on the board of Entity B but Entity A does not have the ability to require that those members serve on the Entity B board, Entity A does not have a majority voting interest in the board of Entity B.

CRITERIA TO DETERMINE IF CONSOLIDATION IS REQUIRED OR PERMITTED

8-6.   If a controlling financial interest through ownership of a majority voting interest exists, consolidation (as discussed in paragraphs 8-4 and 8-5) is required.

8-7.   If a majority voting interest in the board of the other entity exists (either the governing board of the reporting organization appoints or approves appointment to the governing board of the other organization, or a majority of the other organization's governing board are required to consist of individuals who are also board members, officers, or employees of the reporting organization) and an economic interest exists, consolidation is required.

8-8.   If control exists in a form other than (a) a controlling financial interest through ownership of a majority voting interest, (b) control though a majority ownership interest by other than ownership of a majority voting interest, or (c) control through a majority voting interest in the board of the other entity and an economic interest exists, consolidation is permitted but not required.

EJAC encourages consolidation when it enhances full and meaningful disclosure to financial statement users such as if the reporting organization provides a significant portion of the revenue or guarantees the liabilities of the other organization. However, if control and an economic interest exist but consolidated financial statements are not presented, SOP 94-3 requires that the notes to the financial statements should include:

- identification of the other organization(s) and the nature of the relationship(s) with the reporting organization that results in control

- summarized financial data of the other organization(s), including:

  - total assets, liabilities, net assets, revenues, and expenses

  - resources that are held for the benefit of the reporting organization or that are under its control

- description and quantification of any transactions between the other organization(s) and the reporting organization and other disclosures required by FASB Statement No. 57

8-9.   Consolidation is precluded if control (other than a controlling financial interest through ownership of a majority ownership interest) or an economic interest (but not both) exists, unless the entities have been following guidance established in SOP 78-10. (This provision of SOP 78-10 was grandfathered as discussed in the *AICPA NPO Guide 2000,* pages 122 and 128.) Even if consolidation is required, separate subsidiary-only financial statements may be presented, but these should disclose the nature of the control relationships and include any disclosures required by FASB Statement No. 57. FASB Statement No. 94 precludes the use of parent-company-only financial statements for use as the general purpose financial statements of the primary reporting entity. (See Appendix G of this guide for AICPA flowcharts and decision trees for reporting of related entities.)

8-10.   On February 3, 1999, the FASB released an exposure draft (revised) of a proposed FASB Statement, *Consolidated Financial Statements: Purpose and Policy—Revision of Exposure Draft issued October 16, 1995,* that, in addition to other matters, would supersede FASB Statement No. 94.

This proposed statement would establish standards that specify when entities should be included in consolidated financial statements and how consolidated financial statements should be prepared. It would apply to business enterprises and not-for-profit organizations that control other entities regardless of the legal form of the controlling and controlled entities. Its outcome is uncertain at this time. In January, 2001, FASB announced it was suspending deliberations on this draft. *(Canadian ministries, see 9-21.)*

AFFILIATION OR JOINT MINISTRIES AGREEMENTS

8-11.   Organizations sometimes choose to operate in cooperation with other entities (joint venture) under an affiliation or joint ministries agreement. Such ministries might conduct the same ministry, use the same strategy and materials, even share substantially the same name, but be independent without mutual control. Affiliated organizations, including those in other ministry-funding/ missionary-sending countries, must be consolidated if certain kinds of control and an economic interest exist (as previously discussed). If they not consolidated, however, combined financial statements still may be considered meaningful to present the worldwide activities and financial position of the affiliated (joint ministries) organizations. Also, the disclosures set forth in FASB Statement No. 57 may be required.

8-12.   If a joint ministries agreement is in substance a joint venture or partnership, the reporting organization should include in its financial statements either its pro rata share of assets, liabilities, net assets, revenue, and expenses or other appropriate share of equity or stipulated financial elements. (See Appendix H for a sample Joint Ministries Agreement.)

DEVELOPING ORGANIZATIONS

8-13.   Developing organizations established by Christian ministries are normally not consolidated after operating control and financial responsibility have been transferred to another independent governing body, even though identity and doctrinal distinctions may continue to be shared. However, during the establishment phase, the ministry that established the developing organization usually controls it, and consolidation may be required unless control is likely to be temporary, in which case consolidation is prohibited. When control of a subsidiary (including its assets, liabilities, and operations) is transferred to another independent, governing body, accounting for the transfer requires consideration of the circumstances surrounding the transfer to determine the proper reporting. Some transfers clearly are simply contributions of the subsidiary to the other governing body and are reported under FASB Statement No. 116 as expenses by the transferor in its statement of changes in net assets (or, if restricted net assets are transferred, are reported as other reductions in net assets). (Under FASB Statement No. 117, it is permissible, if desired, to report the expense below an "operating" subtotal in that statement.) The transfer is likely to be reported as a contribution if the transferor engages in many such transfers, and/or if the transfer does not in substance change the transferor's reporting entity. (Transfers: (1) to owners, (2) that are for the purchase of goods or services, or the settlement of liabilities, or (3) in which one party is acting as an agent, intermediary, or trustee, are not contemplated by this paragraph.)

However, if the transfer in substance results in a new reporting entity for the transferor, the transferor should report the transfer as a change in reporting entity. Paragraph 8-23 discusses changes in the reporting entity.

REVENUE-PRODUCING OPERATIONS

8-14.   Christian ministries are frequently involved in related ministry operations that produce revenue, either as a direct activity or through a related entity. Christian bookstores, camps, retreat centers, conventions, publications, and education are examples of such ministries. Ministries may also conduct unrelated business activities. Activities conducted directly by a Christian ministry should always be included in its financial reports. If activities are conducted by another entity, that entity should either be consolidated or the financial statements of the ministry should include certain disclosures about it, as previously discussed.

OPERATIONS IN OTHER LOCATIONS AND COUNTRIES

8-15.   A Christian ministry conducting operations in various locations (domestic or worldwide) that are under the control of the reporting organization and otherwise meet the conditions for consolidation should have comprehensive branch reporting that is integrated with the primary entity's records. Branch or field-based assets, liabilities, revenues, and expenses should be included in the primary financial reports of the reporting organization, if material. The financial statements should disclose assets held in other countries and revenues from foreign sources.

8-16.   In the past, some ministries conducting operations in other countries have bought, held, or sold assets, rented property and equipment, or otherwise used their assets to generate revenues without including these assets and transactions in their financial statements. Organizations may set up foreign corporations in other countries that are in substance controlled by the ministry. Such revenues and related assets and liabilities, even in other countries, should be included in the organization's financial statements, if material. *(Canadian ministries, see 9-5.)*

Examples include branch/field offices, camps, bookstores, medical clinics, rental properties, etc. FASB Statement No. 5, *Accounting for Contingencies,* paragraph 32, addresses the issue of expropriation regarding such assets that are directly owned by the organization. If there exists "probable intent by a government to expropriate assets," then a reserve for a loss contingency should be recorded if the amount can be reasonably estimated.

Even if capital assets in other countries have a limited useful life due to unusual circumstances, they should be capitalized and depreciated over that useful life. Examples include political conditions that make expropriation likely; other circumstances limiting sale or exchange making abandonment probable; or intent to turn over (grant) the assets to a national entity at some point in time. The notes to the financial statements should disclose conditions that limit the useful life of assets and the useful lives used for depreciation.

FOR-PROFIT ENTITIES

8-17. Christian ministries may also be involved in the long-term ownership of for-profit entities, either to generate income or for ministry purposes. Caution should be exercised to ensure consideration of all tax implications between the for-profit and not-for-profit entity.

The provisions of SOP 94-3, *Reporting of Related Entities by Not-for-Profit Organizations,* and FASB Statement No. 94, *Consolidation of All Majority-Owned Subsidiaries,* should be followed. Generally, a majority voting ownership interest will result in consolidation; interests of 20-50% are generally reported on the equity method; and interests of under 20% are reported according to general investment accounting policies. As an option, the SOP permits reporting investments of less than 50 percent ownership interest on the market value basis, if that policy was permitted by an *AICPA Guide* previously applicable to the organization and followed for all investments of less than 50 percent ownership interest.

CONSOLIDATED FINANCIAL STATEMENTS
AND DISCLOSURES

8-18. Care should be exercised in the procedures used to consolidate financial information, to be certain that all interorganizational transactions are properly eliminated, preventing the overstatement of assets, liabilities, revenues, and expenses. For example, sales from a consolidated affiliate to the reporting organization should be eliminated against the affiliate's activities, leaving only truly external resource revenues and expenditures for the consolidated entity. The notes to the financial statements should state that all material interorganizational amounts have been eliminated. Organizations may also wish to present such eliminations in an eliminations column in the consolidating schedules.

8-19. The notes to the financial statements should identify the related organizations that have been consolidated in the statements.

Affiliated or related organizations not consolidated should also be disclosed.

8-20.   Related party transactions should be carefully considered and material transactions reported for those occurring between entities not consolidated, as discussed in FASB Statement No. 57, *Related Party Disclosures.*

MERGERS OF NOT-FOR-PROFIT ORGANIZATIONS

8-21.   Mergers are becoming more common among not-for-profit organizations. Care should be taken to properly evaluate financial, operational, and accounting implications and to prepare an effective transition plan. Investment of resources in due diligence, thorough evaluation, and a well-developed transition plan are critical to affect the desired result without undue surprises and costs.

Mergers may constitute:

- the curtailment of one entity and granting of assets to another

- the purchase of one entity or its assets by another

- a pooling of interests (which is the most common)

8-22.   Accounting literature discusses accounting methods for business combinations. Although some attributes of the pooling of interests method do not apply to not-for-profit mergers—primarily because most not-for-profit organizations do not have stock ownership—the pooling method may be the most meaningful presentation. In this method, the assets, liabilities, net assets, revenue, and expenses of each organization are combined for reporting purposes as of the date of the merger.

In September 1999, the FASB released an exposure draft of a proposed Statement of Financial Accounting Standards, *Business Combinations and Intangible Assets.* This proposed Statement is divided into two parts. The first part addresses the method of accounting for business combinations and would amend APB Opinion No. 16, *Business Combinations,* to provide that all combinations be accounted for using the purchase method. The second part addresses the accounting for intangible assets (including goodwill) whether acquired singly, in a group, or as part of a business combination, and would supersede APB No. 17, *Intangible Assets*. The second part of this proposed Statement would apply to both not-for-profit and for-profit organizations, and to intangible assets (including goodwill) acquired in transactions initiated after the issuance date of the final statement. The proposed Statement would amend or supersede other existing accounting pronouncements.

The FASB is addressing issues specific to combinations of not-for-profit organizations as a separate subproject, conducted concurrently with the main business combinations project.

8-23.   Sometimes one organization will split into two or more organizations, such as in a reverse merger or if an existing entity transfers control of a subsidiary to another independent, governing body, as discussed in paragraph 8-13. As noted in paragraph 8-13, when a subsidiary is transferred to another independent, governing body, accounting for the transfer requires consideration of the circumstances surrounding the transfer to determine the proper reporting.

If the substance of the transaction results in a change in the reporting entity for the transferor, paragraphs 12 and 34-35 of APB No. 20, *Accounting Changes,* require restatement of the financial statements of all prior periods presented, to show financial statements for the new reporting entity for all periods presented. (In single-year statements, the only number(s) to be restated would be the beginning net assets.) If comparative prior-period statements are presented, the effect of the change in the reporting entity on changes in net assets reported on the statement of activities. Also, any reported performance indicator, should be disclosed for all periods presented.

To comply with the disclosure requirements of paragraph 35 of APB 20, which do not contemplate the net asset reporting model of FASB Statement No. 117, EJAC also recommends that in the period in which the reporting entity changes, the effect of the restatement on net assets of the reporting entity be disclosed by reconciling net assets as previously reported to the corresponding amount(s) after the split-up. This reconciliation can be presented either on the face of the statement of activity or in a note. In addition, APB No. 20

requires that a note to the financial statements describe the nature of the change and the reason for it.

In many cases, judgment will be required to determine whether such a transfer results in a change in the reporting entity. Organizations should consider all relevant facts and circumstances, including the size of the transfer relative to the total assets and activities of the transferor.

Canadian Principles and Practices

Contents

PRINCIPLES FOR REGISTERED CHARITIES 201

PRINCIPLES FOR CHARITABLE GIFTS 202

ACCOUNTING PRACTICES 203

Special Trust Funds 204

Contingent Beneficial Interest in a Special Trust 205

Consolidation of Special Trusts 206

Accounting for Revenue 208

Endowment Funds 210

Unrestricted Revenue 212

Administered Revenue 212

Fund Accounting 214

Inter-fund Transfers 216

Pledges 217

Gifts-in-Kind 217

Notional Revenues 217

Life Insurance 218

Chapter 9

Canadian Principles and Practices

9-1.   The first eight chapters of this book are written from an American perspective. This chapter highlights several important differences that apply to Christian ministries that are Canadian registered charities.   References to chapter nine are included where appropriate in the previous chapters.

PRINCIPLES FOR REGISTERED CHARITIES

9-2.   In the Canadian context the charitable sector is a subset of the not-for-profit sector. Legal restrictions in Canada require a registered charity to devote all resources to the pursuit of exclusively charitable purposes carried on by *itself*. The charity must demonstrate that it has "direction and control" over all expenditures. This can only be done through a written agreement such as an Agency Agreement or a Joint Ministry Agreement. (See Appendix H.) Compliance with the terms of such agreements must be clearly evident. The Canadian Income Tax Act also deems registered charities to have direction and control when they make grants to "qualified donees" (e.g., other registered charities with compatible objects and post-secondary educational institutions outside Canada that are listed in Schedule VIII of the Canadian Income Tax Act).

9-3.   Canadian registered charities are either charitable trusts (unincorporated organizations) or corporate trusts (incorporated organizations). The board of an unincorporated charity consists of trustees who are subject to all the duties imposed on trustees by law. For an incorporated charity, the corporation is the trustee and the directors have duties similar to those of trustees. In either case, the organization *itself* must not be the primary concern. The concern of the board must be that the trust property be used exclusively to pursue charitable purposes. These purposes must be *exclusively* of benefit to the public at large.

9-4.   An analogy of executors of estates is helpful to understand the "trustee nature" of Canadian registered charities. An executor may not have a self-interest in the property of the estate. The property must be administered exclusively for the benefit of the beneficiaries. The executor is entitled to reimbursement for out-of-pocket expenses incurred in administering the estate. However, the executor is not entitled to any remuneration for services rendered without specific legislative authority or court approval. Similarly, a Canadian registered charity is entitled to reimbursement of out-of-pocket expenses (e.g., salaries and supplies), but is not entitled to use any other portion of the charitable property under its administration for the benefit of itself or its board members.

9-5.　　Because of the foregoing principle, Canadian registered charities are not permitted to operate businesses or engage in any activities that do not advance their charitable objects. The charity may not engage in an unrelated for-profit business (unless it is operated substantially by volunteers) or control a for-profit entity. This impacts function-based accounting. Allocating resources to the promotion of the organization for its own sake is inappropriate.

9-6.　　All function-based reporting requires that administrative and fund-raising costs be allocated to the purpose or program for which they are incurred. The allocation of such "overhead" expenses must be reasonable. Examples are percentage of (a) space occupied, (b) employee time, (c) cost, or (d) a combination of these. The selected method should be applied consistently from year to year. Canadian taxing authorities require registered charities to report their management and fund-raising costs separately, but reporting on the financial statements should by done by function. Charities that allocate by function should use a matrix showing primary program service costs (including program administration and promotion), general management costs and fund-raising costs.

PRINCIPLES FOR CHARITABLE GIFTS

9-7.　　Canadian courts have consistently held that a contribution made to a registered charity that is to be treated as a gift for income tax purposes must be "a voluntary transfer of property without valuable consideration." The courts have also held that the word "transfer" in the definition means that the donor may not retain any right or control over the contribution after the charity accepts it.

Consideration refers to anything of value the donor receives in return for the contribution, whether directly or indirectly.

9-8.　　If a donor makes a gift to a Canadian registered charity with conditions, the donor does not have the legal right or power to change those conditions after the gift has been completed.　For example, if a donor designates a gift to support a ministry conducted by a specific missionary, the donor may not be asked for permission to use the funds for an alternative ministry if the original designation cannot be complied with.　The completion of a charitable gift made to a Canadian registered charity is similar to a testamentary gift.　A testamentary gift can be made only when the donor has died.　A donor is considered to be dead regarding the gift once it is completed.　A gift is completed when the registered charity has accepted the transfer of the property with the attached conditions, if any.　To be claimed as a tax benefit, a gift must be acknowledged with an official receipt for income tax purposes.　(To use designated funds for another purpose, application must be made to the court of the province where the gift was made.)

9-9.　　As noted above, based on common law, a Canadian registered charity may not give anything of value in return for a contribution.　However, the Canadian tax authority administratively permits fund-raising incentives to be given to donors, provided the fair market value of the item does not exceed the lesser of 10% of the gift or $50. If the incentive is consumed during a fund-raising event, there are no restrictions.　Consequently, fund-raising incentives should be allocated to specific purposes or programs, or they may be allocated in accordance with the method described in paragraph 9-6.　(For further details see Canada Customs and Revenue Agency Interpretation Bulletins IT-110R3 and IT-111R2.)

ACCOUNTING PRACTICES

9-10.　Sections 4400 to 4450 of the *Handbook of the Canadian Institute of Chartered Accountants* (the CICA) contain recommendations for the presentation of information in the financial statements issued by not-for-profit organizations in Canada. GAAP is followed by Canadian chartered accountants who express opinions on financial statements issued by not-for-profits.　The CICA has not issued recommendations specifically for the subsector that is made up of registered charities. Where the recommendations do not conflict with the legal principles outlined in paragraphs 9-2 through 9-9 above, Canadian registered charities should follow them. Where the CICA recommendations conflict with the legal principles applicable to registered charities, Canadian Council of Christian Charities recommends that they not be followed. Accounting recommendations that are not in compliance with fundamental legal principles by definition cannot be GAAP.

9-11.   The CICA recommendations deal with the accounting treatment of internally and externally restricted funds. However, there are no recommendations that deal with trust funds that are held in whole or in part for the benefit or purposes of other entities or persons. They also do not deal with the fundamental distinction between restricted funds and special trusts. All trust funds are restricted funds, but not all restricted funds are trust funds. If the board of a registered charity decides to set aside its unrestricted funds for a specific project within its charitable purposes, such a fund is a restricted fund but not a trust fund.

9-12.   For a trust to be established by a transfer of property there must be (a) a settlor or settlors, (b) a trustee or trustees, and (c) a beneficiary or beneficiaries. The settlor must be the absolute owner of the property to be transferred and must be free to use the property in any manner whatsoever. When a charity earmarks unrestricted funds for a specific project, these conditions would not be satisfied. Therefore, internally restricted funds cannot be a trust that is separate from the general funds of a charity.

Special Trust Funds

9-13.   Where the board of a registered charity establishes a separate fund for which it solicits contributions from the public, the fund is externally restricted. It would be a special trust fund with specific objects. Such a fund may be restricted for a limited time or for a specific purpose within the charitable objects of the charity. To avoid potential court costs, it is prudent for the directors to require donors to agree before the gift is made that funds left over after the specified period has elapsed or the needs of the specific project have been met will be used where needed most. The specific wording when the fund was established, and the specific restrictions on contributions made to the fund, should dictate the accounting treatment.

9-14. A trustee may exercise full or partial direction over a fund if discretionary power to direct or redirect the use of the property of the fund is given. A registered charity has control over a fund if it has discretionary investment power between receipt of the capital and its use for the designated purpose. If it receives a gift, but is not given discretionary investment powers, the gift is a special trust in addition to being a restricted fund. If the charity is not given the power to pool the funds with its general or other special purpose funds, the funds must be segregated from all its other funds. For example, if a registered charity receives grants from the government to fund the delivery of its general services, the board has discretion over which aspects of its general services will be financed with the grants. However, if the government makes a grant for a specific service with the added stipulation that any income earned by investing the grant are to be added to the capital, the board of the registered charity has no discretionary authority over the use of the original grant or related income. Such a grant constitutes a special trust until the grant and its investment income are either used for the designated service or are returned to the government if the board is not able to use them as designated.

9-15. Funds that are similar to the funds described in the previous paragraph should be reported as restricted special trust funds in the financial statements of a charity.

Contingent Beneficial Interest in a Special Trust

9-16. A registered charity is the contingent beneficiary of a fund if one or more of the charity's objects are the exclusive residual beneficiaries of special trust capital contributed. For example, if a charity receives funds which it is required to invest for the benefit of a named beneficiary until a specified event occurs, but where the capital may be encroached upon, or to pay an annuity for life to an individual beneficiary, ownership of the remainder capital does not vest in the charity for its charitable purposes until the specified event has occurred (e.g., the death of the individual). Unless the conditions for vesting have been, or are certain to be, satisfied, the charity's charitable purposes are at most a contingent beneficiary.

9-17. A registered charity may receive a gift that it is required to disburse to a third party after a specified time or event. While the capital is held by the charity, the income is payable to the charity for its charitable purposes. In this example, the charity's charitable purposes never become the beneficiary of the capital of the special trust.

9-18. A registered charity may receive a gift for the benefit of multiple capital and/or income beneficiaries, where the capital and/or income distribution is subject to predetermined conditions. Even when the charity's charitable purpose is one of the capital or income beneficiaries, the charity's charitable purpose does not receive the benefit of its share of the income or capital until such conditions have been satisfied.

9-19. In the examples cited in the previous three paragraphs, it would not be appropriate to report any of the funds as restricted trust funds on the balance sheet of the reporting charity; however, it would be appropriate to include a full report of such funds in the notes to the financial statements or as an attached schedule.

9-20. Clearly a registered charity's financial reports should not include special trust funds where the funds are not available, either currently or in the future, for carrying out its charitable purposes. Although the CICA recommendations for not-for-profits may require inclusion of such funds in financial statements because of the definition of controlled and related entities, registered charities should not follow this practice.

Consolidation of Special Trusts

9-21. CICA Section 4450 deals with the consolidation of financial statements. According to definition 4450.02, where a not-for-profit has control or significant influence over or an economic interest in an entity, it should consolidate the financial accounts of the entity with those of the not-for-profit. Control exists where it has continuing power to determine its strategic operating, investing and financing policies without the cooperation of others. Significant influence over an entity is the ability to affect these policies. An economic interest in another entity exists if the other entity holds resources that must be used to produce revenue or provide services for the registered charity, or if the charity is responsible for the liabilities of the other entity.

9-22. Under the CICA 4450 recommendations, a presumption of control exists where the reporting not-for-profit has the right to appoint the majority of the voting members of the other entity, unless there is clear evidence that control does not exist.

9-23. CICA 4450.09 states that significant influence over another entity exists where there is representation on the board of directors, existence of an economic interest, participation in policy-making processes, material inter-entity transactions or interchange of managerial personnel.

9-24. Normally a registered charity that is the trustee of a special trust fund has the power to appoint the original or replacement trustees of the trust. Clearly the charity that is the trustee of a trust has an economic interest in the trust. Even if the charity has neither a capital nor an income interest in the trust, it is responsible for carrying out the charitable purposes of the trust because as trustee it is subject to all the duties of trustees. Frequently the charity will participate in the policy-making processes because it has fiduciary duties as trustee of the trust. Although there may be no financial transfers between the charity and the special trust because of the fiduciary duties of the trustee, the managerial personnel of the charity and the special trust are likely to be the same individuals.

9-25. All but one of the CICA criteria for consolidating the financial statements of the special trust with the financial statements of the reporting charity apply. An auditor who does not take the issue of beneficial ownership into account may insist on having such special trusts consolidated on the registered charity's statement of financial position.

9-26. Financial statements that apply the CICA recommendations in Section 4450, in relation to restricted funds which are legally special trust funds, may not be reliable. By consolidating special trust funds with restricted funds, the impression is created that the reporting charity is the ultimate beneficial owner of the special trust assets. In some cases, the charity's charitable purposes may not benefit from either the income or capital of the special trust in which the funds are held. In other situations, the charity's charitable purposes may benefit from the income or capital in a special trust, only if certain conditions are met first.

9-27. Nothing in the CICA standards prevents a registered charity from treating all contributions, including those for its general charitable purposes, as externally restricted funds. The financial statements of a charity that generates some of its revenue by providing goods or services should clearly show how contributed funds were used in accordance with the restrictions imposed by specific donor direction or by trust law.

9-28. For the reasons stated, registered charities should not apply CICA 4450 recommendations relating to the consolidation of the financial reports for restricted funds which are special trust funds, unless the capital and income benefits are for its charitable purposes. It is appropriate to report such special trust funds as segregated funds on a schedule attached to the financial statements, and to include a note in the financial statements describing the special trust funds and any related contingent benefits or liabilities.

9-29. Registered charities are encouraged to prepare financial reports according to the principles described in this chapter. Unless the CICA handbook is amended to reflect the appropriate treatment of restricted funds that are special trust funds not beneficially owned by the reporting charity, following the recommendations in this chapter will likely result in a qualified audit opinion. It is more important to provide the readers of financial statements with accurate and reliable information that complies with the underlying legal principles, than to receive an unqualified audit opinion.

Accounting for Revenue

9-30. CICA Subsection 4410.02(b) identifies only three types of contributions—restricted, endowment and unrestricted. These categories are not sufficient to properly account for many types of gifts received by a registered charity. The following table indicates the possible sources of revenue of a registered charity:

Sources of Revenue of a Registered Charity

	Restricted		Unrestricted	
Sources of Revenue	Purpose	Time	Earned	General
Contributions	X	X		X
Members' dues			X	X
Income from investments	X	X	X	X
Sale of goods or services			X	

9-31.　CICA 4410.02(b) defines contributions as follows:

A contribution is a nonreciprocal transfer to a not-for-profit organization of cash or other assets or a nonreciprocal settlement or cancelation of its liabilities. Government funding provided to a not-for-profit organization is considered to be a contribution.

There are three types of contributions identified for purposes of this Section:

(i) A *restricted contribution* is a contribution subject to externally imposed stipulations that specify the purpose for which the contributed asset is to be used. A contribution restricted for the purchase of a capital asset or a contribution of the capital asset itself is a type of restricted contribution.

(ii) An *endowment contribution* is a type of restricted contribution subject to externally imposed stipulations specifying that the resources contributed be maintained permanently, although the constituent assets may change from time to time.

(iii) An *unrestricted contribution* is a contribution that is neither a restricted contribution nor an endowment contribution.

9-32. CICA 4410.02(c) provides the following definition of restricted revenue:

> *Restrictions* are stipulations imposed that specify how resources must be used. External restrictions are imposed from outside the organization, usually by the contributor of the resources. Internal restrictions are imposed in a formal manner by the organization itself, usually by resolution of the board of directors. Restrictions on contributions may only be externally imposed. Net assets or fund balances may be internally or externally restricted. Internally restricted net assets or fund balances are often referred to as reserves or appropriations.

9-33. There is nothing specifically wrong with the definition of restricted contributions in CICA 4410.02(b)(i) and it can be applied to registered charities. However, it is incomplete because of the definition of unrestricted contributions in 4410.02(b)(iii). All payments made to a charity that meet CICA's definition of contribution *are* externally restricted within the meaning of 4410.02(b). External restrictions are imposed not only by the contributor, but also by law. For example, contributions may not be used to secure a loan made by a third party (like a bank) to the charity, unless the donor specifically made the contribution for that purpose.

9-34. When a donor makes a contribution to be used for the charitable purposes of the charity, the contribution comes under the authority and protection of the public's representative, the Attorney General of the province where the gift is made. Contributions may only be used to achieve a specific objective of the charity, or its general objectives, depending on the directions of the donor.

9-35. For the reasons stated in the previous paragraphs, a registered charity must decide whether accounting entries which are in accordance with CICA 4410.02(b)(iii) properly reflect the legal trust restrictions imposed on contributions.

Endowment Funds

9-36. Although the definition of endowment contribution in CICA 4410.02(b)(ii) covers one valid type of endowment contribution, it fails to recognize that many endowment contributions do not have the perpetuity requirement. They may be restricted until a specific objective has been achieved or until a specific time has elapsed. For example, the Canadian Council of Christian Charities encourages its certified members to place two restrictions on endowment contributions. The first restriction is that the endowment contribution must be held for a minimum of ten years. This restriction excludes the endowment contribution from the charity's disbursement quota calculation for income tax purposes. The second recommended restriction is that the endowment contribution may be transferred, by exclusive action of the board, to general restricted fund purposes when the specific objective for which the endowment income is to be used is no longer an objective of the charity, or where, in the charity's exclusive opinion, the endowment is uneconomical to maintain. This restriction prevents the accumulation of endowment funds which may become *ultra virus* to the objectives of the charity or which are not economical to maintain. It may be argued that contributions that are not required to be held in perpetuity should be recorded as restricted funds and not as endowment funds. However, such treatment would negate the importance of distinguishing between specifically restricted and endowment funds.

9-37. CICA's requirement that endowment funds must be maintained permanently is less constraining than would first appear. Its *Not-for-profit Financial Reporting Guide,* published in 1998, p. 103, states that:

> The endowment fund balance (i.e., net assets held for endowment) will include externally restricted amounts that must be maintained permanently. (Note: The endowment fund balance may also include internally restricted amounts.)

The note in parentheses indicates that endowment funds need not consist exclusively of funds to be maintained in perpetuity. The board of the charity can decide to transfer funds that are internally restricted, within the restrictions imposed by the original source of such funds. The statement of financial position at 4400(a)(iii) of the *CICA Accounting Recommendations,* March 1996, also reflects this treatment.

9-38. It is recommended that registered charities accept endowment contributions only where the board has the discretion to transfer the contributions to other objectives at the later of the elapse of ten years, or when the objective for which the endowment contribution was made is no longer an objective of the charity. It is also recommended that charities account for such restricted contributions as endowment funds.

Unrestricted Revenue

9-39. Truly unrestricted revenue of a registered charity consists of payments exclusively received for the supply of goods or services, or income earned from the investment of such revenue. Registered charities are encouraged to distinguish between these earned unrestricted revenues and the general unrestricted fund (contributions received for general charitable purposes and related investment income). Under common law, charities may not use future donation revenue as security for operating loans. Only earned revenue may be used for such purposes. The solution is to separate the funds.

Administered Revenue

9-40. In addition to the foregoing types of revenue, a registered charity may be the trustee and administrator of funds for which it is reasonably certain to be neither the income nor capital beneficiary. Such funds are not dealt with in the CICA recommendations. They would be specifically restricted trust funds not held to meet the objectives of the reporting charity. An example would be a trust fund established to assist affiliated charities from whom contributions are solicited for the trust. Here the trustee has the administrative and investment control of the specifically restricted trust fund, but the charity receives no benefit as an income or capital beneficiary. Such a fund should be recorded as a segregated fund in the financial statements, not as part of its fund balances and net assets.

9-41. Segregated funds also include all trusts for which the registered charity is the irrevocable remainder beneficiary, but the contributor is a "life tenant" with the right to encroach on capital.

Another example would be trust funds the charity holds for named third-party beneficiaries, where the charity is the sole or partial income beneficiary.

9-42. CICA 4400.29 states that:

> Under the restricted method of accounting for contributions, endowment contributions are accumulated in the endowment fund balance. Other restricted contributions are accumulated in the statement of financial position as part of the appropriate restricted fund balance. If there is no appropriate restricted fund, restricted contributions are accumulated as deferred contributions in the general fund.

This description fails to address the many types of contributions that exist. For example, a charity may accept a contribution with the condition that the income beneficiary (or life tenant) may encroach on the capital contributed, and the charity is the beneficiary of the remainder after the occurrence of a specific event, usually the death of the income beneficiary. The remainder amount cannot be determined with any degree of certainty at the time the trust is funded. Therefore, registered charities should record specifically restricted trust funds for which the charity is neither the capital nor income beneficiary, or for which the remainder to be received by the charity cannot be determined with any degree of certainty, in an appropriate, segregated fund.

9-43. The previous paragraph could be viewed as being at variance with CICA 4400.29 and 4410.65-4410.67. These state that "restricted contributions for which no corresponding restricted fund is presented should be recognized in the general fund in accordance with the deferral method." The types of contributions referred to could include those with a significant level of uncertainty as to the benefit to be received by the charity, or contributions from which the charity is precluded from being a beneficiary. To record such contributions in a general fund, which implies beneficial ownership, would be misleading.

Fund Accounting

9-44. The majority of registered charities use the fund method of accounting. CICA 4400.02(d) defines the fund method of accounting as follows:

> The *restricted fund method* of accounting for contributions is a specialized type of fund accounting which involves the reporting of details of financial statement elements by fund in such a way that the organization reports total general funds, one or more restricted funds, and an endowment fund, if applicable. Reporting of financial statement elements segregated on a basis other than the use restrictions (e.g., by program or geographic location) does not constitute the restricted fund method.

9-45. The restricted fund method of accounting for not-for-profits as defined in CICA 4400.02(d) is a modification of the traditional fund accounting method. It restricts the funds to three types—one general fund, multiple restricted funds, and one endowment fund. However, more than one general fund may exist. Where this is the case, each general fund would report an excess or deficiency of revenue over expenses for the reporting period.

9-46. Registered charities are encouraged to use four categories of funds: earned general (or owned), general contribution (or unrestricted for objects), specifically restricted, and endowment. The segregated (or trusteed and administered) funds would not be part of the statement of financial position and must be tracked separately.

9-47. All revenue from the supply of goods and services and income generated by such revenue are recorded in the earned fund. The earned fund balance would include net assets available to satisfy obligations incurred to meet past expenditures in pursuit of a charity's objectives (e.g., operating loan payments) and future expenditures.

9-48. Unrestricted contributions are recorded in a general contribution fund. General contribution fund balances would include assets that are only available to meet future expenditures in pursuit of a charity's objectives (e.g., not to secure loans or to make operating loan payments).

9-49. All specifically restricted contributions and revenues are recorded in an appropriate specifically restricted fund. Such revenues are restricted until the specified expenditure has occurred.

9-50. All endowment contributions, whether they are to be held in perpetuity or not, are reported as revenue of the endowment fund. Any investment income earned by the endowment fund that must be added by direction of the donor, or that cannot be immediately transferred to other funds, is also reported as revenue of the endowment fund. The endowment fund balance would reflect the net assets of the fund that are restricted for a specified purpose or a specified period of time, and that are not currently available for the general objectives of the registered charity.

9-51. All segregated fund contributions and related investment income are reported as revenue of the appropriate segregated fund. The segregated fund balance would reflect the net position of each specific fund. These are not available for the objectives of the registered charity and would not be recorded as assets or liabilities on the statement of financial position.

9-52. CICA 4400.41 states that:

The statement of changes in net assets should present changes in the following for the period:

(a) net assets invested in capital assets;

(b) net assets subject to restrictions requiring that they be maintained permanently as endowments;

(c) other restricted net assets;

(d) unrestricted net assets; and

(e) total net assets.

9-53. Consistent with a number of the foregoing paragraphs, a registered charity should follow CICA 4400.41 with the following modifications:

The statement of changes in net assets of a registered charity should present changes in the following for the period:

(a) net assets invested in capital assets;

(b) net assets subject to restrictions requiring that they be maintained in perpetuity (or for the longer of ten years, or until the objective of the restriction no longer exists) as endowments;

(c) specifically restricted net assets;

(d) generally restricted net assets (net from undesignated contributions);

(e) unrestricted net assets (net from supply of goods and services); and

(f) total net assets.

There are no segregated fund net assets since such assets and liabilities are not recorded on the statement of financial position. Therefore, no segregated funds can flow through to the balance of funds section of the financial statements.

Inter-fund Transfers

9-54. Inter-fund transfers should be fully explained in the notes so the reader can obtain an accurate "picture" of the financial position of each of the funds and of the charity as a whole. The notes should demonstrate that the transfers comply with all external restrictions, both legal and donor imposed, and show which assets are unencumbered. For example, the board of the charity may transfer funds from the unrestricted fund (as defined in paragraph 9-39) to any other fund. However, the board does not have the legal authority to transfer generally or specifically restricted funds to the unrestricted fund, except as specifically permitted under trust law or the restriction imposed by the donor at the time the contribution is made.

Pledges

9-55. CICA recommends that a pledge (i.e., a promise to make a contribution) be recorded as revenue when the collection of the pledge can be reasonably assured. A pledge does not constitute a contribution of a resource because there is no transfer of property at the time the pledge is made. If a pledge is treated as an obligation and recorded as a receivable, the subsequent payment of cash may be the settlement of a contractual agreement, not a voluntary transfer of property. If pledges are treated as receivables by the charity, the donor may never be entitled to an official receipt for income tax purposes. Therefore, Canadian registered charities should *never* record pledges that are eligible for official income tax receipts as revenue.

Gifts-in-Kind

9-56. Canadian income tax law requires registered charities to determine the fair market value of "gifts-in-kind" for which official income tax receipts are provided. If the value of the gift is $1,000 or less, the charity may have a qualified person not dealing at "arm's length" with the charity provide an appraisal. Where the value of the gift-in-kind is greater than $1,000, a person who is qualified and who deals at arm's length with both the donor and the charity must provide the written appraisal. The receipt issued to the donor must include the fair value determined by the appraiser, the name of the appraiser and a description of the property received. The donor must file the receipt for income tax purposes and the charity must report this value in its accounting records.

Notional Revenues

9-57. Canadian income tax law requires registered charities to report on a cash basis on the annual return. By administrative practice registered charities are permitted to report on an accrual basis, but only for timing differences. Therefore, Canadian registered charities should not record revenue in their financial statements for the value of notional benefits, such as voluntary services and interest saved on low- or no-interest loans payable.

Life Insurance

9-58.   Gifts of whole life insurance policies are acceptable gifts for registered charities. If the donor makes the gift of the policy with the commitment to make future premium payments, if any are still required, the charity may retain the policy and provide official receipts for income tax purposes to the donor for the actual premiums paid. However, where a donor does not make the required premium payment, the charity cannot legally make the payment out of other resources, including the cash surrender value of the policy itself. In this event, the charity must cash in the value of the policy or convert it to a paid-up policy.

Bibliography

This bibliography is intended to provide information about publications cited in this Guide, as well as other sources of information that may be useful to readers.

 PROFESSIONAL GUIDES
(see ordering information at introduction, page xix)

American Institute of Certified Public Accountants. Audit and Accounting Guide, *Not-for-Profit Organizations*. New York. 2000.

American Institute of Certified Public Accountants. Audit and Accounting Guide. *Health Care Organizations.* New York. 2000.

American Institute of Certified Public Accountants. *Technical Practice Aids.* New York. 2000.

American Institute of Certified Public Accountants. Statement of Position 98-2, *Accounting for Joint Costs of Informational Materials and Activities of Not-for-Profit Organizations That Include a Fund-Raising Appeal.* New York. 1987.

Financial Accounting Standards Board. Statement of Financial Accounting Concepts No. 4, *Objectives of Financial Reporting by Nonbusiness Organizations.* Stamford, Conn. 1980.

Financial Accounting Standards Board. Statement of Financial Accounting Concepts No. 6, *Elements of Financial Statements.* Stamford, Conn. 1985.

Financial Accounting Standards Board. Statement of Financial Accounting Standards No. 7, *Using Cash Flow Information and Present Value in Accounting Measures.* Norwalk, Conn. 2000.

Financial Accounting Standards Board. Statement of Financial Accounting Standards No. 93, *Recognition of Depreciation by Not-for-Profit Organizations.* Stamford, Conn. 1987.

Financial Accounting Standards Board. Statement of Financial Accounting Standards No. 116, *Accounting for Contributions Received and Contributions Made.* Norwalk, Conn. 1993.

Financial Accounting Standards Board. Statement of Financial Accounting Standards No. 117, *Financial Statements of Not-for-Profit Organizations.* Norwalk, Conn. 1993.

Financial Accounting Standards Board. Statement of Financial Accounting Standards No. 124, *Accounting for Certain Investments Held by Not-for-Profit Organizations.* Norwalk, Conn. 1999.

Financial Accounting Standards Board. Statement of Financial Accounting Standards No. 136, *Transfers of Assets to a Not-for-Profit Organization or Charitable Trust That Raises or Holds Contributions for Others.* Norwalk, Conn. 1999.

OTHER GUIDES AND PROFESSIONAL PAPERS

Accounting Standards Committee. *Accounting by Charities: a Discussion Paper*. London, England. 1984.

AICPA Financial Statement Presentation and Disclosure Practices for Not-for-Profit Organizations. New York. AICPA. 1999.

Anthony, R. N. *Financial Accounting in Nonbusiness Organizations: An Exploratory Study of Conceptual Issues.* Norwalk, Connecticut: Financial Accounting Standards Board, 1978.

The Charity Commission. *Accounting by Charities—Statement of Recommended Practices No. 2, Exposure Draft.* London, U.K. 1993.

National Health Council, Inc. and National Assembly of National Voluntary Health and Welfare Organizations, Inc. *Standards of Accounting and Financial Reporting for Voluntary Health and Welfare Organizations.* New York, 1998. 4th Edition.

Voluntary Organizations Steering Committee. *Canadian Standards of Accounting and Financial Reporting for Voluntary Organizations.* The Canadian Council on Social Development, 1967.

Voluntary Organizations Steering Committee. *Programme Budgeting for Canadian Voluntary Organizations.* The Canadian Council on Social Development, 1969.

BOOKS—ACCOUNTING AND REPORTING

Anthony, R. and D. Young. *Management Control in Nonprofit Organizations.* Burr Ridge, Illinois: 1994. 5th Edition.

Blazek, Jody. *Tax and Financial Planning for Tax-Exempt Organizations: Forms, Checklists, Procedures.* New York: John Wiley & Sons, 1993 (1994, 1995, 1996, 1997 and 1998 Supplements).

Gross, M. J., R. F. Larkin and J. H. McCarthy. *Financial and Accounting Guide for Not-for-Profit Organizations.* New York: John Wiley & Sons, 2000 (2001 Supplement). 6th Edition.

Hay, L. and E. Wilson. *Accounting for Governmental and Nonprofit Entities.* Burr Ridge, Illinois: 1994. 9th Edition.

Henke, E. O. *Accounting for Nonprofit Organizations.* Cincinnati, Ohio: South-Western Publishing Co., 1989. 5th Edition.

Larkin, R. F. and M. DiTommaso. *Not-for-Profit GAAP.* New York: John Wiley & Sons, 2001.

Lindsey, S. W., C. A. Hartfield, M. L. Benson, and K. W. Fransen. *Guide to Nonprofit GAAP.* Fort Worth, Texas: Practitioners Publishing Company, 2000. 5th Edition.

Sumariwalla, R. and W. Lewis. *Unified Financial Reporting System for Not-for-Profit Organizations.* San Francisco: Jossey-Bass, 2000.

BOOKS—FINANCIAL MANAGEMENT AND LEGAL ISSUES

Bryce, H. *Financial and Strategic Management for Nonprofit Organizations.* Englewood Cliffs, New Jersey: 1992.

Bryson, John M. *Strategic Planning for Public and Nonprofit Organizations.* Revised edition. San Francisco: Jossey-Bass, 1995.

Busby, Dan. *The Zondervan Church and Nonprofit Organization Tax & Fianncial Guide.* Grand Rapids, Michigan: 2000. 2001 edition.

Conners, Tracy. *The Nonprofit Handbook.* New York: McGraw-Hill, 1988. 2nd Edition.

Conners, Tracy. *The Nonprofit Handbook—Management.* New York: John Wiley & Sons, 1997. 2nd Edition.

Crumroy, Otto F., Jr., Stan Kukawka, Frank M. Whitman. *Church Administration and Finance Manual.* Harrisburg, Pennsylvania: Morehouse Publishing, 1998.

Herman, Robert D. and Associates. *The Jossey-Bass Handbook of Nonprofit Leadership and Management.* San Francisco: Jossey-Boss, 1994.

Herzlinger, R. and D. Nitterhouse. *Financial Accounting and Managerial Control for Nonprofit Organizations.* Cincinnati, Ohio: South-Western Publishing Co., 1994.

Hopkins, Bruce. *The Law of Fund-Raising.* New York: John Wiley & Sons, 1996 (1998, 2000 Supplements). 2nd Edition.

Hopkins, Bruce. *The Law of Tax-Exempt Organizations.* New York: John Wiley & Sons, 1998 (1999, 2000, 2001 Supplements). 7th Edition.

Hopkins, Bruce. *Starting and Managing a Nonprofit Organization.* New York: John Wiley & Sons, 2000. 3rd Edition.

Hopkins, Bruce. *The Tax Law of Charitable Giving.* New York: John Wiley & Sons, 2000. 2nd Edition.

Zeibell, M. and D. DeCoster. *Management Control Systems in Nonprofit Organizations.* Orlando, Florida: Harcourt Brace Jovanovich, 1991.

Appendix A—Glossary

A number of accounting terms used throughout this guide are commonly used by not-for-profit organizations. Because these terms have specialized meanings, this glossary is included to help the reader better understand these terms. Many of the terms are based on those in the glossaries included in the AICPA *Audit and Accounting Guide for Not-for-Profit Organizations* and FASB Statement Nos. 116 and 117.

accrual accounting – Recognizing assets, liabilities, income, and expenses as earned or incurred rather than as cash or similar assets received or paid.

agent – One who acts on behalf of another. See custodian funds.

American Institute of Certified Public Accountants (AICPA) – The national professional association for CPAs in the U.S. whose objectives include establishing accounting standards, which it sets through its Accounting Standards Executive Committee (AcSEC). AcSEC standards issued as Statements of Position (commonly referred to as "SOP") and Audit and Accounting Guides are considered generally accepted accounting principles and must be followed in order for an organization to receive an unqualified opinion from auditors.

annuity gift – A transfer of assets to a not-for-profit organization in connection with a split-interest agreement that is in part a contribution and in part an exchange transaction. The organization accepts the contribution and is obligated to make periodic stipulated payments to the donor or a third-party beneficiary for a specified period of time, usually either a specified number of years or until the death of the donor or third-party beneficiary.

annuity trust – An annuity gift (q.v.) set up as a trust under which the income payments are a stated percentage of the initial value. See charitable remainder trust.

auxiliary activity or organization – An activity or organization providing a service that may or may not be part of the basic program of the organization.

bargain sale – A sale of property or other assets at a price which is less than the fair market value. This transaction is part sale and part gift.

board designated – See designated net assets.

Canadian Institute of Chartered Accountants (CICA) – The national professional association for Chartered Accountants (CA) in Canada.

charitable lead trust – A trust established in connection with a split-interest agreement in which the not-for-profit organization receives distributions during the agreement's term. Upon termination of the trust, the remaining trust assets are paid to the donor or to third-party beneficiaries designated by the donor.

charitable remainder trust – A trust established in connection with a split-interest agreement in which the donor or a third-party beneficiary receives specified distributions during the agreement's term. Upon termination of the trust, a not-for-profit organization receives the assets remaining in the trust. See annuity trust, unitrust.

class(es) – The characteristic type of resources or net assets based upon donor-imposed restrictions or lack thereof; e.g., permanently restricted, temporarily restricted, unrestricted.

conditional promise to give – A promise to give that depends on the occurrence of a specified future and uncertain event to bind the promisor.

consolidated financial statements – Financial statements which include added-together data for two or more related entities.

contribution – An unconditional transfer of cash or other assets to an entity or a settlement or cancelation of its liabilities in a voluntary nonreciprocal transfer by another entity acting other than as an owner.

corpus – The principal amount of a gift or trust.

custodian funds – Resources received and held by an organization as a fiscal agent for others.

deferred gift – The term deferred gifts refers to a variety of giving arrangements in which ultimate receipt of the benefits of a gift is deferred until some later date or event.

deferred revenue – Revenue received or recorded before it is earned—that is, before the conditions are met, in whole or in part, for which the revenue is received or is to be received.

designated net assets – Unrestricted net assets subject to self-imposed limits by action of the governing board. Designated net assets may be earmarked for future programs, investment, contingencies, purchase or construction of fixed assets, or other uses.

deputized fund-raising – Charities using this concept generally determine an amount each staff member is responsible to raise. Funds are often recorded in a support account for each worker. Charges are made against the support account that funds the staff member's particular sphere of the organization's ministry.

donor-imposed condition – A donor stipulation that specifies a future and uncertain event whose occurrence or failure to occur gives the promisor a right of return of the assets it has transferred, or releases the promisor from its obligation to transfer its assets.

donor-imposed restriction – A donor stipulation that specifies a use for the contributed asset that is more specific than broad limits resulting from the nature of the organization, the environment in which it operates, and the purposes specified in its articles of incorporation or bylaws, or comparable documents for an unincorporated association. A restriction on an organization's use of the asset contributed may be temporary or permanent.

encumbrances – Commitments in the form of orders, contracts, and similar items that will become payable when goods are delivered or services rendered. Encumbrances are a part of net assets, not liabilities.

endowment – A gift in which a donor has stipulated in the donative instrument that the principal is to be maintained inviolate and in perpetuity, and only the income from the investment of the assets may be expended. If, at some future date or event, it will no longer be required to maintain the assets in perpetuity, the amounts would be called term endowment (q.v.). Also see quasi-endowment.

equity – See net assets.

exchange transaction – Transactions in which each party receives and sacrifices commensurate value (usually purchases and sales).

expendable net assets – Assets that are available currently to finance an organization's program services and supporting activities, including both unrestricted and restricted amounts.

extraordinary items – Transactions and other events that are material in nature, of a character significantly different from the typical or customary business activities, not expected to recur frequently, and not normally considered in evaluating the ordinary operating results of an entity.

faith promise – A commitment between an individual and God to contribute to an organization, subject to God's future provision. See paragraphs 4-37 and 4-50.

field ministry – The assignment location of a missionary away from his or her home or sending country.

Financial Accounting Standards Board – An independent not-for-profit organization whose mission includes establishing financial accounting standards. Financial Accounting Standards Board (commonly referred to as the "FASB") Standards are considered generally accepted accounting principles and must be followed in order for an organization to receive an unqualified opinion from auditors.

functional classification – A classification of expenses according to the purpose for which costs are incurred. The primary functional categories are program services and supporting activities. Functional classification is contrasted to object or natural classification of expenses, such as salaries and wages, employee benefits, supplies, etc.

fund – An accounting entity established for the purpose of accounting for resources used for specific activities or objectives in accordance with special regulations, restrictions, or limitations. Funds of similar character are likely to be grouped for simplification of reporting. Also see class.

fund balance(s) – The balance held in a particular fund—may be unrestricted, temporarily restricted, or permanently restricted.

fund group – A group of funds of similar character; for example, operating funds, endowment funds, and annuity and life income funds.

fund-raising activities – Activities undertaken to induce potential donors to contribute money, securities, services, materials, facilities, other assets, or time. They include publicizing and conducting fund-raising campaigns; maintaining donor mailing lists; conducting special fund-raising events; preparing and distributing fund-raising manuals, instructions, and other materials; and conducting other activities involved with soliciting contributions from individuals, foundations, governments, and others.

funds held in trust by others – Resources held and administered, at the direction of the resource provider, by an outside trustee for the benefit of the organization.

furlough expenses – Costs relating to the temporary leave from field ministries by missionary personnel. The purposes of furlough are varied, but most organizations request their personnel use furlough time to report to supporting constituency, rest and recuperation, continuing education, fund-raising, and/or special home ministries. Also referred to by some organizations as home service or home assignment.

generally accepted accounting principles (GAAP) – Broad concepts or guidelines and detailed practices, including all conventions, rules, and procedures that together make up accepted accounting practices at a given time.

gift annuity – See annuity gift.

home ministry – See ministry to constituency.

investment pool – Assets of several funds pooled or consolidated for investment purposes.

lead trust – A trust established for a specified term, during which the income goes to a charity and at the end of which the principal reverts to the donor or a designee.

life income agreement – An agreement whereby money or other property is given to an organization on the condition that the organization binds itself to pay, periodically to the donor or other designated individual, the income earned by the assets donated to the organization for the lifetime of the donor or of the designated individual.

life tenant – One who possesses a life-use right to property.

ministry to constituency – (For organizations other than local churches) Expenses related to encouraging people at home to minister, in the name of Jesus Christ, to the spiritual needs of others at home and elsewhere throughout the world. This category of expenses recognizes the need of each Christian organization to challenge people to go, give, and pray for the fields of need around the world.

natural expense classification – See object classification of expenses.

net assets – The excess or deficiency of assets over liabilities, classified according to the presence or absence of donor-imposed restrictions.

net investment (equity) in land, buildings, and equipment – The total carrying value (after accumulated depreciation) of all property, plant, and equipment used in the ministry, less directly related liabilities. This is exclusive of real properties that are held for investment purposes.

nonreciprocal transfer – A transaction in which an entity incurs a liability or transfers an asset to another entity (or receives an asset or cancelation of a liability) without directly receiving (or giving) value in exchange.

object classification of expenses – A method of classifying expenditures according to their natural classification, such as salaries and wages, employee benefits, supplies purchased, services, etc.

permanent restriction – A donor-imposed restriction that stipulates that resources be maintained permanently, but permits the organization to use up or expend part or all of the income (or other economic benefits) derived from the donated assets.

permanently restricted net assets – The part of the net assets of a not-for-profit organization resulting (a) from contributions and other inflows of assets whose use by the organization is limited by donor-imposed stipulations that neither expire by passage of time nor can be fulfilled or otherwise removed by actions of the organization; (b) from other asset enhancements and diminishments subject to the same kinds of stipulations; and (c) from reclassifications from (or to) other classes of net assets as a consequence of donor-imposed stipulations.

personal gifts – A transfer of money or other property from one individual to another individual, voluntarily, without any obligation, and without consideration for services rendered.

pledge – A promise to make a contribution to an organization in the amount and form stipulated.

pooled fund-raising – Funds raised to support a group of workers instead of a particular worker. There might be just one group—all the self-supported workers. Or, the group might be a team of workers in several mission fields.

pooled income fund – A remainder trust under which the income payout is the actual income earned by the trust.

program services – The activities that fulfill the purposes or mission for which the organization exists and which result in the distribution of goods and services to beneficiaries, customers, or members. Those services are the major purpose for the major output of the organization and often relate to several major programs.

promises to give – A written or oral agreement to contribute cash or other assets to another entity. A promise to give may be either conditional or unconditional.

quasi-endowment – Unrestricted net assets that the governing board of an organization has determined are to be retained and invested. The governing board has the right to decide at any time to expend the principal of such funds. Quasi-endowments remain unrestricted net assets *after* the designation. Also see designated net assets.

reclassifications – Transfers of amounts from one class to another, usually as a result of the release or lapsing of restrictions; e.g., from temporarily restricted to unrestricted.

remainder trust – See charitable remainder trust.

remainderman – The recipient of the corpus (remaining principal) of a trust upon termination.

restricted net assets – Resources whose use is restricted by an outside agency or person, as contrasted with those over which the organization has complete control and discretion. Contributions from a donor who has stipulated that the principal remain intact in perpetuity are also referred to as "pure" or "term" endowments.

pure endowment – A donor-restricted contribution that must be maintained for a specified term.

restriction – A limit on the time or purpose of use of a gift created by a donor stipulation (q.v.).

revenue – Income from delivering or producing goods, rendering services, or other earning activities of an organization such as dues, sales, fees, interest, dividends, or rental income.

revolving loan funds – Funds held for the purpose of making and remaking loans upon repayment.

split-interest agreement – Trust or other arrangements initiated by donors under which not-for-profit organizations receive benefits that are shared with either the donor or third-party beneficiaries. These gifts include lead interests (see lead trust) and remainder interests (see charitable remainder trust, annuity gift, pooled income fund, and unitrust).

stipulation – A statement by a donor which creates a condition or restriction on the use of the transferred resources (q.v.).

support – The conveyance of property from one person or organization to another without consideration; for example, donations, gifts, grants, or bequests. See contribution.

supporting activities – Activities other than program services. The primary supporting activities are management and general, fund-raising, and membership development activities.

temporarily restricted – Donor restricted for a stated period of time or until a stated event.

term endowment – A donor-restricted contribution that must be maintained for a specified term.

transfer – Moving net assets from one fund to another. Transfers do not increase or decrease the total resources of an organization.

unitrust – A charitable remainder trust (q.v.) under which the income payments are calculated as a stated percentage of the current value annually.

unrestricted net assets – The part of net assets of a not-for-profit organization that is neither permanently restricted nor temporarily restricted by donor-imposed stipulations.

voluntary health and welfare organizations – Organizations formed for the purpose of performing voluntary services for various segments of society. They are tax exempt (organized for the benefit of the public), supported by the public, and operated on a "not-for-profit" basis. Most voluntary health and welfare organizations concentrate their efforts and expend their resources in an attempt to solve health and welfare problems of our society and, in many cases, those of specific individuals. As a group, voluntary health and welfare organizations include those not-for-profit organizations that derive their revenue primarily from voluntary contributions from the general public to be used for general or specific purposes connected with health, welfare, or community services.

Appendix B—Accounting for Support and Revenue Supplemental Information

Exhibit 1—Purchase of Goods or Services vs. Restricted Grants

(Reference: paragraph 4-6 to 4-8)

Factors to be considered in distinguishing contracts for the purchase of goods or services from restricted grants

Following is a list of factors which may be helpful to:

- not-for-profit organizations, in deciding how to account for the receipt of payments which might be considered as being either for the purchase of goods or services from the organization or as restricted-purpose gifts or grants to the organization (the reason this distinction is important is that advance payments of gifts are recorded as revenue immediately upon receipt, while advance payments of the purchase price of goods or services are deferred until the goods or services are furnished to the buyer)

- auditors, in assessing the reasonableness of the client's decision

Additional discussion of this distinction can be found in the instructions to IRS Form 990, lines 1a-c; and in IRS Regulation 1.509(a)-3(g).

No one of these factors is normally determinative by itself; all relevant factors should be considered together.

Factors whose presence would indicate the payment is for the purchase of goods or services	**Factors whose presence would indicate the payment is a restricted grant for a specific purpose**

Factors related to the agreement between the payor and the payee:

1. The expressed intent is for the payee to provide goods/services to the payor or to other specifically identified recipients as determined by the payor.

   The expressed intent is to make a gift to the payee to advance the programs of the payee.

2. There is a specified time and/or place for delivery of goods/services to the payor or other recipient.

   Time and/or place of delivery of any goods/services is largely at the discretion of the payee.

3. There are provisions for economic penalties, beyond the amount of the payment, against the payee for failure to meet the terms of the agreement.

   Any penalties are expressed in terms of required delivery of goods/services or are limited to return of unspent amounts.

4. The amount of the payment per unit is computed in a way which explicitly provides for a "profit" margin for the payee.

   The payment is stated as a flat amount or a fixed amount per unit based only on the cost (including overhead) of providing the goods/service.

5. The total amount of the payment is based only on the quantity of items delivered.

   The payment is based on a line item budget request, including an allowance for actual administrative costs.

6. The tenor of the agreement is that the payor receives approximately equivalent value in return for the payment.

   The payor does not receive approximately equivalent value.

Factors whose presence would indicate the payment is for the purchase of goods or services	Factors whose presence would indicate the payment is a restricted grant for a specific purpose

Factors related to the goods/services (items) covered by the payment:

7. The items are closely related to commercial activity regularly engaged in by the payor.	The items are related to the payee's program activities.
8. There is substantial benefit to the payor itself from the items.	The items are normally used to provide goods/services considered of social benefit to society as a whole, or to some defined segment thereof (e.g., children, persons having a disease, students), which might not otherwise have ready access to the items.
9. If the payor is a governmental unit, the items are things the government itself has explicitly undertaken to provide to its citizens; the government has arranged for another organization to be the actual service provider.	The government is in the role of subsidizing provision of services to the public by a nongovernmental organization.
10. The benefits resulting from the items are to be made available only to the payor, or to persons or entities designated by the payor.	The items, or the results of the activities funded by the payment, are to be made available to the general public or to any person who requests and is qualified to receive them. Determination of specific recipients is made by the payee.
11. The items are to be delivered to the payor or to other persons or entities closely connected with the payor.	Delivery is to be made to persons or entities not closely connected with the payor.

Factors whose presence would indicate the payment is for the purchase of goods or services	**Factors whose presence would indicate the payment is a restricted grant for a specific purpose**
12. Revenue from sale of the items is considered unrelated business income (IRC Sec. 512) to the payee.	Revenue is not unrelated income to the payee.
13. In the case of sponsored research, the payor determines the plan of research and the desired outcome and retains proprietary rights to the results.	The research plan is determined by the payee; desired outcomes are expressed only in general terms (e.g., to find a cure for a disease), and the rights to the results remain with the payee or are considered in the public domain.
14. The payment supports applied research.	The payment supports basic research.

Appendix B—Accounting for Support and Revenue Supplemental Information

Exhibit 2—Purpose-Restricted or Not

(Reference: paragraph 4-12)

Factors to be considered in deciding whether a particular gift (for operating purposes) should be classified as purpose-restricted or not

Following is a list of factors which may be present in the grant document, donor transmittal letter or other gift instrument, or in the donee's appeal for gifts to be considered by:

- not-for-profit organizations, in deciding how to classify operating gifts

- auditors, in assessing the appropriateness of the client's decision

In some cases, no one of these factors will be determinative by itself; all applicable factors should be considered together.

These factors are intended to facilitate consideration of the appropriate classification of operating gifts which may be purpose-restricted. This list is not intended to deal with how to account for gifts nor with questions regarding time-restricted gifts or nonoperating gifts, although some factors may be helpful in those areas.

Factors whose presence would indicate the gift is purpose-restricted	**Factors whose presence would indicate the gift may not be purpose-restricted**
1. The purpose of the gift is very specifically set forth. (Note 1)	The purpose is described in general or vague terms.

Note: This factor, if judged to be present, would normally be considered determinative.

2. The donor expects a detailed report of how the gift was used.	No special reporting to the donor is expected.
3. Refund to the donor of any unspent amount is specifically called for.	No mention is made of the disposition of any unspent amount.
4. The recipient would likely not have conducted the activity at all, or to the same extent, in the absence of the gift.	The recipient would likely have conducted the activity anyway.
5. The donor specifies that the gift can only be used to expand existing activity.	Factor not present.
6. The terms of the gift are set forth in a formal written document.	The terms are set forth only orally or informally.
7. The activities funded by the gift are similar to activities funded by previous gifts from the same donor, where the previous gifts were clearly restricted.	Factor not present.

Factors whose presence would indicate the gift is purpose-restricted	Factors whose presence would indicate the gift may not be purpose-restricted
8. The expressed intention of the recipient in soliciting the gift was to solicit restricted gifts.	The solicitation was silent as to the use of the gift or described the use in general terms.
9. In describing the purpose of the gift, the solicitation or the gift instrument includes words such as: restricted must; will only expect certain promise; agree	These documents include words such as: general; operating should any; if intend; hope several plan
10. Based on the overall tone of the language describing the gift, it can reasonably be inferred that the donor's expectation is that the gift is restricted. (See other factors.)	The overall tone does not lead to such an inference.
11. For management control and reporting purposes, the recipient organization is divided into operating units to conduct different programs; (Note 2) the gift is explicitly directed to one of those units.	Factor not present.
12. The terms of the gift include non-programmatic "compliance"-type requirements (often found with government grants). (Note 3)	Factor not present.

Notes:

1. The purpose may be described in various ways. Examples include:

   - geographic location (e.g., a country, city, neighborhood, etc.)

   - population to be served or otherwise benefited (e.g., the visually handicapped, children)

   - anticipated outcome of the activity (e.g., reduction in teenage pregnancy, planting a certain number of churches)

   - precise use of the particular gift (e.g., to pay the salary of a named missionary, to buy Bibles for a specified church)

2. Examples include:

   - An organization serving handicapped children runs a daycare center and a summer camp.

   - A university has a law school and a medical school.

   - A missionary organization has separate units which operate a literacy program and an evangelism program.

3. Examples include compliance with regulations governing:

   - purchasing and hiring

   - affirmative action and civil rights

   - lobbying and political activity

   - drug-free workplace

   - cash management

   - allowable costs and overhead rates

   - subgrants

   - fixed assets

   - audits and financial reports

Appendix B—Accounting for Support and Revenue Supplemental Information

Exhibit 3—Bona Fide Pledge

(Reference: paragraph 4-37)

Factors to be considered in assessing whether a donor has made a bona fide pledge to a donee

Following is a list of factors which may be helpful to:

- donees, in assessing whether a pledge has, in fact, been made

- auditors, in assessing the appropriateness of the client's judgment

This list of factors is not intended to be used in deciding on proper accounting (for either the pledge asset or the related revenue/net assets—this is discussed in paragraph 4-37), or to assess collectibility, although some of the factors may be helpful in making those decisions as well.

In many cases no one of these factors is necessarily determinative by itself; all relevant factors should be considered together.

Factors whose presence may indicate a bona fide pledge was made	**Factors whose presence may indicate a bona fide pledge was not made**

Factors related to the solicitation process:

1. There is evidence that the recipient explicitly solicited formal pledges.

    The "pledge" was unsolicited, or the solicitation did not refer to pledges.

2. Public announcement (Note 1) of the pledge has been made by donor or donee.

    No public announcement has been made.

3. Partial payment on the pledge has been made (or full payment after balance sheet date).

    No payments have yet been made, or payments have been irregular, late, or less than scheduled amounts.

Factors related to the "pledge" itself:

4. There is written evidence supporting the pledge.

    There is no written evidence. (Note 2)

5. The evidence was created by the donor.

    The evidence was created by the donee alone.

6. The evidence clearly supports the existence of an unconditional promise to give.

    The written evidence is unclear as to its intent.

Note: This factor, if present, would normally be considered determinative.

7. The evidence includes words such as:
    promise
    agree
    will
    binding; legal

    The evidence includes words such as:
    intend; plan
    hope
    may; if
    expected

Factors whose presence may indicate a bona fide pledge was made	**Factors whose presence may indicate a bona fide pledge was not made**
8. Based on factors 1, 2, 3, and 4, the pledge appears to be legally enforceable. Consult an attorney if necessary. (Note also factor 1 under factors relating to the donee.)	Legal enforceability is questionable or explicitly denied.
9. There is a clearly defined payment schedule, stated in terms of either calendar dates or the occurrence of specified events, whose occurrence is reasonably probable.	A payment schedule is not clearly defined or events are relatively unlikely to occur.
10. The calendar dates or events comprising the payment schedule will (are expected to) occur within a relatively short time (Note 3) after the balance sheet date (or in the case of events, have already occurred).	The time (period) of payment contemplated by the donor is relatively far in the future.
11. The amount of the pledge is clearly specified or readily computable.	The amount is not clear or readily computable.
12. The donor has clearly specified a particular purpose for the gift; e.g., endowment, fixed assets, loan fund, retirement of long-term debt, specific program activity. The purpose is consistent with ongoing donee activities.	The purpose is vague or not specified, or inconsistent with donee activities.

Factors whose presence may indicate a bona fide pledge was made	**Factors whose presence may indicate a bona fide pledge was not made**

Factors related to the donor:

13. There is no reason to question the donor's ability or intent to fulfill the pledge.

    Collectibility of the gift is questionable.

14. The donor has a history of making and fulfilling pledges to the donee of similar or larger amounts.

    Factor not present.

Factors related to the donee:

15. The donee has indicated that it would take legal action to enforce collection if necessary, or has a history of doing so.

    It is unlikely (based on donee's past practices) or uncertain whether the donee would enforce the "pledge."

16. The donee has already taken specific action in reliance on the pledge or publicly (1) announced that it intends to do so (4).

    No specific action has been taken or is contemplated.

Notes:

1. The announcement would not necessarily have to be made to the general public; announcement in media circulated among the constituency of either the donor or donee would suffice. Examples include newsletters, fund-raising reports, annual reports, a campus newspaper, etc. In the case of announcements by the donee, there should be a reasonable presumption that the donor is aware of the announcement and has not indicated any disagreement with it.

2. See discussion of oral pledges in paragraph 4-47.

3. What constitutes a relatively short time has to be determined in each case. The longer the time contemplated, the more weight will have to be given to other factors in assessing the existence of a pledge. In most circumstances, periods longer than three to five years would likely be judged relatively long.

4. Types of specific action contemplated include:

- commencing acquisition, construction or lease of capital assets or signing binding contracts to do so

- making public announcement of the commencement or expansion of operating programs used by the public (e.g., the opening of a new clinic, starting a new concert series, a special museum exhibit)

- indicating to another funder that the pledge will be used to match part of a challenge grant from that funder

- soliciting other pledges or loans for the same purpose by explicitly indicating that "X has already pledged"

- committing proceeds of the pledge in other ways such as awarding scholarships, making pledges to other charities, hiring new staff, etc. (where such uses are consistent with either the donee's stated purposes in soliciting the pledge or the donor's indicated use of the pledge)

- forbearing from soliciting other available major gifts (e.g., not submitting an application for a foundation grant) because, with the pledge in question, funding for the purpose is considered complete

- using the pledge as collateral for a loan

Appendix B—Accounting for Support and Revenue Supplemental Information

Exhibit 4—Conditional or Restricted

(Reference: paragraph 4-12 and 4-40; FASB Statement No. 116, paragraphs 7, 22-23, 57-71, 75-81)

Factors to be considered in deciding whether a gift or pledge subject to donor stipulations is conditional or restricted

- Donors place many different kinds of stipulations on pledges and other gifts. Some stipulations create legal *restrictions* which limit the way in which the donee may use the gift. Other stipulations create *conditions* which must be fulfilled before a donee is entitled to receive (or keep) a gift.

  In FASB Statement No. 116, FASB defines a condition as an uncertain future event which must occur before a promise based on that event becomes binding on the promisor. In some cases, it is not immediately clear whether a particular stipulation creates a condition or a restriction. (Some gifts are both conditional and restricted.) Accounting for the two forms of gift is quite different, so it is important that the nature of a stipulation be properly identified so that the gift is properly categorized.

- Following is a list of factors to be considered by:

  - recipients (and donors) of gifts, in deciding whether a pledge or other gift which includes donor stipulations is conditional or restricted

  - auditors, in assessing the appropriateness of the client's decision

- In many cases, no one of these factors will be determinative by itself; all applicable factors should be considered together.

Factors whose presence in the communication from the donor or the donee-prepared pledge card would indicate the gift may be conditional	**Factors whose presence in the grant document, donor's transmittal letter, or other gift instrument, or in the appeal by the recipient would indicate the gift may be restricted**

Factors related to the terms of the gift/pledge:

1. The document uses words such as:
    if*
    subject to*
    when
    revocable*
	The document uses words such as:
	    must
	    for
	    purpose
	    irrevocable

2. Neither the ultimate amount nor the timing of payment of the gift are clearly determinable in advance of payment.	At least one aspect of the amount and/or timing is clearly specified.
3. The pledge is stated to extend for a very long period of time (for example, over 10 years) or is open-ended. (Often found with pledges to support a needy child overseas, or a missionary in the field).	The time is short and/or specific as to its end.
4. The donor stipulations in the document refer to *outcomes* expected as a result of the activity (with the implication that if the outcomes are not achieved, the donor will expect the gift to be refunded, or will cancel future installments of a multi-period pledge.[1a] * (Such gifts are likely also restricted.)	The donor stipulations focus on the *activities* to be conducted. Although hoped-for outcomes may be implicit or explicit, there is not an implication that achievement of particular outcomes is a requirement.[1b] *

Factors whose presence in the communication from the donor or the donee-prepared pledge card would indicate the gift may be conditional	Factors whose presence in the grant document, donor's transmittal letter, or other gift instrument, or in the appeal by the recipient would indicate the gift may be restricted
5. There is an explicit requirement that amounts not expensed by a specified date must be returned to the donor.	There is no such refund provision, or any refund is required only if money is left after completion of the specified activities.
6. The gift is in the form of a pledge.	The gift is a transfer of cash or other non-cash assets.
7. Payment of amounts pledged will be made only on a cost-reimbursement basis. (D)	Payment of the gift will be made up front, or according to a payment schedule, without the necessity for the donee to have yet incurred specific expenses.
8. The gift has an explicit matching requirement (D), or additional funding beyond that already available will be required to complete the activity.	Factor not present.

Factors related to the circumstances surrounding the gift:

9. The action or event described in the donor's stipulations is largely outside the control of the management or governing board of the donee. [2a] *	The action or event is largely within the donee's control. [2b] *
10. The activity contemplated by the gift is one which the donee has not yet decided to do, and it is not yet certain whether the activity will actually be conducted.*	The donee is already conducting the activity, or it is fairly certain that the activity will be conducted.*

Factors whose presence in the communication from the donor or the donee-prepared pledge card would indicate the gift may be conditional	Factors whose presence in the grant document, donor's transmittal letter, or other gift instrument, or in the appeal by the recipient would indicate the gift may be restricted
11. There is a lower probability that the donor stipulations will eventually be met.	There is a higher probability.
12. The activities to be conducted with the gift money are similar to activities normally conducted on a for-profit basis by the donee or by other organizations.	The activities are not similar.
13. As to any tangible or intangible outcomes which are to be produced as a result of the activities, these products will be under the control of the donor. (In such cases, the payment may not be a gift at all; rather it may be a payment for goods or services.)	Any outcomes will be under the control of the donee.

Notes:

D. Presence of this factor would normally be considered determinative. Absence of the factor is not necessarily determinative.

*   Factors which would generally be considered more important.

Factors whose presence in the communication from the donor or the donee-prepared pledge card would indicate the gift may be conditional

Factors whose presence in the grant document, donor's transmittal letter, or other gift instrument, or in the appeal by the recipient would indicate the gift may be restricted

1a. Examples of outcomes contemplated by this factor include:

- Successful creation of a new vaccine;
- Production of a new television program;
- Commissioning a new musical composition;
- Establishing a named professorship;
- Reduction in the teenage pregnancy rate in a community;
- Construction of a new building;
- Mounting a new museum exhibit.

1b. Examples of activities contemplated by this factor include (but see Factor 10**):

- Conduct of scientific or medical research;
- Broadcasting a specified television program;
- Performing a particular piece of music;
- Paying the salary of a named professor;
- Counseling teenagers judged at risk of becoming pregnant;
- Operating a certain facility;
- Providing disaster relief.

2a. Examples of events contemplated by this factor include:

- Actions of uncontrolled third parties, e.g.:
  - other donors making contributions to enable the donee to meet a matching requirement of this gift;
  - a government granting approval to conduct an activity (e.g.,

2b. Examples of events contemplated by this factor include (but see Factor 10**):

- Eventual use of the gift for the specified purpose (e.g., those listed in Note 1b above), or retention of the gift as restricted endowment;
- Naming a building for a specified person;

awarding a building or a land use permit, or a permit to operate a medical facility);

- an owner of other property required for the activity making the property available to the organization (by sale or lease);

• Natural and man-made disasters.

** There is a presumption here that the right column of Factor 10 applies.

• Future action of this donor (such as agreeing to renew a multi-period pledge in subsequent periods);
• The future willingness and ability of a donor of personal services to continue to provide those services (see FASB Statement No. 116, paragraph 70, third sentence).

(Events outside of the donee's control, but which are virtually assured of happening anyway at a known time and place [e.g., astronomical or normal meteorological events], and the mere passage of time, are not conditions.)

• Filing with the donor routine performance reports on the activities being conducted.

Appendix B—Accounting for Support and Revenue Supplemental Information

Exhibit 5—True Recipient of Donated Services

(Reference: paragraph 4-58 and 4-61)

Factors to be considered in determining who is the true recipient of donated services

The program of some not-for-profit organizations is to facilitate the provision of donated services of volunteers to third parties, which may be individuals or other not-for-profit organizations. Examples include organizations which recruit volunteers such as management personnel (management support organizations), lawyers (legal services providers), religious workers (missionary organizations), technical personnel such as doctors or nurses, Bible translators, readers to the blind, or construction tradespeople.

Following is a list of factors which may be helpful, in those cases, to:

- facilitating organizations, in assessing who is the real recipient of donated services which meet the criteria of FASB Statement No. 116 for recording

- auditors, in assessing the appropriateness of the client's judgment

This list of factors is not intended to be used in deciding on whether the services meet the criteria in FASB Statement No. 116 for recording nor for determining a proper value for the services.

In many cases no one of these factors is necessarily determinative by itself; all relevant factors should be considered together.

Factors whose presence may indicate the reporting organization is the recipient of the volunteer services	Factors whose presence may indicate the reporting organization is not the true recipient of the services, and thus should not record a value for the services
1. The services support activities which are an integral part of the organization's own stated program.	The services support activities which are peripheral or incidental to the organization's program.
2. The organization is considered liable for errors or omissions on the part of the volunteers.	The organization is not so liable.
3. The organization pays for workers' compensation and/or liability insurance covering the volunteers.	Factor not present.
4. The organization assigns the volunteers to specific tasks.	Another organization makes specific work assignments.
5. The organization exercises ongoing supervision and control over the volunteers' daily activities.	Another organization exercises this control, or the volunteers work largely without day-to-day supervision.
6. The organization maintains ongoing involvement in the activities of the volunteers.	Ongoing involvement is limited or absent.
7. The volunteer recruiting activity is funded by government or foundation grants awarded to the reporting organization, which specifically refer to the organization as the beneficiary of the services.	Factor not present.

Factors whose presence may indicate the reporting organization is the recipient of the volunteer services	Factors whose presence may indicate the reporting organization is not the true recipient of the services, and thus should not record a value for the services
8. The ultimate beneficiaries of the services are persons who likely view the reporting organization as the service provider.*	The ultimate beneficiaries likely view another organization or the volunteers individually as the service provider(s).
8a. The volunteer does not know the identity of the ultimate beneficiary(ies) of the services.	The volunteer does know the identity of the beneficiary(ies).
9. The services are performed on premises owned, rented, or controlled by the reporting organization.	The services are performed on premises controlled by another organization, by the volunteer personally, or on public property.
10. The organization owns any tools, equipment, or other assets used by the volunteers in their work.	Any assets used are owned by the volunteers personally or by another organization.

* Factors considered to be generally more significant.

Appendix B—Accounting for Support and Revenue Supplemental Information

Exhibit 6—Contributed Services Requiring Specialized Skills

(Reference: paragraph 4-62; FASB Statement No. 116, paragraph 9)

Factors to be considered in assessing whether contributed services are considered to require specialized skills

Following is a list of factors which may be helpful to:

- recipients of contributed services of volunteers, in assessing whether the skills utilized by the volunteers in the performance of their services are considered to be "specialized" within the meaning of paragraph 9 of FASB Statement No. 116

- auditors, in assessing the appropriateness of the client's judgment

This list of factors is not intended to be used in determining how to value or account for such services.

In some cases no one of these factors is necessarily determinative by itself; all relevant factors should be considered together.

Factors whose presence is often indicative that skills are "specialized"

Characteristics of the commercial work environment:

1. Persons who regularly hold themselves out to the public as qualified practitioners of such skills are required by law or by professional ethical standards to possess a license, other professional

certification, or specified academic credentials. Alternatively, if possession of such license/certification/credentials is optional, the person performing the services does possess such formal certification.

2. Practitioners of such skills are required, by law or professional ethics, to have obtained a specified amount of technical pre-job or on-the-job training, to obtain specified amounts of continuing professional education, a specified amount of practical work experience, or to complete a defined period of apprenticeship in the particular type of work.

3. There is a union or professional association whose membership consists specifically of practitioners of the skills, as opposed to such groups whose members consist of persons who work in a broad industry, a type of company, or a department of a company. Admission to membership in such an organization requires demonstrating one or more of these other factors. (Whether or not the person whose skills are being considered actually belongs to such an organization is not a factor in assessing whether the skills are considered to be specialized; it may be relevant in assessing whether the person possesses the skills.)

4. Practitioners of such skills are generally regarded by the public as being members of a particular "profession."

5. There is a formal disciplinary procedure administered by a government or by a professional association, to which practitioners of such skills are subject, as a condition of offering their skills to the public for pay.

6. Practice of the skills by persons who do so in their regular work is ordinarily done in an environment in which there is regular formal review or approval of work done by supervisory personnel or by professional peers.

Characteristics of persons performing the services:

7. Proper practice of the skills requires the individual to possess specific artistic or creative talent and/or a body of technical knowledge not generally possessed by members of the public at large.

8. The skills are measurable against objective criteria (e.g., typing speed expressed in words per minute and number of mistakes made).

9. Practice of the skills requires the use of technical tools or equipment. The ability to properly use such tools or equipment requires training or experience not generally possessed by members of the public at large.

Appendix B—Accounting for Support and Revenue Supplemental Information

Exhibit 7—Need to Purchase Services

(Reference: paragraph 4-62)

**Factors to be considered in determining whether or not
an organization would typically need
to purchase services if not provided by donation**

Following is a list of factors which may be helpful to:

- not-for-profit organizations, in deciding whether or not contributed services meet the third part of the criterion in paragraph 9b of FASB Statement No. 116

- auditors, in assessing the reasonableness of the client's decision

No one of these factors is normally determinative by itself; all relevant factors and the strength of their presence should be considered together.

Factors whose presence would indicate the services would typically need to be purchased

Factors whose presence would indicate the services would typically not need to be purchased

1. The activities in which the volunteers are involved are an integral part of the reporting organization's ongoing program services (as stated in its IRS Form 1023/4, fund-raising material, and annual report), or of management or fund-raising activities that are essential to the functioning of the organization's programs.

The activities are not part of the reporting organization's program, or of important management or fund-raising activities, or are relatively incidental to those activities; the services primarily benefit the program activities of another organization.

2. Volunteer work makes up a significant portion of the total effort expended in the program service in which the volunteers are used.

Volunteer work is a relatively small part of the total effort of the program.

3. The program service in which the volunteers function is a significant part of the overall program services of the organization.

The program activity is relatively insignificant in relation to the organization's overall program activities.

4. The reporting organization has an objective basis for assigning a value to the services.

No objective basis is readily available.

5. The organization has formal agreements with third parties to provide the program services which are conducted by the volunteers.

Factor not present.

Factors whose presence would indicate the services would typically need to be purchased	**Factors whose presence would indicate the services would typically not need to be purchased**
6. The reporting organization assigns volunteers to specific duties.	Assignment of specific duties to volunteers is done by persons or entities other than the reporting organization, or the volunteers largely determine for themselves what is to be done within broad guidelines.
7. The volunteers are subject to ongoing supervision and review of their work by the reporting organization.	The activities of the volunteers are conducted at geographic locations distant from the organization.
8. The organization actively recruits volunteers for specific tasks.	Volunteers are accepted but not actively recruited or, if recruited, specific tasks are not mentioned in the recruiting materials.
9. If the work of the volunteers consists of creating or enhancing nonfinancial assets, the assets will be owned and/or used primarily by or under the control of the reporting organization after the volunteer work is completed. If the assets are subsequently given away by the organization to charitable beneficiaries, the organization decides who is to receive the assets.	The assets will immediately be owned or used primarily by other persons or organizations.

Factors whose presence would indicate the services would typically need to be purchased	Factors whose presence would indicate the services would typically not need to be purchased
10. If there *were* to be a net increase in net assets resulting from the recording of a value for the services (even though in practice there usually is not), the increase would better meet the criteria for presentation as revenue, rather than as a gain, as set forth in FASB Concepts Statement No. 6, paragraphs 78-79, 82-88, and 111-113.	The net increase would better meet the criteria of a gain, rather than revenue.
11. Management represents to the auditor that it would hire paid staff to perform the services if volunteers were not available.	Management represents that it would not hire paid staff; or it is obvious from the financial condition of the organization that it is unlikely that financial resources would be available to pay for the services.

Auditors are reminded that management representations, alone, do not normally constitute sufficient competent evidential matter to support audit assertions; however, they may be considered in conjunction with other evidence.

Factors particularly relevant in situations where the volunteer services are provided directly to charitable or other beneficiaries of the reporting organization's program services (e.g., Legal Aid society), rather than to the organization itself:

Factors whose presence would indicate the services would typically need to be purchased	**Factors whose presence would indicate the services would typically not need to be purchased**
12. The reporting organization assumes responsibility for the volunteers with regard to workers' compensation and liability insurance, errors or omissions in the work, and satisfactory completion of the work.	The organization has explicitly disclaimed such responsibility.
13. The reporting organization maintains ongoing involvement with the activities of the volunteers.	The organization functions mainly as a clearinghouse for putting volunteers in touch with persons or other organizations needing help, but has little ongoing involvement.

Appendix C — Illustrative Financial Statements

The following are illustrative financial statements that display many of the elements discussed in the text. Note that they are *not* prescriptive but illustrative. The displays are also not intended to present all required disclosures.

Care should be taken to display the most meaningful presentation for each organization based on the needs of the financial statement users within the prescriptive requirements of all FASB and AICPA pronouncements.

Exhibit 1—Sample Large Christian Organization

Statement of Financial Position

(Summary Alternative)

	December 31,	
	20x2	20x1
ASSETS		
Current Assets:		
Cash and cash equivalents	$ 121,400	$ 127,000
Short-term investments (Note 3)	107,100	121,700
Receivables:		
Loans	2,000	2,000
Pledges (Note 4)	56,900	44,000
Grants	5,800	4,600
Other	600	800
From affiliated organizations	1,000	1,000
Inventory	7,000	6,100
Prepaid expenses and deferred charges	13,800	9,600
	315,600	316,800
Noncurrent Investments (Note 3)	639,400	547,200
Land, Buildings, and Equipment—net (Note 5)	174,800	168,500
Total Assets	$ 1,129,800	$ 1,032,500
LIABILITIES AND NET ASSETS		
Current Liabilities:		
Accounts payable and accrued expenses	$ 82,900	$ 83,900
Current portion of mortgage payable	610	560
Current portion of annuities payable	2,100	1,900
Amounts held for missionaries	16,000	13,500
	101,610	99,860
Mortgage Payable, 6% due 20xx—net of current portion (Note 6)	2,590	3,040
Annuities Payable—net of current portion (Note 7)	27,900	21,600
Trust liabilities (Note 8)	35,000	35,000
Total liabilities	167,100	159,500

(continued on next page)

Exhibit 1—Sample Large Christian Organization

Statement of Financial Position – *continued*
(Summary Alternative)

(continued)

	December 31,	
	20x2	20x1
Net Assets:		
Permanently restricted endowment	194,800	191,700
Temporarily restricted by donors for use in future periods (nonexpendable):		
Irrevocable trusts	40,000	26,000
Term endowments	55,000	27,000
	95,000	53,000
Specific purpose (expendable):		
Bible schools	4,000	-
Specific ministry support	102,400	110,000
Acquisition of fixed assets	4,800	2,300
	111,200	112,300
Total temporarily restricted net assets	206,200	165,300
Unrestricted:		
Equity in property and equipment	171,600	164,900
Annuity reserves required by state law	5,000	5,000
Designated by governing board for:		
Annuity reserves	10,000	10,000
Long-term investment	179,600	139,000
Purchase of new equipment	10,400	-
Self-insured reserves	15,200	75,800
Undesignated—available for general activities	169,900	121,300
Total unrestricted net assets	561,700	516,000
Total net assets	962,700	873,000
Total Liabilities and Net Assets	$ 1,129,800	$ 1,032,500

See notes to financial statements

Exhibit 1—Sample Large Christian Organization

Statement of Financial Position
(Detailed Alternative)

December 31,

ASSETS	20x2				20x1			
	Expendable*	Plant	Non-Expendable**	Total	Expendable	Plant	Non-Expendable	Total
Current Assets:								
Cash and cash equivalents	$ 121,400	$	$	$ 121,400	$ 127,000	$	$	$ 127,000
Short-term investments (Note 3)	107,100			107,100	121,700			121,700
Receivables:								
Loans	2,000			2,000	2,000			2,000
Pledges (Note 4)	56,900			56,900	44,000			44,000
Grants	5,800			5,800	4,600			4,600
Other	600			600	800			800
From affiliated organizations	1,000			1,000	1,000			1,000
Inventory	7,000			7,000	6,100			6,100
Prepaid expenses and deferred charges	13,800			13,800	9,600			9,600
	315,600			315,600	316,800			316,800
Noncurrent Investments (Note 3)	279,600		359,800	639,400	239,000		308,200	547,200
Land, Buildings, and Equipment— net (Note 5)		174,800		174,800		168,500		168,500
Total Assets	$ 595,200	$ 174,800	$ 359,800	$ 1,129,800	$ 555,800	$ 168,500	$ 308,200	$ 1,032,500

(continued on next page)

Exhibit 1—Sample Large Christian Organization

Statement of Financial Position – *continued*
(Detailed Alternative)

December 31,

	20x2				20x1			
	Expendable*	Plant	Non-Expendable**	Total	Expendable	Plant	Non-Expendable	Total
LIABILITIES AND NET ASSETS								
Current Liabilities:								
Accounts payable and accrued expenses	$ 82,900	$ -	$ -	$ 82,900	$ 83,900	$ -	$ -	$ 83,900
Current portion of mortgage payable	-	610	-	610	-	560	-	560
Current portion of annuities payable	-	-	2,100	2,100	-	-	1,900	1,900
Amounts held for missionaries	16,000	-	-	16,000	13,500	-	-	13,500
	98,900	610	2,100	101,610	97,400	560	1,900	99,860
Mortgage Payable, 6% due 20xx— net of current portion (Note 6)	-	2,590	-	2,590	-	3,040	-	3,040
Annuities Payable—net of current portion (Note 7)	-	-	27,900	27,900	-	-	21,600	21,600
Trust liabilities (Note 8)	-	-	35,000	35,000	-	-	35,000	35,000
Total liabilities	98,900	3,200	65,000	167,100	97,400	3,600	58,500	159,500

(continued on next page)

Exhibit 1—Sample Large Christian Organization

Statement of Financial Position – *continued*
(Detailed Alternative)

December 31,

	20x2				20x1			
	Expendable*	Plant	Non-Expendable**	Total	Expendable	Plant	Non-Expendable	Total
Net Assets:								
Permanently restricted								
endowment	-	-	194,800	194,800	-	-	191,700	191,700
Temporarily restricted by donors for:								
Nonexpendable:								
Irrevocable trusts			40,000	40,000			26,000	26,000
Term endowments			55,000	55,000			27,000	27,000
			95,000	95,000			53,000	53,000
Expendable:								
Bible schools	4,000			4,000	-			-
Specific ministry support	102,400			102,400	110,000			110,000
Acquisition of fixed assets	4,800			4,800	2,300			2,300
	111,200		-	111,200	112,300		-	112,300
Total temporarily restricted	111,200	-	95,000	206,200	112,300	-	53,000	165,300

(continued on next page)

Exhibit 1—Sample Large Christian Organization

Statement of Financial Position – *continued*
(Detailed Alternative)
December 31,

	20x2				20x1			
	Expendable*	Plant	Non-Expendable**	Total	Expendable	Plant	Non-Expendable	Total
Unrestricted:								
Equity in property and equipment	-	171,600	-	171,600	-	164,900	-	164,900
Required annuity reserves	-	-	5,000	5,000	-	-	5,000	5,000
Designated by governing board for:								
Annuity reserve	10,000	-	-	10,000	10,000	-	-	10,000
Long-term investment	179,600	-	-	179,600	139,000	-	-	139,000
Purchase of new equipment	10,400	-	-	10,400	-	-	-	-
Self-insured reserves	15,200	-	-	15,200	75,800	-	-	75,800
Undesignated—available for general activities	169,900	-	-	169,900	121,300	-	-	121,300
Total unrestricted	385,100	171,600	5,000	561,700	346,100	164,900	5,000	516,000
Total net assets	496,300	171,600	294,800	962,700	458,400	164,900	249,700	873,000
Total Liabilities and Net Assets	$ 595,200	$ 174,800	$ 359,800	$ 1,129,800	$ 555,800	$ 168,500	$ 308,200	$ 1,032,500

* "Expendable" or "Operating"
** "Nonexpendable" or "Annuities, Trusts, and Endowments"

See notes to financial statements

Exhibit 1—Sample Large Christian Organization

Statement of Activities

Years Ended December 31,

	20x2					20x1				
		Temporarily Restricted		Permanently			Temporarily Restricted		Permanently	
Support and Revenue:	Unrestricted	Expendable	Nonexpendable	Restricted	Total	Unrestricted	Expendable	Nonexpendable	Restricted	Total
Public support:										
Contributions	$388,700	$1,313,100	$45,000	$200	$1,747,000	$337,400	$1,426,800	$	$4,000	$1,768,200
Donated materials and services	23,600	-	-	-	23,600	17,400			-	17,400
Special events contributions (Note 10)	10,500	-	-	-	10,500	-			-	-
Special events direct benefits cost (Note 10)	(2,500)	-	-	-	(2,500)	-	-	-	-	-
Legacies and bequests	47,100	7,500	-	400	55,000	46,500	15,000		12,000	73,500
Total public support	467,400	1,320,600	45,000	600	1,833,600	401,300	1,441,800	-	16,000	1,859,100
Revenue:										
Sales of materials and services	400	-	-	-	400	300	-	-	-	300
Investment income (Note 11)	27,000	700	-	2,500	30,200	24,700	500	-	27,800	53,000
Change in value of annuities and trusts (Note 12)	1,500	-	2,000	-	3,500	1,000		1,500	-	2,500
Miscellaneous revenue	6,700	-	-	-	6,700	5,500	-	-	-	5,500
Total revenue	35,600	700	2,000	2,500	40,800	31,500	500	1,500	27,800	61,300
Total Support and Revenue	503,000	1,321,300	47,000	3,100	1,874,400	432,800	1,442,300	1,500	43,800	1,920,400

(continued on next page)

Exhibit 1—Sample Large Christian Organization

Statement of Activities – continued

Years Ended December 31,

	20x2					20x1				
	Unrestricted	Temporarily Restricted Expendable	Temporarily Restricted Nonexpendable	Permanently Restricted	Total	Unrestricted	Temporarily Restricted Expendable	Temporarily Restricted Nonexpendable	Permanently Restricted	Total
Reclassifications:										
Assessments against restricted gifts	118,000	(118,000)	-	-	-	130,000	(130,000)	-	-	-
Capital expenditures that fulfill purpose restrictions	4,700	(4,700)	-	-	-	14,000	(14,000)	-	-	-
Expiration of time restrictions	5,000	-	(5,000)	-	-	-	-	-	-	-
Satisfaction of purpose restrictions	1,200,000	(1,200,000)	-	-	-	1,313,400	(1,313,400)	-	-	-
Total reclassifications	1,327,700	(1,322,700)	(5,000)	-	-	1,457,400	(1,457,400)	-	-	-
Expenses:										
Program services:										
Bible schools and seminaries	445,000				445,000	429,300				429,300
Church growth and evangelism	548,000				548,000	609,000				609,000
Media ministries	86,000				86,000	60,300				60,300
Medical and relief	235,000				235,000	265,600				265,600
Ministry to constituency	203,000				203,000	220,000				220,000
Total program services	1,517,000				1,517,000	1,584,200				1,584,200

(continued on next page)

Exhibit 1—Sample Large Christian Organization

Statement of Activities – continued

Years Ended December 31,

	20x2					20x1				
		Temporarily Restricted		Permanently			Temporarily Restricted		Permanently	
	Unrestricted	Expendable	Nonexpendable	Restricted	Total	Unrestricted	Expendable	Nonexpendable	Restricted	Total
Supporting activities:										
General and administrative	175,000	-	-	-	175,000	163,800	-	-	-	163,800
Fund-raising	93,000	-	-	-	93,000	84,600	-	-	-	84,600
	268,000	-	-	-	268,000	248,400	-	-	-	248,400
Total Expenses	1,785,000	-	-	-	1,785,000	1,832,600	-	-	-	1,832,600
Effect of Foreign Currency Translation	-	300	-	-	300	-	(200)	-	-	(200)
Change in Net Assets:										
Unrestricted	45,700	-	-	-	45,700	57,600	-	-	-	57,600
Temporarily restricted	-	(1,100)	42,000	-	40,900	-	(15,300)	1,500	-	(13,800)
Permanently restricted	-	-	-	3,100	3,100	-	-	-	43,800	43,800
	45,700	(1,100)	42,000	3,100	89,700	57,600	(15,300)	1,500	43,800	87,600
Net Assets, Beginning of Year	516,000	112,300	53,000	191,700	873,000	458,400	127,600	51,500	147,900	785,400
Net Assets, End of Year	$561,700	$111,200	$95,000	$194,800	$962,700	$516,000	$112,300	$53,000	$191,700	$873,000

See notes to financial statements

Exhibit 1—Sample Large Christian Organization

Statement of Cash Flows
(Detailed Alternative—Direct Method)

Years Ended December 31,

	20x2				20x1			
	Expendable*	Plant	Non-Expendable**	Total	Expendable	Plant	Non-Expendable	Total
Cash Flows from Operating Activities:								
Cash received from donors:								
Unrestricted	$ 454,500	$ -	$ -	$ 454,500	$ 421,800	$ -	$ -	$ 421,800
Temporarily Restricted	1,318,000	4,100	41,100	1,363,200	1,423,300	10,400	-	1,433,700
	1,772,500	4,100	41,100	1,817,700	1,845,100	10,400	-	1,855,500
Expiration of time restrictions	5,000	-	-	5,000	-	-	-	-
Cash received from earned income	36,000	-	-	36,000	33,600	-	-	33,600
	1,813,500	4,100	41,100	1,858,700	1,878,700	10,400	-	1,889,100
Cash paid to suppliers and employees	(1,026,400)			(1,026,400)	(1,121,200)			(1,121,200)
Cash paid to mission fields	(762,000)	-	-	(762,000)	(709,600)	-	(19,000)	(728,600)
	(1,788,400)	-	-	(1,788,400)	(1,830,800)	-	(19,000)	(1,849,800)
Net Cash Provided (Used) by Operating Activities	25,100	4,100	41,100	70,300	47,900	10,400	(19,000)	39,300

(continued on next page)

Exhibit 1—Sample Large Christian Organization

Statement of Cash Flows – *continued*
(Detailed Alternative—Direct Method)

Years Ended December 31,

	20x2				20x1			
	Expendable*	Plant	Non-Expendable**	Total	Expendable	Plant	Non-Expendable	Total
Cash Flows from Investing Activities:								
Acquisition of property and equipment	(8,000)	(4,700)	-	(12,700)	(17,200)	(14,000)	-	(31,200)
Proceeds from disposal of fixed assets	-	1,000	-	1,000	-	-	-	-
Purchase of investments	(54,600)	-	(57,100)	(111,700)	(2,800)	-	(73,700)	(76,500)
Proceeds from sale of investments	17,000	-	3,000	20,000	2,800	-	56,200	59,000
Effect of exchange rate changes on cash	300	-	-	300	(200)	-	-	(200)
Net Cash Used by Investing Activities	(45,300)	(3,700)	(54,100)	(103,100)	(17,400)	(14,000)	(17,500)	(48,900)

(continued on next page)

Exhibit 1—Sample Large Christian Organization

Statement of Cash Flows – continued
(Detailed Alternative—Direct Method)

Years Ended December 31,

	20x2				20x1			
	Expendable*	Non-Expendable**	Plant	Total	Expendable	Non-Expendable	Plant	Total
Cash Flows From Financing Activities:								
Proceeds from contributions restricted								
for long-term purposes	-	18,000	-	18,000		27,700	-	27,700
Expiration of time restrictions		(5,000)	-	(5,000)		-	-	-
Cash received from earned								
income	-	2,000	-	2,000		10,500	-	10,500
Payments to annuitants	-	(2,000)	-	(2,000)		(1,700)	-	(1,700)
Proceeds from mortgage	-	-	-	-		-	4,000	4,000
Payments on mortgage	-	-	(400)	(400)		-	(400)	(400)
Net Cash Provided (Used)								
by Financing Activities	-	13,000	(400)	12,600		36,500	3,600	40,100
Net Increase (Decrease) in Cash	(20,200)	-	-	(20,200)	30,500	-	-	30,500
Cash and Short-term Investments:								
Beginning of year	248,700	-	-	248,700	218,200	-	-	218,200
End of year	$ 228,500	$ -	$ -	$ 228,500	$ 248,700	$ -	$ -	$ 248,700

(continued on next page)

Exhibit 1—Sample Large Christian Organization

Statement of Cash Flows — *Continued*
(Detailed Alternative—Direct Method)

Years Ended December 31,

	20x2				20x1			
	Expendable*	Plant	Non-Expendable**	Total	Expendable	Plant	Non-Expendable	Total
Reconciliation of Change in Net Assets to Net Cash Used by Operating Activities:								
Change in net assets				$ 89,700				$ 87,600
Adjustments to reconcile change in net assets to net cash provided by operating activities:								
Depreciation				5,400				4,800
Net change in receivables, inventory, and prepaids				(17,450)				(15,200)
Contributions and investment income for annuity or endowment				(7,450)				(37,900)
Actuarial loss on annuity obligation				100				-
Net Cash Provided by Operating Activities				$ 70,300				$ 39,300

See notes to financial statements

Exhibit 1—Sample Large Christian Organization

Statement of Cash Flows

(Summary Alternative—Indirect Method)

	Years Ended December 31,	
	20x2	20x1
Cash Flows from Operating Activities:		
Change in net assets	$ 89,700	$ 87,600
Adjustments to reconcile change in net assets to net cash provided by operating activities:		
Depreciation	5,400	4,800
Net change in receivables, inventory, prepaid expenses, and payables	(17,500)	(15,200)
Loss on investments	7,600	300
Actuarial loss on annuity obligation	100	-
Investment income restricted for long-term purposes	3,000	(10,500)
Contributions restricted for long-term purposes	(18,000)	(27,700)
Net Cash Provided by Operating Activities	70,300	39,300
Cash Flows from Investing Activities:		
Acquisition of fixed assets	(12,700)	(31,200)
Proceeds from disposal of fixed assets	1,000	-
Purchases of investment securities	(111,700)	(76,500)
Proceeds from sale of investment securities	20,000	59,000
Effect of exchange rate changes on cash	300	(200)
Net Cash Used by Investing Activities	(103,100)	(48,900)
Cash Flows from Financing Activities		
Proceeds from contributions restricted for acquisition of building	18,000	27,700
Payments of annuity obligation	(2,000)	(1,700)
Interest and dividends restricted for reinvestment	(3,000)	10,500
Other financing activities:		
Proceeds from mortgage	-	4,000
Payments on mortgage	(400)	(400)
Net Cash Provided by Financing Activities	12,600	40,100
Net Increase (Decrease) in Cash	(20,200)	30,500
Cash and Short-Term Investments, Beginning of Year	248,700	218,200
Cash and Short-Term Investments, End of Year	$ 228,500	$ 248,700

See notes to financial statements

Exhibit 1—Sample Large Christian Organization

Notes to Financial Statements
December 31, 20x2

1. Nature of Organization:

The Sample Large Christian Organization is a nonprofit corporation dedicated to spreading the Gospel through establishing, developing, and promoting all aspects of church ministry and missionary activity worldwide. [Organizations should adapt this note to adequately describe their own activities.]

The organization is exempt from income tax under Section 501(c)(3) of the U.S. Internal Revenue Code and comparable state law, and contributions to it are tax deductible within the limitations prescribed by the code. The organization has been classified as a publicly supported organization which is not a private foundation under Section 509(a) of the code.

2. Significant Accounting Policies:

The financial statements have been prepared on the accrual basis. The preparation of financial statements in conformity with generally accepted accounting principles requires management to make estimates and assumptions that affect the reported amounts and disclosures. Actual results could differ from these estimates. The fair value of financial instruments approximates their carrying value. The significant accounting policies followed are described as follows:

Principles of Combination

The financial statements include the worldwide ministries of the organization and all of its affiliated organizations described in Note 1. Intra-organization transactions and balances are eliminated for financial statement purposes. [Organizations should adapt this note to specifically identify the affiliated organizations and to provide summary financial information about affiliated activities that have not been combined.]

Classes of Revenue and Net Assets

The financial statements report amounts separately by class

of net assets:

a) Unrestricted amounts are those currently available for use in the organization's ministries under the direction of the board, those designated for specific uses, and those resources invested in land, buildings, and equipment.

b) Expendable temporarily restricted amounts are those which are restricted by donors for specific operating purposes or for the acquisition of land, buildings, and equipment.

c) Nonexpendable temporarily restricted amounts are those not currently available for use in the organization's ministries until commitments regarding their use have been fulfilled or used in future periods, or lifetime beneficiary interests have ceased.

d) Permanently restricted amounts are those restricted by donors in perpetuity as endowments or irrevocable trusts.

All contributions are considered available for unrestricted use, unless specifically restricted by the donor or subject to other legal restrictions.

Cash and Cash Equivalents

Cash and cash equivalents consist of cash held in interest-bearing accounts (checking and savings) and short-term investments in money market accounts and certificates of deposit with original maturities of less than 90 days.

Inventory

Inventory consists of ministry-related books and literature held for future distribution and data processing supplies. They are valued at the lower of cost or market on the first-in, first-out method.

Investments

Investments in equity securities with readily determinable fair values and all debt securities are reported at fair value with gains and losses included in the statements of activities. All other investments (such as real property) are reported at the lower of cost or fair value.

Land, Buildings, Equipment and Depreciation

Expenditures for land, building, and equipment in excess of $1,000 are capitalized at cost. Donated assets to be used in the ministry are capitalized at their fair market value on the date of the gift. Depreciation of buildings and equipment is computed on the straight-line method over the estimated useful lives of the assets (30 years for buildings, 10 years for furniture and equipment, 5 years for computer equipment, and 3 years for vehicles).

Annuities and Trust Liabilities

The liability for annuities and trusts is based upon actuarially determined present values considering the income beneficiaries and applicable discount rates based upon federal tables. Trust liabilities also include any remainder interest due to other charitable organizations. An actuarial adjustment is recognized in the statement of activities for changes in the value.

Public Support, Revenue, Reclassifications, and Expenses

Revenue is recognized when earned and support when contributions are made, which may be when cash is received, unconditional promises are made, or ownership of other assets is transferred. Pledges are recorded in the balance sheet when the organization is notified of the pledge, and allowances are provided for amounts estimated as uncollectible. Bequests are recorded as income at the time the organization has an established right to the bequest and the proceeds are measurable.

Gifts of cash and other assets are reported as restricted support if they are received with donor stipulations that limit the use of the donated amounts. When a stipulated time restriction ends or purpose restriction is satisfied, temporarily restricted net assets are reclassified to unrestricted net assets and reported in the statement of activities as net assets released from restrictions. However, if a restriction is fulfilled in the same time period in which the contribution is received, the organization reports the support as unrestricted.

Gifts of property and equipment are reported as unrestricted support unless explicit donor stipulations specify how the donated assets must be used. Absent explicit donor stipulations about how long those long-lived assets must be maintained, expirations of donor restrictions are reported when the donated or acquired long-lived assets are placed in service.

Expenses are recorded when costs are incurred.

Allocation of Expenses

The costs of providing the various program services and supporting activities of the organization have been summarized on a functional basis in the statement of activities. Accordingly, certain costs have been allocated among the program services and supporting activities.

In 20x2, the organization conducted activities that included fund-raising appeals, as well as program and management and general components. These activities consisted of direct mail campaigns. The joint costs ($10,500) of these joint activities were allocated as follows: $2,900 was allocated to fund-raising expense, $4,600 was allocated to church growth and evangelism expense, $2,700 was allocated to medical ministry, and $300 was allocated to management and general expense.

Foreign Operations

In connection with its worldwide ministry, the organization maintains certain supporting facilities in various countries outside the United States. As of December 31, 20x2, assets in other countries totaled approximately $150,000, and liabilities in other countries were approximately $50,000. Total support and revenue received from foreign sources totaled approximately $48,000 for the year ended December 31, 20x2.

Account balances relating to foreign operations are reflected in the financial statements in United States dollars.

3. Investments:

Investments consist of the following:

| | December 31, | | | |
| | 20x2 | | 20x1 | |
	Cost	Fair Value	Cost	Fair Value
Short-term Investments:				
Unrestricted:				
Certificates of deposit with original maturities of less than 90 days	$ 96,000	$ 96,000	$ 112,100	$ 112,100
Government issue money market funds	11,100	11,100	9,600	9,600
	$ 107,100	$ 107,100	$ 121,700	$ 121,700
Noncurrent Investments:				
Expendable:				
Common stock	$ 160,000	$ 150,000	$ 110,000	$ 110,000
Corporate bonds	134,600	129,600	130,000	129,000
	294,600	279,600	240,000	239,000
Nonexpendable— permanent endowment:				
Investment cash	400	400	1,000	1,000
Common stock	113,000	110,000	114,000	110,000
Corporate bonds	86,400	84,400	78,700	80,700
	199,800	194,800	193,700	191,700
Nonexpendable— assets held in trust:				
Investment cash	10,000	10,000	5,000	5,000
Common stock	65,000	53,000	30,500	30,500
Government bonds	87,500	102,000	65,000	81,000
	162,500	165,000	100,500	116,500
	$ 656,900	$ 639,400	$ 534,200	$ 547,200

Because investment cash of nonexpendable net asset classes is not available for use in operations, it is included with investments on the balance sheet.

4. Pledges Receivable:

Unconditional promises expected to be collected within one year are reported at net realizable value. Those expected in more than one year are reported at the present value of their estimated future cash flows using a risk-free interest rate at the date of the pledge to determine the discounts. Amortization of the discounts is included in contribution revenue.

	December 31,		December 31,	
	20x2		20x1	
Unconditional promises receivable (pledges) before unamortized discount and allowance for uncollectible amounts	$	73,800	$	55,000
Less unamortized discount		(11,700)		(7,000)
		62,100		48,000
Less allowance for uncollectibles		(5,200)		(4,000)
Net pledges receivable	$	56,900	$	44,000
Amounts due in:				
Less than one year	$	22,600		
One to five years		44,100		
More than five years		7,100		
	$	73,800		

Discount rates ranged from 5.5% to 6.5% for the pledges due in more than one year.

5. Land, Buildings, Equipment and Depreciation:

At December 31, 20x2 and 20x1, such assets were as follows:

	December 31,		December 31,	
	20x2		20x1	
Land	$	37,600	$	37,600
Buildings		100,000		94,600
Office furniture and equipment		58,800		54,500
Automobile		8,000		8,000
		204,400		194,700
Less accumulated depreciation		(29,600)		(26,200)
	$	174,800	$	168,500

Depreciation in the amount of $5,400 and $4,800 has been allocated to program services and supporting activities in the statement of activities for the years 20x2 and 20x1, respectively.

Management has reviewed the assets in other countries, totaling $76,300 and $68,500 for the years ended December 31, 20x2 and 20x1, respectively, and has determined that they are under the control and ownership of the organization. While for this reason such items are recognized as assets of the organization, it should be noted that the political situation in many countries is subject to rapid change. Therefore, the reader should be aware that while the organization believes the assets are properly stated at the date of this report, subsequent changes could occur that would adversely affect the realizable value of the assets in other countries. In addition, it should be understood that the carrying value of assets may not be representative of the amount that would be realized should the assets be sold or donated to other local ministries.

6. Mortgage Payable:

The mortgage is secured by the affiliate's land and headquarters building. It is payable in monthly installments of $100 to the State Bank. Annual maturities of mortgage payable for the next five years are as follows:

20x3	$	610
20x4		690
20x5		750
20x6		790
20x7		360
	$	3,200

7. Annuities Payable:

The organization has established a gift annuity plan whereby donors may contribute assets to the organization in exchange for the right to receive a fixed dollar annual return during their lifetimes. A portion of the transfer is considered to be a charitable contribution for income tax purposes.

The difference between the amount provided for the gift annuity and the liability for future payments, determined on an actuarial basis, is recognized as unrestricted contributions income at the date of the gift, unless the gift portion is restricted. Income earned on annuity investments and distributions paid are credited and charged, respectively, against unrestricted revenue, unless the annuity agreement stipulates to the disposition of any remaining actuarial value.

The annuity liability is revalued annually based upon actuarially computed present values. Resulting actuarial gain or loss is recorded as other unrestricted revenue in the statement of activities. Reserves required by state law in excess of the computed liability are reported as unrestricted net assets.

8. Trust Liabilities:

As trustee, the organization administers revocable (grantor) trusts that provide for a beneficial interest to the organization at the grantor's death. Because the trusts are revocable at the discretion of the grantor, the principal amounts provided are recorded as liabilities. All trust income, deductions, and credits are reportable by the grantor for tax purposes. At the grantor's death, the remaining trusts assets will be recorded as contributions income.

As trustee, the organization administers irrevocable trusts, charitable remainder unitrusts, and charitable remainder annuity trusts. These trusts provide for the payment of lifetime distributions to the grantor or other designated beneficiaries. At the death of the lifetime beneficiaries, the trusts provide for the distribution of assets to designated charitable remaindermen. The portion of the trusts attributable to the future interest of the organization is recorded on the statement of activities as temporarily restricted nonexpendable contributions in the period received. Certain trusts contain provisions to distribute assets to remaindermen other than the organization. The trust liabilities include the present value of the life interest payable to the trust recipient and any remainder interest due other remaindermen (charitable organizations).

Trust liabilities include:

	December 31,	
	20x2	20x1
Revocable trusts	$ 3,000	$ 3,000
Irrevocable trusts	32,000	32,000
	$ 35,000	$ 35,000

Irrevocable trust obligations are actuarially determined based on the present value of future payments due income beneficiaries using discount rates determined at the time each trust was established, which range from 6.2 to 7.8%, and federal mortality tables for the life expectancy.

9. Donated Materials and Services:

Donated materials and equipment are reflected as contributions in the accompanying statements at their estimated values at date of receipt.

Donated services include skilled services provided by volunteers in medical, media, and educational programs. Skilled services were valued using equivalent missionary compensation amounts for comparable services or published rates based on studies available for the type and location of the service.

10. Special Events:

During 20x2, the organization conducted a dinner rally designed to inform supporters about current operations and to expose potential new donors to the organization. Support received from the dinner rally totalled $10,500, less $2,500 in costs for the direct benefits provided. All costs related to publicity, travel, related salaries, and administration of the event have been included in fund-raising expenses.

11. Investment Income:

Investment income (exclusive of annuities and trusts) consists of:

| | Years Ended December 31, | |
	20x2	20x1
Realized gains (losses)	$ (19,800)	$ 12,000
Valuation adjustment for unrealized gains (losses)	12,200	(12,300)
Interest and dividends	37,800	53,300
	$ 30,200	$ 53,000

12. Change in Value of Annuities and Trusts:

Change in value of annuities and trusts consists of:

| | Years Ended December 31, | |
	20x2	20x1
Investment income-interest and dividends	$ 11,000	$ 8,500
Realized and unrealized gains and losses	2,000	3,000
Actuarial adjustments	(2,500)	(2,000)
Payments to income beneficiaries	(7,000)	(7,000)
	$ 3,500	$ 2,500

13. Pension Plan:

The organization has a defined benefit pension plan covering substantially all of its employees. The benefits are based on years of service and the employees' compensation during the last five years of employment. The organization's funding policy is to contribute principally the normal cost each year. Contributions are intended to provide not only for benefits attributed to service to date, but also for those expected to be earned in the future.

The following table sets forth the plan's funded status and amounts recognized in the balance sheet at December 31, 20x2:

Actuarially present value of benefit obligations:

Accumulated benefit obligation, including vested benefits of $2,870	$ (3,350)
Projected benefit obligation for service rendered to date	$ (5,000)
Plan assets at fair value, primarily lists stocks and U.S. bonds	4,750
Projected benefit obligation in excess of plan assets	(250)
Unrecognized net gain from past experience different from that assumed and effects of changes in assumptions	(530)
Prior service costs not yet recognized in net periodic pension cost	190
Unrecognized net obligation at January 1, 20x1 being recognized over 15 years.	770
Prepaid pension cost included in deferred charges	$ 180

	December 31,	
	20x2	20x1
Net pension cost included the following components:		
Service costs (benefits earned during the period)	$ 260	$ 250
Interest cost on projected benefit obligation	390	320
Actual return on plan assets	(450)	(400)
Net amortization and deferral	100	100
Net periodic pension costs	$ 300	$ 270

The weighted-average discount rate and rate of increase in future compensation levels used in determining the actuarial present value of the projected benefit obligation were 9% and 6%, respectively, in both years. The expected long-term rate of return on assets was 10% in 20x2 and 9% in 20x1.

Exhibit 1—Sample Large Christian Organization

Schedule of Functional Expenses

Year Ended December 31, 20x2
(With Comparative Totals for the Year Ended December 31, 20x1)

	Program Services						Supporting Activities				Comparative Totals for 20x1
	Bible Schools and Seminaries	Church Growth and Evangelism	Media Ministries	Medical and Relief	Ministry to Constituency	Total	General and Administrative	Fund-Raising	Total	Total	
Salaries:											
Homeland personnel	$ -	$ -	$ -	$ -	$16,600	$16,600	$37,000	$34,000	$71,000	$87,600	$82,400
Field personnel	167,000	184,000	22,000	103,000	94,000	570,000	44,000	-	44,000	614,000	605,000
Health and Pension Benefits	16,000	19,000	2,000	10,500	13,000	60,500	8,000	3,000	11,000	71,500	66,000
Payroll Taxes	11,000	13,000	1,500	7,000	6,000	38,500	4,000	1,500	5,500	44,000	41,500
Housing and Other Allowances	24,000	27,000	4,500	15,500	21,000	92,000	12,000	3,500	15,500	107,500	102,000
Total Salaries and Benefits	218,000	243,000	30,000	136,000	150,600	777,600	105,000	42,000	147,000	924,600	896,900
Advertising and Promotion	14,000	3,000	500	1,000	3,000	21,500	1,500	6,500	8,000	29,500	26,100
Conferences and Meetings	23,000	20,000	1,000	2,000	3,200	49,200	4,000	1,000	5,000	54,200	48,500
Cost of Goods Used	22,500	14,000	4,500	9,000	9,000	59,000	-	9,000	9,000	68,000	66,000
Depreciation	-	-	-	-	-	-	4,200	1,200	5,400	5,400	4,800
Direct Project Costs	29,000	28,000	13,400	5,000	18,000	93,400	20,800	1,800	22,600	116,000	197,800
Donated Materials and Services	6,000	-	2,600	15,000	-	23,600	-	-	-	23,600	17,400
Equipment and Rental	-	500	600	6,000	-	7,100	1,000	-	1,000	8,100	8,000
Grants to Other Organizations	-	180,000	17,000	20,000	-	217,000	-	-	-	217,000	243,600
Insurance	1,000	1,000	500	300	-	2,800	4,500	-	4,500	7,300	7,100
Legal and Audit	1,500	1,500	-	1,700	-	4,700	7,000	-	7,000	11,700	7,000

(continued on next page)

Exhibit 1—Sample Large Christian Organization

Schedule of Functional Expenses – continued

Year Ended December 31, 20x2
(With Comparative Totals for the Year Ended December 31, 20x1)

	Program Services						Supporting Activities				Comparative Totals for 20x1
	Bible Schools and Seminaries	Church Growth and Evangelism	Media Ministries	Medical and Relief	Ministry to Constituency	Total	General and Administrative	Fund-Raising	Total	Total	
Maintenance and Repairs	9,800	2,500	1,000	1,000	-	14,300	4,000	-	4,000	18,300	19,400
Occupancy Costs (rent, rates, and taxes)	18,200	4,000	1,500	4,000	-	27,700	2,500	-	2,500	30,200	28,800
Office Supplies	24,000	2,500	2,500	1,500	1,600	32,100	7,000	13,000	20,000	52,100	46,400
Other Expenses	2,700	2,000	500	500	1,700	7,400	-	500	500	7,900	5,500
Outfit Supplies and Expenses	9,500	15,000	1,500	14,000	4,000	44,000	-	-	-	44,000	41,500
Postage and Shipping	2,300	1,000	1,500	2,000	2,900	9,700	2,500	1,200	3,700	13,400	15,800
Printing Supplies and Expenses	25,000	5,000	3,400	1,000	4,500	38,900	4,500	10,800	15,300	54,200	52,100
Telephone and Telegraph	10,500	3,000	1,500	5,000	1,000	21,000	3,000	2,500	5,500	26,500	25,500
Travel, Transportation, and Shipping	20,000	19,000	1,500	7,000	3,500	51,000	2,000	3,000	5,000	56,000	59,000
Utilities	8,000	3,000	1,000	3,000	-	15,000	1,500	500	2,000	17,000	15,400
Total Expenses, 20x2	$445,000	$548,000	$86,000	$235,000	$203,000	$1,517,000	$175,000	$93,000	$268,000	$1,785,000	
Total Expenses, 20x1	$429,300	$609,000	$60,300	$265,600	$220,000	$1,584,200	$163,800	$84,600	$248,400		$1,832,600

See notes to financial statements

Exhibit 1—Sample Large Christian Organization

Schedule of Program Services by Country

	Bible Schools and Seminaries	Church Growth and Evangelism	Media Ministries	Medical and Relief	Ministry to Constituency	Total
	Year Ended December 31, 20x2					
Austria	$ -	$71,000	$9,000	$ -	$ -	$80,000
Bolivia	-	56,000	11,000	72,000	-	139,000
Ecuador	195,000	65,000	12,000	29,000	-	301,000
Japan	165,000	53,000	11,000	-	-	229,000
Korea	-	85,000	8,000	19,000	-	112,000
Mali	-	67,000	10,000	28,000	-	105,000
Peru	85,000	72,000	13,000	87,000	-	257,000
Spain	-	79,000	12,000	-	-	91,000
Canada	-	-	-	-	95,000	95,000
United States	-	-	-	-	108,000	108,000
	$445,000	$548,000	$86,000	$235,000	$203,000	$1,517,000

See notes to financial statements

Exhibit 2a—Sample Small Ministry
Full Accrual

Balance Sheet

	December 31,		December 31,	
		20x2		20x1
ASSETS				
Current Assets:				
Cash and cash equivalents	$	4,157	$	5,737
Pledges receivable (Note 3)		-		4,000
Supplies		342		186
Total current assets		4,499		9,923
Noncurrent assets:				
Equipment (Note 4)		8,000		
Accumulated depreciation		(800)		-
		7,200		-
Total Assets	$	11,699	$	9,923
LIABILITIES AND NET ASSETS				
Current liabilities:				
Accounts payable	$	242	$	-
Payroll taxes payable		703		658
Total liabilities		945		658
Net Assets:				
Temporarily restricted:				
Time restricted				2,000
Restricted for equipment purchase		-		6,000
Total temporarily restricted		-		8,000
Unrestricted:				
Undesignated		3,554		1,265
Represented by equipment		7,200		-
Total Unrestricted		10,754		1,265
Total Net Assets		10,754		9,265
Total Liabilities and Net Assets	$	11,699	$	9,923

See notes to financial statements

Exhibit 2a—Sample Small Ministry
Full Accrual

Statement of Activities

	December 31,	
	20x2	20x1
Changes in Unrestricted Net Assets:		
Revenues		
Contributions	$ 70,631	$ 35,401
Contributed services (Note 5)	8,640	-
Interest income	112	-
Total unrestricted revenues	79,383	35,401
Net assets released from restrictions:		
Satisfaction of equipment acquisition		
restrictions	6,000	
Satisfaction of time restrictions	2,000	-
	8,000	-
Total revenues, gains, and other support	87,383	35,401
Expenses:		
Program services:		
Program A	49,436	26,031
Program services contributed	8,640	-
Supporting activities:		
Management and general	11,397	4,695
Fund-raising	8,421	3,410
Total expenses	77,894	34,136
Increase (Decrease) in unrestricted net assets	9,489	1,265
Changes in Temporarily Restricted Net Assets:		
Contributions	-	8,000
Net assets released from restrictions	(8,000)	-
Increase (Decrease) in temporarily restricted		
net assets	(8,000)	8,000
Change in Net Assets	1,489	9,265
Net Assets, Beginning of Year	9,265	-
Net Assets, End of Year	$ 10,754	$ 9,265

See notes to financial statements

Exhibit 2a—Sample Small Ministry
Full Accrual

Statement of Cash Flows

	December 31,	
	20x2	20x1
Cash Flows from Operating Activities:		
Cash received from donors	$ 70,631	$ 37,401
Interest received	112	-
Cash paid to employees and suppliers	(68,323)	(33,664)
Net cash provided by operating activities	2,420	3,737
Cash Flows from Investing Activities:		
Cash paid for equipment	(8,000)	-
Net cash used by investing activities	(8,000)	-
Cash Flows from Financing Activities:		
Proceeds from contributions restricted for:		
Purchase of equipment	4,000	2,000
Net cash provided by financing activities	4,000	2,000
Increase (Decrease) in Cash & Cash Equivalents	(1,580)	5,737
Cash and Cash Equivalents:		
Beginning of year	5,737	-
End of Year	$ 4,157	$ 5,737
Reconciliation of Change in Net Assets to Net Cash from Operating Activities:		
Change in net assets	$ 1,489	$ 9,265
Adjustments to reconcile change in net assets to net cash provided by operating activities:		
Increase in accounts payable	287	658
Depreciation	800	-
Decrease (increase) in pledges receivable	4,000	(4,000)
Contributions restricted for the purchase of equipment	(4,000)	(2,000)
Increase in supplies inventory	(156)	(186)
Net Cash Provided by Operating Activities	$ 2,420	$ 3,737

See notes to financial statements

Exhibit 2a—Sample Small Ministry Full Accrual

Notes to Financial Statements
December 31, 20x2

1. Nature of Organization:

Sample Small Ministry is an organization committed to presenting the Gospel of Jesus Christ to children through children's after-school Bible classes and youth rallies. [Organizations should adapt this note to adequately describe their own activities.]

The organization is exempt from income tax under Section 501(c)(3) of the U.S. Internal Revenue Code and comparable state law, and contributions to it are tax deductible within the limitations prescribed by the code. The organization has been classified as a publicly supported organization which is not a private foundation under Section 509(a) of the code.

2. Significant Accounting Policies:

The financial statements of Sample Small Ministry have been prepared on the accrual basis. The preparation of financial statements in conformity with generally accepted accounting principles requires management to make estimates and assumptions that affect the reported amounts and disclosures. Actual results could differ from these estimates. The fair value of financial instruments approximates their carrying value. The significant accounting policies followed are described below to enhance the usefulness of the financial statements to the reader.

Classes of Revenue and Net Assets

The financial statements report amounts separately by class of net assets.

a) **Unrestricted** amounts are those currently available at the discretion of the board for use in the organization's operations and those resources invested in equipment.

b) **Temporarily restricted** amounts are those which are stipulated by donors for specific operating purposes or for the acquisition of equipment.

All contributions are considered available for unrestricted use, unless specifically restricted by the donor or subject to other legal restrictions.

Cash and Cash Equivalents

Cash and cash equivalents consist of cash held in checking, savings and money market accounts and certificates of deposit with original maturities of less than 90 days.

Equipment and Depreciation

Expenditures for equipment in excess of $1,000 are capitalized at cost. Donated assets to be used in the ministry are capitalized at their fair market value on the date of the gift. Depreciation of equipment is computed on the straight-line method over the estimated useful lives of the assets (10 years for furniture and equipment, 5 years for computer equipment, and 3 years for vehicles).

Revenues and Expenses

Unrestricted contributions are recognized when cash or ownership of donated assets is unconditionally promised to the organization.

Temporarily restricted contributions are recognized as contribution income in the statement of activities when cash or ownership of donated assets is unconditionally promised to the organization and subsequently released to the unrestricted fund when expenses have been incurred in satisfaction of those restrictions.

Other income is recognized when earned. Expenses are recognized when incurred in accordance with the accrual basis of accounting.

The organization reports gifts of land, buildings, and equipment as unrestricted support unless explicit donor stipulations specify how the donated assets must be used. Gifts of long-lived assets with explicit restrictions that specify how the assets are to be used, and gifts of cash or other assets that must be used to acquire long-lived assets are reported as restricted support. Absent explicit donor stipulations about how long those long-lived assets must be maintained, the organization reports expirations of donor restrictions when the donated or acquired long-lived assets are placed in service.

Allocation of Expenses

The costs of providing the various program services and supporting activities of the organization have been summarized on a functional basis in the statement of activities. Accordingly, certain costs have been allocated among the program services and supporting activities.

Salaries and benefits are allocated 75% to program, 12.5% to management and general, and 12.5% to fund-raising.

3. Pledges Receivable:

During 20x1, a donor pledged $8,000, of which $6,000 was for office furniture and computer equipment and $2,000 was for the 20x2 operating budget. The donor paid $4,000 in 20x1; the balance of $4,000 was paid in 20x2.

4. Equipment

On June 30, 20x2, used office and computer equipment was purchased for $8,000. Straight-line depreciation has been used; the estimated life is five years.

5. Contributed Services:

A substantial number of unpaid volunteers have made significant contributions of their time. The value of this contributed time is not reflected in these statements because they do not meet the recognition criteria in FASB Statement No. 116.

In addition, during 20x2 the organization received contributed services from a local child psychologist and a local seminary professor who prepares and reviews club curriculum. Both individuals donated between five to seven hours of their time monthly to the organization during 20x2. Support arising from these contributed services has been recognized in the financial statements at the fair value of the services received totalling $8,640 and $-0- for the years ended December 31, 20x2 and 20x1, respectively.

Exhibit 2a—Sample Small Ministry
Full Accrual

Schedule of Functional Expenses
Year Ended December 31, 20x2

	Program A	Contributed Program Services	Management and General	Fund-raising	Total
Salaries, wages and benefits	$38,520	$8,640	$ 6,420	$6,420	$60,000
Travel	1,250	-	-	870	2,120
Supplies	1,881	-	-	-	1,881
Printing	2,866	-	207	191	3,264
Professional services	-	-	3,000	-	3,000
Occupancy	4,500	-	750	750	6,000
Depreciation	-	-	800	-	800
Interest	-	-	15	-	15
Telephone	419	-	205	190	814
Totals	$ 49,436	$ 8,640	$ 11,397	$ 8,421	$ 77,894

Exhibit 2b—Sample Small Ministry
Modified Cash Basis

Statement of Assets, Liabilities, and Net Assets

	December 31,	
	20x2	20x1
ASSETS		
Current Assets:		
Cash and cash equivalents	$ 4,157	$ 5,737
Pledges receivable	n/a	n/a
Supplies	342	186
Total current assets	4,499	5,923
Noncurrent assets:		
Equipment (Note 2)	8,000	
Accumulated depreciation	(800)	-
	7,200	-
Total Assets	$ 11,699	$ 5,923
LIABILITIES AND NET ASSETS		
Current liabilities:		
Withheld payroll taxes not remitted	$ 945	$ 658
Total liabilities	945	658
Net Assets:		
Temporarily restricted:		
Time restricted		2,000
Restricted for equipment purchase	-	2,000
Total temporarily restricted	-	4,000
Unrestricted:		
Undesignated	3,554	1,265
Represented by equipment	7,200	-
Total Unrestricted	10,754	1,265
Total Net Assets	10,754	5,265
Total Liabilities and Net Assets	$ 11,699	$ 5,923

See notes to financial statements

Exhibit 2b—Sample Small Ministry
Modified Cash Basis

Statement of Revenues, Expenditures, and Net Assets

	December 31,	
	20x2	20x1
Changes in Unrestricted Net Assets:		
Revenues		
Contributions	$ 70,631	$ 35,401
Contributed services (Note 2)	-	-
Interest income	112	-
Total unrestricted revenues	70,743	35,401
Net assets released from restrictions:		
Satisfaction of equipment acquisition restrictions	6,000	
Satisfaction of time restrictions	2,000	-
	8,000	-
Total revenues, gains, and other support	78,743	35,401
Expenses:		
Program services:		
Program A	49,436	26,031
Program services contributed	-	-
Supporting activities:		
Management and general	11,397	4,695
Fund-raising	8,421	3,410
Total expenses	69,254	34,136
Increase (Decrease) in unrestricted net assets	9,489	1,265
Changes in Temporarily Restricted Net Assets:		
Contributions	4,000	4,000
Net assets released from restrictions	(8,000)	-
Increase (Decrease) in temporarily restricted net assets	(4,000)	4,000
Change in Net Assets	5,489	5,265
Net Assets, Beginning of Year	5,265	-
Net Assets, End of Year	$ 10,754	$ 5,265

See notes to financial statements

Exhibit 2b—Sample Small Ministry Modified Cash Basis

Notes to Financial Statements
December 31, 20x2

1. Nature of Organization:

Sample Small Ministry is an organization committed to presenting the Gospel of Jesus Christ to children through children's after-school Bible classes and youth rallies. [Organizations should adapt this note to adequately describe their own activities.]

The organization is exempt from income tax under Section 501(c)(3) of the U.S. Internal Revenue Code and comparable state law, and contributions to it are tax deductible within the limitations prescribed by the code. The organization has been classified as a publicly supported organization which is not a private foundation under Section 509(a) of the code.

2. Significant Accounting Policies:

The significant accounting policies followed are described below to enhance the usefulness of the financial statements to the reader.

Basis of Accounting

The financial statements of the organization are prepared on the modified cash basis of accounting. Income is recognized when received rather than when earned, and expenses are recognized when paid rather than when the obligation is incurred.

Classes of Revenue and Net Assets

The financial statements report amounts separately by class of net assets.

a) **Unrestricted** amounts are those currently available at the discretion of the board for use in the organization's operations and those resources invested in equipment.

b) **Temporarily restricted** amounts are those which are

stipulated by donors for specific operating purposes or for the acquisition of equipment.

All contributions are considered available for unrestricted use, unless specifically restricted by the donor or subject to other legal restrictions.

Cash and Cash Equivalents

Cash and cash equivalents consist of cash held in checking, savings and money market accounts and certificates of deposit with original maturities of less than 90 days.

Equipment and Depreciation

Expenditures for equipment in excess of $1,000 are capitalized at cost. Donated assets to be used in the ministry are capitalized at their fair market value on the date of the gift. Depreciation of equipment is computed on the straight-line method over the estimated useful lives of the assets (10 years for furniture and equipment, 5 years for computer equipment, and 3 years for vehicles).

Revenues and Expenses

Unrestricted contributions are recognized when cash or ownership of donated assets is received by the organization.

Temporarily restricted contributions are recognized as contribution revenues in the statement of revenues, expenditures, and net assets when cash or ownership of donated assets is unconditionally transferred to the organization. They are subsequently released to the unrestricted fund when expenses have been incurred in satisfaction of those restrictions.

Other income is recognized when received. Contributed services are not recognized. Expenses are recognized when paid.

The organization reports gifts of land, buildings, and equipment as unrestricted support unless explicit donor stipulations specify how the donated assets must be used. Gifts of long-lived assets with explicit restrictions that specify how the assets are to be used and gifts of cash or other assets that must be used to acquire long-lived assets are reported as restricted support. Absent explicit donor stipulations about how long those long-lived assets must be maintained, the organization reports expirations of donor restrictions when the donated or acquired long-lived assets are placed in service.

Contributed Services

A substantial number of unpaid volunteers have made significant contributions of their time to hold weekly children's Bible clubs. In addition, the organization receives contributed services from a local child psychologist and a local seminary professor who prepares and reviews club curriculum. Both individuals donated between five to seven hours of their time monthly to the organization during 20x2. Support arising from these contributed services has not been recognized in the financial statements as it is the organization's policy not to recognize contributed time.

Allocation of Expenses

The costs of providing the various program services and supporting activities of the organization have been summarized on a functional basis in the statement of activities. Accordingly, certain costs have been allocated among the program services and supporting activities.

Salaries and benefits are allocated 75% to program, 12.5% to management and general, and 12.5% to fund-raising.

3. Equipment

On June 30, 20x2, used office and computer equipment was purchased for $8,000. Straight-line depreciation has been used; the estimated life is five years.

Exhibit 2b—Sample Small Ministry
Modified Cash Basis

Schedule of Functional Expenses
Year Ended December 31, 20x2

	Program A	Management and General	Fund-raising	Total
Salaries, wages and benefits	$38,520	$ 6,420	$6,420	$51,360
Travel	1,250	-	870	2,120
Supplies	1,881	-	-	1,881
Printing	2,866	207	191	3,264
Professional services	-	3,000	-	3,000
Occupancy	4,500	750	750	6,000
Depreciation	-	800	-	800
Interest	-	15	-	15
Telephone	419	205	190	814
Totals	$49,436	$11,397	$8,421	$69,254

See notes to financial statements

Exhibit 2c—Sample Small Ministry
Cash Basis

Statement of Assets, Liabilities, and Net Assets

	December 31,	
	20x2	20x1
ASSETS		
Current Assets:		
Cash and cash equivalents	$ 4,157	$ 5,737
Total current assets	4,657	5,737
Total Assets	$ 4,157	$ 5,737
NET ASSETS		
Net Assets:		
Temporarily restricted:		
Time restricted	$ -	$ 2,000
Restricted for equipment purchase	-	2,000
Total temporarily restricted	-	4,000
Unrestricted:		
Undesignated	4,157	1,737
Total Unrestricted	4,157	1,737
Total net assets	4,157	5,737
Total Liabilities and Net Assets	$ 4,157	$ 5,737

See notes to financial statements

Exhibit 2c—Sample Small Ministry
Cash Basis

Statement of Revenues, Disbursements, and Cash Balances

	Years Ended December 31,	
	20x2	20x1
Changes in Unrestricted Net Assets:		
Revenues		
Contributions	$ 70,631	$ 35,401
Interest income	112	-
Total unrestricted revenues	70,743	35,401
Net assets released from restrictions:		
Satisfaction of equipment acquisition restrictions	6,000	
Satisfaction of time restrictions	2,000	-
	8,000	-
Total revenues, gains, and other support	78,743	35,401
Expenses:		
Program services:		
Program A	43,399	25,723
Program services equipment	6,000	-
Supporting activities:		
Management and general	18,549	4,613
Fund-raising	8,375	3,328
Total expenses	76,323	33,664
Increase (Decrease) in unrestricted net assets	2,420	1,737
Changes in Temporarily Restricted Net Assets:		
Contributions	4,000	4,000
Net assets released from restrictions	(8,000)	-
Increase (Decrease) in temporarily restricted net assets	(4,000)	4,000
Change in Net Assets	(1,580)	5,737
Net Assets, Beginning of Year	5,737	-
Net Assets, End of Year	$ 4,157	$ 5,737

See notes to financial statements

Exhibit 2c—Sample Small Ministry
Cash Basis

Notes to Financial Statements
December 31, 20x2

These financial statements are presented on the cash basis of accounting to illustrate that method of accounting and financial reporting. Some organizations are not required to prepare financial statements on the accrual basis in conformity with generally accepted accounting principles and choose not to do so.

1. Nature of Organization:

Sample Small Ministry is an organization committed to presenting the Gospel of Jesus Christ to children through children's after-school Bible classes and youth rallies.

2. Significant Accounting Policies:

The significant accounting policies followed are described below to enhance the usefulness of the financial statements to the reader.

Cash Basis of Accounting

The financial statements of the organization are maintained using the cash basis of accounting, where receipts and disbursements are recognized when cash is received or paid, as opposed to the accrual basis of accounting, where revenue and expenses are recognized when earned or incurred.

Classes of Revenue and Net Assets

The financial statements report amounts separately by class of net assets.

a) **Unrestricted** amounts are those currently available at the discretion of the board for use in the organization's operations and those resources invested in equipment.

b) **Temporarily restricted** amounts are those which are stipulated by donors for specific operating purposes or for the acquisition of equipment.

All contributions are considered available for unrestricted use, unless specifically restricted by the donor or subject to other legal restrictions.

Cash and Cash Equivalents

Cash and cash equivalents consist of cash held in checking, savings and money market accounts and certificates of deposit with original maturities of less than 90 days.

Equipment

Expenditures for equipment are expensed as incurred.

Revenues and Expenses

Unrestricted contributions are recognized when cash or ownership of donated assets is unconditionally received by the organization.

Temporarily restricted contributions are recognized when cash or ownership of donated assets is unconditionally transferred to the organization and subsequently released to the unrestricted fund when expenses have been incurred in satisfaction of those restrictions.

Expenses are recognized when paid. Contributed services are not recognized.

Contributed Services

A substantial number of unpaid volunteers have made significant contributions of their time to hold weekly children's Bible clubs. In addition, the organization receives contributed services from a local child psychologist and a local seminary professor who prepares and reviews club curriculum. Both individuals donated between five to seven hours of their time monthly to the organization during 20x2. Support arising from these contributed services has not been recognized in the financial statements.

Allocation of Expenses

Salaries and benefits are allocated 75% to program, 12.5% to management and general, and 12.5% to fund-raising.

Exhibit 2c—Sample Small Ministry
Cash Basis

Schedule of Functional Expenses
Year Ended December 31, 20x2

	Program A	Management and General	Fund-raising	Total
Salaries, wages and benefits	$38,487	$ 6,414	$6,414	$51,315
Travel	1,150	-	870	2,020
Supplies	2,037	-	-	3,037
Printing	2,866	207	191	3,264
Professional services	-	3,000	-	3,000
Occupancy	4,500	750	750	6,000
Equipment purchased	-	8,000	-	8,000
Interest	-	15	-	15
Telephone	359	163	150	672
Totals	$ 49,399	$ 18,549	$ 8,375	$ 76,323

Exhibit 2d—Sample Small Ministry
Comparative Information

Balance Sheet
December 31, 20x2 and 20x1

	Full Accrual		Modified Cash		Cash Basis	
ASSETS	20x2	20x1	20x2	20x1	20x2	20x1
Current Assets:						
Cash and cash equivalents	$ 4,157	$ 5,737	$ 4,157	$ 5,737	$ 4,157	$ 5,737
Pledges receivable (Note 3)	-	4,000	n/a	n/a	n/a	n/a
Supplies	342	186	342	186	n/a	n/a
Total current assets	4,499	9,923	4,499	5,923	4,157	5,737
Noncurrent assets:						
Equipment	8,000		8,000		n/a	n/a
Accumulated depreciation	(800)	-	(800)	-	n/a	n/a
	7,200	-	7,200	-	n/a	n/a
Total Assets	$ 11,699	$ 9,923	$ 11,699	$ 5,923	$ 4,157	$ 5,737
LIABILITIES AND NET ASSETS						
Current liabilities:						
Accounts payable	$ 242	$ -	$ -	$ -	$ n/a	$ n/a
Payroll taxes payable	703	658	945	658	n/a	n/a
Total liabilities	945	658	945	658	n/a	n/a
Net Assets:						
Temporarily restricted:						
Time restricted		2,000		2,000		2,000
Restricted for equipment						
purchase	-	6,000	-	2,000	-	2,000
Total temporarily restricted	-	8,000	-	4,000	-	4,000
Unrestricted:						
Undesignated	3,554	1,265	3,554	1,265	4,157	1,737
Represented by equipment	7,200	-	7,200	-	n/a	n/a
Total Unrestricted	10,754	1,265	10,754	1,265	4,157	1,737
Total Net Assets	10,754	9,265	10,754	5,265	4,157	5,737
Total Liabilities and Net Assets	$ 11,699	$ 9,923	$ 11,699	$ 5,923	$ 4,157	$ 5,737

Note to reader: This exhibit portrays financial statement displays for three different bases of accounting. An organization would present its financial statements on one of the three bases.

Exhibit 2d—Sample Small Ministry Comparative Information

Statement of Activities
December 31, 20x2 and 20x1

	Full Accrual		Modified Cash		Cash Basis	
	20x2	20x1	20x2	20x1	20x2	20x1
Changes in Unrestricted Net Assets:						
Revenues						
Contributions	$ 70,631	$ 35,401	$ 70,631	$ 35,401	$ 70,631	$ 35,401
Contributed services	8,640	-	-	-	-	-
Interest income	112	-	112	-	112	-
Total unrestricted revenues	79,383	35,401	70,743	35,401	70,743	35,401
Net assets released from restrictions:						
Satisfaction of equipment acquisition restrictions	6,000		6,000		6,000	
Satisfaction of time restrictions	2,000	-	2,000	-	2,000	-
	8,000	-	8,000	-	8,000	-
Total revenues, gains, and other support	$ 87,383	$ 35,401	$ 78,743	$ 35,401	$ 78,743	$ 35,401
Expenses:						
Program services:						
Program A	49,436	26,031	49,436	26,031	49,399	25,723
Program services contributed	8,640	-	-	-	-	-
Supporting activities:						
Management and general	11,397	4,695	11,397	4,695	18,549	4,613
Fund-raising	8,421	3,410	8,421	3,410	8,375	3,328
Total expenses	77,894	34,136	69,254	34,136	76,323	33,664
Increase in unrestricted net assets	9,489	1,265	9,489	1,265	2,420	1,737
Changes in Temporarily Restricted Net Assets:						
Contributions	-	8,000	4,000	4,000	4,000	4,000
Net assets released from restrictions	(8,000)	-	(8,000)	-	(8,000)	-
Increase (Decrease) in temporarily restricted net assets	(8,000)	8,000	(4,000)	4,000	(4,000)	4,000
Change in Net Assets	1,489	9,265	5,489	5,265	(1,580)	5,737
Net Assets, Beginning of Year	9,265	-	5,265	-	5,737	-
Net Assets, End of Year	$ 10,754	$ 9,265	$ 10,754	$ 5,265	$ 4,157	$ 5,737

Exhibit 2d—Sample Small Ministry
Comparative Information

Statement of Cash Flows
December 31, 20x2 and 20x1

	Full Accrual		Modified Cash		Cash Basis	
	20x2	20x1	20x2	20x1	20x2	20x1
Cash Flows from Operating Activities:						
Cash received from donors	$ 70,631	$ 37,401	$ 70,631	$ 37,401	$ 70,631	$ 37,401
Interest received	112	-	112	-	112	-
Cash paid to employees and suppliers	(68,323)	(33,664)	(68,323)	(33,664)	(76,323)	(33,664)
Net cash provided by operating activities	2,420	3,737	2,420	3,737	(5,580)	3,737
Cash Flows from Investing Activities:						
Cash paid for equipment	(8,000)	-	(8,000)	-	n/a	n/a
Net cash used by investing activities	(8,000)	-	(8,000)	-	n/a	n/a
Cash Flows from Financing Activities:						
Proceeds from contributions restricted for:						
Purchase of equipment	4,000	2,000	4,000	2,000	4,000	2,000
Net cash provided by financing activities	4,000	2,000	4,000	2,000	4,000	2,000
Net Increase (Decrease) in Cash & Cash Equivalents	(1,580)	5,737	(1,580)	5,737	(1,580)	5,737
Cash and Cash Equivalents:						
Beginning of year	5,737	-	5,737	-	5,737	-
End of Year	$ 4,157	$ 5,737	$ 4,157	$ 5,737	$ 4,157	$ 5,737

Continued on next page

Exhibit 2d—Sample Small Ministry
Comparative Information

Statement of Cash Flows – *continued*
December 31, 20x2 and 20x1

	Full Accrual		Modified Cash		Cash Basis	
	20x2	20x1	20x2	20x1	20x2	20x1
Reconciliation of Change in Net Assets to Net Cash from Operating Activities:						
Change in net assets	$ 1,489	$ 9,265	$ 5,489	$ 5,265	$ (1,580)	$ 5,737
Adjustments to reconcile change in net assets to net cash provided (used) by operating activities:						
Increase in accounts payable	287	658	287	658	n/a	n/a
Depreciation	800	-	800	-	n/a	n/a
Decrease (increase) in pledges receivable	4,000	(4,000)	n/a	n/a	n/a	n/a
Contributions restricted for the purchase of equipment	(4,000)	(2,000)	(4,000)	(2,000)	(4,000)	(2,000)
Increase in supplies inventory	(156)	(186)	(156)	(186)	n/a	n/a
Net Cash Provided (Used) by Operating Activities	$ 2,420	$ 3,737	$ 2,420	$ 3,737	$ (5,580)	$ 3,737

Exhibit 2d—Sample Small Ministry
Comparative Information

Statement of Functional Expenses
Year Ended December 31, 20x2

Full Accrual

	Program A	Contributed Program Services	Management and General	Fund-raising	Total
Salaries, wages and benefits	$38,520	$8,640	$ 6,420	$6,420	$60,000
Travel	1,250	-	-	870	2,120
Supplies	1,881	-	-	-	1,881
Printing	2,866	-	207	191	3,264
Professional services	-	-	3,000	-	3,000
Occupancy	4,500	-	750	750	6,000
Depreciation	-	-	800	-	800
Interest	-	-	15	-	15
Telephone	419	-	205	190	814
Totals	$ 49,436	$ 8,640	$ 11,397	$ 8,421	$ 77,894

Modified Cash

	Program A	Management and General	Fund-raising	Total
Salaries, wages and benefits	$38,520	$ 6,420	$6,420	$51,360
Travel	1,250	-	870	2,120
Supplies	1,881	-	-	1,881
Printing	2,866	207	191	3,264
Professional services	-	3,000	-	3,000
Occupancy	4,500	750	750	6,000
Depreciation	-	800	-	800
Interest	-	15	-	15
Telephone	419	205	190	814
Totals	$49,436	$11,397	$ 8,421	$69,254

Continued on next page

Exhibit 2d—Sample Small Ministry
Comparative Information

Statement of Functional Expenses – *continued*
Year Ended December 31, 20x2

Cash Basis

	Program A	Management and General	Fund-raising	Total
Salaries, wages and benefits	$38,487	$ 6,414	$6,414	$51,315
Travel	1,150	-	870	2,020
Supplies	2,037	-	-	2,037
Printing	2,866	207	191	3,264
Professional services	-	3,000	-	3,000
Occupancy	4,500	750	750	6,000
Equipment purchased	-	8,000	-	8,000
Interest	-	15	-	15
Telephone	359	163	150	672
Totals	$ 49,399	$ 18,549	$ 8,375	$ 76,323

Exhibit 3—Sample Religious Broadcaster

Statement of Financial Position

	September 30,	
ASSETS	20x2	20x1
Current Assets:		
Cash and cash equivalents	$ 174,300	$ 79,500
Contributions receivable	75,000	74,000
Accounts receivable	50,000	32,500
Prepaid expenses	59,300	66,800
Costs incurred for programs not yet broadcast		
(Note 2)	184,000	-
Other	7,500	-
	550,100	252,800
Assets Held in Trust (Note 3)	40,000	-
Property and Equipment—net (Note 4)	1,354,700	1,204,200
Total Assets	$ 1,944,800	$ 1,457,000
LIABILITIES AND NET ASSETS		
Current Liabilities:		
Accounts payable	$ 160,300	$ 76,100
Deferred broadcast revenue (Note 2)	150,000	-
Current portion of notes payable (Note 5)	1,500	200
	311,800	76,300
Notes Payable (Note 5)	38,200	3,100
Revocable Trusts (Note 3)	40,000	-
Total liabilities	390,000	79,400
Net Assets:		
Unrestricted:		
Undesignated	239,800	161,300
Equity in property and equipment	1,282,000	1,204,300
	1,521,800	1,365,600
Temporarily restricted:		
Expendable (Note 6)	33,000	12,000
Total net assets	1,554,800	1,377,600
Total Liabilities and Net Assets	$ 1,944,800	$ 1,457,000

See notes to financial statements

Exhibit 3—Sample Religious Broadcaster

Statement of Activities

	Years Ended September 30,					
	20x2			20x1		
	Unrestricted	Temporarily Restricted	Total	Temporarily Restricted	Restricted	Total
Support and Revenue:						
Support:						
Contributions	$232,500	$279,500	$512,000	$602,400	$16,100	$618,500
Donated goods	5,700	-	5,700	101,600	-	101,600
Other grants	26,600	-	26,600	56,300	-	56,300
Special events	1,300	-	1,300	8,800	-	8,800
Contributed skilled services	8,900	-	8,900	8,200	-	8,200
	275,000	279,500	554,500	777,300	16,100	793,400
Revenue:						
Broadcast revenue	230,700		230,700	-		-
Rentals	27,200		27,200	23,900		23,900
Interest	1,500		1,500	3,600		3,600
Other	3,300	-	3,300	-	-	-
	262,700	-	262,700	27,500	-	27,500
Net Assets Released from Restrictions:						
Satisfaction of program restrictions	6,800	(6,800)	-	2,650	(2,650)	-
Satisfaction of development project restrictions	216,000	(216,000)	-	-	-	-
Expiration of time restrictions	8,400	(8,400)	-	-	-	-
Assessments against restricted gifts	27,300	(27,300)	-	1,450	(1,450)	-
Total Support and Revenue	796,200	21,000	817,200	808,900	12,000	820,900

Continued next page

Exhibit 3—Sample Religious Broadcaster

Statement of Activities – *continued*

| | Years Ended September 30, | | | | | |
| | 20x2 | | | 20x1 | | |
	Unrestricted	Temporarily Restricted	Total	Temporarily Restricted	Restricted	Total
Expenses:						
Program services:						
Broadcasting ministry:						
KTVR—Ashford	253,300		253,300	148,900		148,900
KLRN—Warren	51,400		51,400	54,000		54,000
KLMT—Springfield	71,400		71,400	50,600		50,600
KTMZ—Jackson	79,900		79,900	53,300		53,300
Evangelism and growth	115,100	-	115,100	109,300	-	109,300
	571,100	-	571,100	416,100	-	416,100
Supporting activities:						
General and administrative	15,200		15,200	12,800		12,800
Fund-raising	31,600	-	31,600	44,500	-	44,500
	46,800	-	46,800	57,300	-	57,300
Total Expenses	617,900	-	617,900	473,400	-	473,400
Excess of Support and Revenue over Expenses before Extraordinary Loss	178,300	21,000	199,300	335,500	12,000	347,500
Extraordinary Loss on Property (Note 4)	(22,100)	-	(22,100)	-	-	-
Change in Net Assets	156,200	21,000	177,200	335,500	12,000	347,500
Net Assets:						
Beginning of year	1,365,600	12,000	1,377,600	1,030,100	-	1,030,100
End of year	$ 1,521,800	$ 33,000	$ 1,554,800	$ 1,365,600	$ 12,000	$ 1,377,600

See notes to financial statements

Exhibit 3—Sample Religious Broadcaster

Statement of Cash Flows

	September 30,	
	20x2	20x1
Cash Flows from Operating Activities:		
Change in net assets	$ 177,200	$ 347,500
Adjustments to reconcile change in net assets to net cash provided by operating activities:		
Donated goods and services provided	(5,700)	(101,600)
Donated goods and services expensed	-	5,300
Depreciation	97,700	78,800
Net change in receivables	(17,500)	(300)
Net change in contribution receivables	(1,000)	10,000
Net change in prepaid items	7,500	(1,300)
Net change in costs incurred for future broadcasts	(184,000)	-
Net change in payables	234,200	6,600
Extraordinary loss	22,100	-
Net Cash Provided by Operating Activities	330,500	345,000
Cash Flows from Investing Activities:		
Acquisitions of property and equipment	(264,700)	(352,900)
Purchase of noncurrent investments	(40,000)	-
Net Cash Used by Investing Activities	(304,700)	(352,900)
Cash Flows from Financing Activities:		
Payments on notes payable	(1,000)	(200)
Contributions for investment in equipment	(7,500)	-
Investment subject to revocable trust	4,000	-
Proceeds from note payable	73,500	-
Net Cash Provided (Used) by Financing Activities	69,000	(200)
Net Increase (Decrease) in Cash	94,800	(8,100)
Cash, Beginning of Year	79,500	87,600
Cash, End of Year	$ 174,300	$ 79,500
Supplemental Disclosures:		
Interest paid	$ 5,100	$ 200
Donated goods and services capitalized	$ 5,700	$ 96,200

See notes to financial statements

Exhibit 3—Sample Religious Broadcaster

Notes to Financial Statements
September 30, 20x2

1. Nature of Organization:

Sample Religious Broadcaster (SRB) is a nonprofit, religious corporation. The organization is an interdenominational ministry committed to the design, establishment and operation of Christian radio broadcasting stations on the U.S./Mexico border. Its purpose is to honor God through the operation of communications ministries; to build the Church by proclaiming and teaching the Gospel of Jesus Christ; and to serve the community with programs of information and education based on Biblical principles. SRB is affiliated with the Association of Gospel Broadcasters (AGB) in the accomplishment of these objectives.

SRB operates four radio stations: KTVR—Ashford, KLRN—Warren, KLMT—Springfield, and KTMZ—Jackson. A FCC license has been received for a station in Loraine which will begin broadcasting in 20x4. An application is before the FCC for a station in Great Bend. Broadcasting is provided in both English and Spanish.

SRB is exempt from income tax under section 501(c)(3) of the U.S. Internal Revenue Code and comparable state law. Contributions to it are tax deductible within the limitations prescribed by the Code. The organization has been classified as a publicly supported organization which is not a private foundation under Code Section 509(a).

2. Significant Accounting Policies:

The financial statements have been prepared on the accrual basis. The preparation of financial statements in conformity with generally accepted accounting principles requires management to make estimates and assumptions that affect the reported amounts and disclosures. Actual results could differ from these estimates. The fair value of financial instruments approximates their carrying values. The significant accounting policies followed are described below to enhance the usefulness of the financial statements to the reader.

Cash and Cash Equivalents

Cash and cash equivalents include cash, checking, and savings accounts and certificates of deposit with original maturities of 90 days or less.

Programs Not Yet Broadcast

Costs incurred for programs not yet broadcast relate to programs that will be aired principally in the next fiscal year. Receipts from other broadcasts relating to programs not yet broadcast are included as deferred revenue. As the programs are broadcast, the costs incurred will be included in operating expenses and the deferred revenue will be included in revenue.

Property, Equipment, and Depreciation

Expenditures for land, buildings, and equipment in excess of $1,000 are capitalized at cost. Donated assets to be used in the ministry are capitalized at their fair market value on the date of the gift. Depreciation of buildings and equipment is computed on the straight-line method over the estimated useful lives of the assets (15-25 years for buildings, towers, and transmitters; 5-15 years for broadcasting equipment; 5 years for furniture and equipment; and 5 years for vehicles).

The organization reports gifts of land, buildings, and equipment as unrestricted support unless explicit donor stipulations specify how the donated assets must be used. Gifts of long-lived assets with explicit restrictions that specify how the assets are to be used and gifts of cash or other assets that must be used to acquire long-lived assets are reported as restricted support. Absent explicit donor stipulations about how long those long-lived assets must be maintained, the organization reports expirations of donor restrictions when the donated or acquired long-lived assets are placed in service.

Classes of Net Assets

The financial statements report amounts separately by class of net assets.

a) Unrestricted amounts are those currently available at the discretion of the board for use in the organization's operations and those resources invested in equipment.

b) Temporarily restricted amounts are those which are stipulated by donors for specific operating purposes, the acquisition of equipment, or for use in future periods.

All contributions are considered available for unrestricted use, unless specifically restricted by the donor or subject to other legal restrictions.

Public Support, Revenue, and Expenses

Unrestricted contributions are recognized when made, which may be when cash is received, unconditionally promised, or ownership of donated assets is transferred to SRB.

Temporarily restricted contributions are recognized when made, which may be when cash is received, unconditionally promised, or ownership of donated assets is transferred to SRB. Temporarily restricted net assets are subsequently released to the unrestricted net asset class when expenses have been incurred in satisfaction of those restrictions.

Contributed Services

A substantial number of unpaid volunteers have made significant contributions of their time to perform clerical work in the organization's offices. In addition, the organization received approximately 200 hours of contributed services with a fair value of $50 per hour from sound engineers who help produce the organization's broadcasting ministry.

Allocation of Expenses

The costs of providing the various program and supporting activities have been summarized on a functional basis in the statement of activities. Accordingly, certain costs have been allocated among the program services and supporting activities.

In 20x2, the organization conducted activities that included fund-raising appeals, as well as program and general and administrative components. Those activities consisted of evangelical radio shows, a special events dinner, and a golf tournament. The costs of conducting those activities included a total of $26,000 of joint costs, which are not specifically attributable to particular components of the activities. Of those joint costs, $18,000 was allocated to broadcasting ministry, $5,000 was allocated to fund-raising expense, and $3,000 was allocated to general and administrative.

3. Revocable Trusts:

As trustee, the organization administers revocable (grantor) trusts that provide for a beneficial interest to the organization at the grantor's death. Because the trusts are revocable at the discretion of the grantor, the principal amounts provided are recorded as liabilities. All trust income, deductions, and credits are reportable by the grantor for tax purposes. At the grantor's death, the remaining trust assets will be recorded as contributions income.

At September 30, 20x2 and 20x1, charitable trusts amounted to $40,000 and $-0-, respectively, and are funded by certificates of deposit restricted for these agreements.

4. Property and Equipment:

Property and equipment consist of the following:

	September 30,	
	20x2	20x1
Land	$ 52,700	$ 74,800
Buildings	1,268,100	1,085,800
Broadcasting equipment	594,200	507,800
Office furniture and equipment	34,100	32,400
Vehicles	5,600	5,600
	1,954,700	1,706,400
Less accumulated depreciation	(600,000)	(502,100)
	$ 1,354,700	$ 1,204,300

Depreciation in the amount of $97,800 and $78,800 for the years ended September 30, 20x2 and 20x1, respectively, has been allocated to program services and supporting activities.

During the year ended September 30, 20x1, SRB constructed a new headquarters building that includes KTVR operations. Costs capitalized as "buildings" totaled $353,700, of which $85,100 consisted of donated goods and services valued at fair value.

During the year ended September 30, 20x1, SRB discovered that title to a portion of adjacent property is not clear. The appraised value of the remaining property has been reduced by $22,100.

5. Notes Payable:

Notes payable consist of the following:

	September 30,	
	20x2	20x1
Note payable represents a contract payable to County Land Board in semiannual amounts of $221, including interest at 6.5%, secured by real property	$ 3,100	$ 3,300
Note payable of $37,450 to finance purchase of warehouse in Springfield, due in monthly installments of approximately $709, including principal and interest at 10%, maturing in January, 20x7	36,600	-
	39,700	3,300
Less current portion	(1,500)	(200)
	$ 38,200	$ 3,100

Maturity of notes payable is as follows:

Year ended September 30,

20x3	$ 1,500
20x4	1,700
20x5	1,900
20x6	2,100
20x7	29,300
Thereafter	3,200
	$ 39,700

6. Temporarily Restricted Net Assets:

Temporarily restricted net assets represent the unspent balance of donor-restricted contributions for the SRB headquarters development project which was substantially completed during fiscal 20x2, and other broadcasting projects. Activity is as follows:

	September 30,	
	20x2	20x1
Beginning balance	$ 12,000	$ -
Contributions	279,500	16,100
Expenditures	(231,200)	(2,650)
Assessments against restricted gifts	(27,300)	(1,450)
	$ 33,000	$ 12,000

Temporarily restricted net assets are available for the following purposes or periods:

	September 30,	
	20x2	20x1
For new Spanish broadcasts	$ 4,500	$ 2,000
For headquarters development	-	10,000
Taping equipment stipulated by donor to be used for a 5-year minimum	7,500	-
For English ministry to immigrants	21,000	-
	$ 33,000	$ 12,000

7. Leases and Other Commitments:

As part of its exempt activities, the organization has incurred certain obligations and commitments relating to its broadcast program materials, offices, and broadcasting operations. The following summarizes the commitments and future minimum payments required under license agreements and operating leases.

	Broadcast Materials Licenses	Property and Equipment	Total
Years ending September 30,			
20x3	$ 31,200	$ 16,800	$ 48,000
20x4	11,000	10,800	21,800
20x5	5,200	10,100	15,300
20x6	5,200	1,800	7,000
20x7	5,200	1,800	7,000
Thereafter	-	14,700	14,700
	$ 57,800	$ 56,000	$ 113,800

Rental expense for years
  ended September 30,

20x2	$ 36,600	$ 29,400	$ 66,000
20x1	$ 30,400	$ 22,600	$ 53,000

8. Transactions with Affiliate:

As described in Note 1, SRB is affiliated with the Association of Gospel Broadcasters (AGB). As an affiliate, certain board members of AGB are required to sit on SRB's board. This does not give AGB a majority voting interest; therefore these financial statements are not consolidated with AGB.

As of September 30, 20x2 and 20x1, the assets of AGB totaled $5,620,514 and $5,440,700; liabilities were $2,780,200 and $2,545,000; and net assets amounted to $2,840,314 and $2,895,700, respectively. Total support and revenue of AGB amounted to $12,678,000 and $12,365,000 for the years ended September 30, 20x2 and 20x1. Expenses totaled $12,733,386 and $12,605,000 for the years ended September 30, 20x2 and 20x1, respectively. In addition, AGB has provided contributions to SRB of $125,258 and $341,856 for the years ended September 30, 20x2 and 20x1, respectively. During 19x2, the organization provided a temporary loan to SRB included in accounts payable at September 30, 20x2.

Exhibit 4—Sample Camp/Conference Center

Balance Sheet
(Detailed Alternative)

June 30,

ASSETS	20x2				20x1			
	Operating Funds	Plant Funds	Endowment and Life Income Funds	Total	Operating Funds	Plant Funds	Endowment and Life Income Funds	Total
Current Assets:								
Cash and cash equivalents	$ 517,800	$ 418,100	$ 85,200	$ 1,021,100	$ 368,300	$ 153,800	$ 63,400	$ 585,500
Investments (Note 3)	63,600	-	968,400	1,032,000	163,400	-	36,600	200,000
Accounts and accrued interest receivable (Note 4)	115,000	-	-	115,000	141,800	-	-	141,800
Inventory (Notes 2 and 5)	365,300	-	-	365,300	353,400	-	-	353,400
Prepaid expenses and other current assets	74,200	-	-	74,200	74,500	-	-	74,500
Assets held in trust (Note 8)	-	-	63,600	63,600	-	-	63,400	63,400
	1,135,900	418,100	1,117,200	2,671,200	1,101,400	153,800	163,400	1,418,600
Land, Buildings, and Equipment—net (Notes 2 and 6)	-	7,436,900	-	7,436,900	-	7,405,200	-	7,405,200
Total Assets	$ 1,135,900	$ 7,855,000	$ 1,117,200	$ 10,108,100	$ 1,101,400	$ 7,559,000	$ 163,400	$ 8,823,800

(continued on next page)

Exhibit 4—Sample Camp/Conference Center

Balance Sheet – *Continued*
(Detailed Alternative)

June 30,

LIABILITIES AND NET ASSETS	20x2 Operating Funds	20x2 Plant Funds	20x2 Endowment and Life Income Funds	20x2 Total	20x1 Operating Funds	20x1 Plant Funds	20x1 Endowment and Life Income Funds	20x1 Total
Current Liabilities:								
Accounts payable	$ 99,800	$ —	$ —	$ 99,800	$ 122,900	$ —	$ —	$ 122,900
Accrued expenses	181,300			181,300	120,500			120,500
Conference deposits	325,200			325,200	318,800			318,800
Total current liabilities	606,300			606,300	562,200			562,200
Charitable Trusts (Note 8)	—	—	63,600	63,600	—	—	63,400	63,400
Total liabilities	606,300	—	63,600	669,900	562,200	—	63,400	625,600
Net Assets (Fund Balances):								
Unrestricted								
Undesignated	313,800	—	5,000	318,800	334,200	—	—	334,200
Net investment in land, buildings, and equipment	—	7,436,900	—	7,436,900	—	7,405,200	—	7,405,200
Temporarily restricted	215,800	418,100	—	633,900	205,000	153,800	—	358,800
Permanently restricted endowment (Note 9)	—	—	1,048,600	1,048,600	—	—	100,000	100,000
Total net assets (fund balances)	529,600	7,855,000	1,053,600	9,438,200	539,200	7,559,000	100,000	8,198,200
Total Liabilities and Net Assets	$ 1,135,900	$ 7,855,000	$ 1,117,200	$ 10,108,100	$ 1,101,400	$ 7,559,000	$ 163,400	$ 8,823,800

See notes to financial statements

Exhibit 4—Sample Camp/Conference Center

Statement of Activities
(Detailed Alternative)

Years Ended June 30,

	20x2				20x1			
	Unrestricted	Temporarily Restricted	Permanently Restricted	Total	Unrestricted	Temporarily Restricted	Permanently Restricted	Total
Operating Income:								
Conference fees	$ 4,691,700	$ -	$ -	$ 4,691,700	$ 4,618,800	$ -	$ -	$ 4,618,800
Bookstore	466,600	-	-	466,600	443,500	-	-	443,500
Clubhouse sales	113,200	-	-	113,200	102,200	-	-	102,200
Crafts	122,200	-	-	122,200	118,400	-	-	118,400
Miscellaneous	14,000	-	-	14,000	17,700	-	-	17,700
Expended restricted contributions for scholarships and other operating costs	119,400	(119,400)		-	208,600	(208,600)		-
Assessments against restricted gifts	35,500	(35,500)		-	9,000	(9,000)		-
Expiration of time restrictions	105,000	(105,000)	-	-	171,900	(171,900)	-	-
Total operating income	5,667,600	(259,900)	-	5,407,700	5,690,100	(389,500)	-	5,300,600

(continued on next page)

Exhibit 4—Sample Camp/Conference Center

Statement of Activities – *Continued*
(Detailed Alternative)

Years Ended June 30,

	20x2				20x1			
	Unrestricted	Temporarily Restricted	Permanently Restricted	Total	Unrestricted	Temporarily Restricted	Permanently Restricted	Total
Operating Costs and Expenses:								
Food service	1,179,800			1,179,800	1,195,900			1,195,900
Adult/Children conferences	1,838,700			1,838,700	1,819,500			1,819,500
Horse ranch	1,158,700			1,158,700	1,109,200			1,109,200
Guest relations	448,900			448,900	451,400			451,400
Accommodations	333,400			333,400	334,000			334,000
Needs list	20,800			20,800	69,500			69,500
Bookstore	375,800			375,800	359,900			359,900
Clubhouse	97,400	-	-	97,400	86,100	-	-	86,100
Total operating costs and expenses	5,453,500	-	-	5,453,500	5,425,500	-	-	5,425,500
Operating Income Over (Under) Costs and Expenses	214,100	(259,900)	-	(45,800)	264,600	(389,500)	-	(124,900)

(continued on next page)

Exhibit 4—Sample Camp/Conference Center

Statement of Activities – *Continued*
(Detailed Alternative)

Years Ended June 30,

	20x2				20x1			
	Unrestricted	Temporarily Restricted	Permanently Restricted	Total	Unrestricted	Temporarily Restricted	Permanently Restricted	Total
Other Income:								
General contributions	130,600	821,300	900,000	1,851,900	151,600	335,000	100,000	586,600
Expended restricted contributions for capital projects	336,300	(336,300)	-	-	949,700	(949,700)	-	-
Income on investments	88,000	50,000	-	138,000	47,100	-	-	47,100
Net realized and unrealized gains on investments	5,000	-	48,600	53,600	-	-	-	-
Total other income	559,900	535,000	948,600	2,043,500	1,148,400	(614,700)	100,000	633,700
Other Costs and Expenses:								
Management and general	509,400	-	-	509,400	467,100	-	-	467,100
Fund-raising	248,300	-	-	248,300	259,300	-	-	259,300
Total other costs and expenses	757,700	-	-	757,700	726,400	-	-	726,400
Change in Net Assets	16,300	275,100	948,600	1,240,000	686,600	(1,004,200)	100,000	(217,600)
Net Assets, Beginning of Year	7,739,400	358,800	100,000	8,198,200	7,052,800	1,363,000	-	8,415,800
Net Assets, End of Year	$ 7,755,700	$ 633,900	$ 1,048,600	$ 9,438,200	$ 7,739,400	$ 358,800	$ 100,000	$ 8,198,200

See notes to financial statements

Exhibit 4—Sample Camp/Conference Center

Balance Sheet

(Prior-Year Summary Alternative)

Year Ended June 30, 20x2
(With Comparative Totals as of June 30, 20x1)

ASSETS	Operating Funds	Plant Funds	Endowment and Life Income Funds	Total	Comparative Totals for 20x1
Current Assets:					
Cash and cash equivalents	$ 517,800	$ 418,100	$ 85,200	$ 1,021,100	$ 585,500
Investments (Note 3)	63,600	-	968,400	1,032,000	200,000
Accounts and accrued interest receivable (Note 4)	115,000	-	-	115,000	141,800
Inventory (Notes 2 and 5)	365,300	-	-	365,300	353,400
Prepaid expenses and other current assets	74,200	-	-	74,200	74,500
Assets held in trust (Note 8)	-	-	63,600	63,600	63,400
	1,135,900	418,100	1,117,200	2,671,200	1,418,600
Land, Buildings, and Equipment— net (Notes 2 and 6)	-	7,436,900	-	7,436,900	7,405,200
Total Assets	$ 1,135,900	$ 7,855,000	$ 1,117,200	$ 10,108,100	$ 8,823,800
LIABILITIES AND NET ASSETS					
Current Liabilities:					
Accounts payable	$ 99,800	$	$	$ 99,800	$ 122,900
Accrued expenses	181,300			181,300	120,500
Conference deposits	325,200	-	-	325,200	318,800
Total current liabilities	606,300	-	-	606,300	562,200
Charitable Trusts (Note 8)	-	-	63,600	63,600	63,400
Total liabilities	606,300	-	63,600	669,900	625,600
Net Assets (Fund Balances):					
Unrestricted					
Undesignated	313,800	-	5,000	318,800	334,200
Net investment in land, buildings, and equipment	-	7,436,900	-	7,436,900	7,405,200
Temporarily restricted	215,800	418,100	-	633,900	358,800
Permanently restricted endowment (Note 9)	-	-	1,048,600	1,048,600	100,000
Total net assets (fund balances)	529,600	7,855,000	1,053,600	9,438,200	8,198,200
Total Liabilities and Net Assets	$ 1,135,900	$ 7,855,000	$ 1,117,200	$ 10,108,100	$ 8,823,800

See notes to financial statements

Exhibit 4—Sample Camp/Conference Center

Statement of Activities
(Prior-Year Summary Alternative)
Year Ended June 30, 20x2
(With Comparative Totals for the Year Ended June 30, 20x1)

	Unrestricted	Temporarily Restricted	Permanently Restricted	Total	Comparative Totals for 20x1
Operating Income:					
Conference fees	$ 4,691,700	$ -	$ -	$ 4,691,700	$ 4,618,800
Bookstore	466,600	-		466,600	443,500
Clubhouse sales	113,200	-		113,200	102,200
Crafts	122,200	-		122,200	118,400
Miscellaneous	14,000	-		14,000	17,700
Expended restricted contributions for scholarships and other costs	119,400	(119,400)		-	-
Assessments against restricted gifts	35,500	(35,500)		-	-
Expiration of time restrictions	105,000	(105,000)	-	-	-
Total operating income	5,667,600	(259,900)	-	5,407,700	5,300,600
Operating Costs and Expenses:					
Food services	1,179,800			1,179,800	1,195,900
Adult/Children conferences	1,838,700			1,838,700	1,819,500
Horse ranch	1,158,700			1,158,700	1,109,200
Guest relations	448,900			448,900	451,400
Accommodations	333,400			333,400	334,000
Needs list	20,800			20,800	69,500
Bookstore	375,800			375,800	359,900
Clubhouse	97,400	-	-	97,400	86,100
Total operating costs and expenses	5,453,500	-	-	5,453,500	5,425,500
Operating Income Over (Under) Costs and Expenses	214,100	(259,900)	-	(45,800)	(124,900)

(continued on next page)

Exhibit 4—Sample Camp/Conference Center

Statement of Activities – *Continued*

(Prior-Year Summary Alternative)

Year Ended June 30, 20x2
(With Comparative Totals for the Year Ended June 30, 20x1)

	Unrestricted	Temporarily Restricted	Permanently Restricted	Total	Comparative Totals for 20x1
Other Income:					
General contributions	130,600	821,300	900,000	1,851,900	586,600
Expended restricted contributions					
for capital projects	336,300	(336,300)	-	-	-
Income on investments	88,000	50,000	-	138,000	47,100
Net realized and unrealized					
gains on investments	5,000	-	48,600	53,600	-
Total other income	559,900	535,000	948,600	2,043,500	633,700
Other Costs and Expenses:					
Management and general	509,400			509,400	467,100
Fund-raising	248,300	-	-	248,300	259,300
Total other costs and					
expenses	757,700	-	-	757,700	726,400
Change in Net Assets	16,300	275,100	948,600	1,240,000	(217,600)
Net Assets, Beginning of Year	7,739,400	358,800	100,000	8,198,200	8,415,800
Net Assets, End of Year	$ 7,755,700	$ 633,900	$ 1,048,600	$ 9,438,200	$ 8,198,200

See notes to financial statements

Exhibit 4—Sample Camp/Conference Center

Statement of Cash Flows

| | Years Ended June 30, | |
	20x2	20x1
Cash Flows from Operating Activities:		
Change in net assets	$ 1,240,000	$ (217,600)
Adjustments to reconcile change in net assets		
to net cash provided by operating activities:		
Depreciation	509,400	467,100
Gain on sale of equipment/investments	(53,600)	(1,800)
Decrease in accounts receivable	26,800	12,400
Decrease in accounts payable	(23,100)	(43,400)
Increase in deposits	6,400	134,900
Decrease (Increase) in inventory,		
prepaid assets, and accrued expenses	49,200	(57,500)
Net Cash Provided by Operating Activities	1,755,100	294,100
Cash Flows from Investing Activities:		
Acquisition of fixed assets	(541,100)	(1,075,600)
Purchase of investments	(900,200)	(300,200)
Proceeds from maturities of investments	121,600	744,700
Proceeds from sale of fixed assets	-	1,800
Net Cash Used by Investing Activities	(1,319,700)	(629,300)
Cash Flows from Financing Activities:		
Proceeds from charitable trusts	200	63,600
Net Cash Provided by Financing Activities	200	63,600
Net Increase (Decrease) in Cash and		
Cash Equivalents	435,600	(271,600)
Cash and Cash Equivalents, Beginning of Year	585,500	857,100
Cash and Cash Equivalents, End of Year	$ 1,021,100	$ 585,500

See notes to financial statements

Exhibit 4—Sample Camp/Conference Center

Notes to Financial Statements
June 30, 20x2

1. Nature of Organization and Tax Status:

Sample Camp/Conference Center is a ministry serving many churches and parachurch organizations by providing interdenominational religious training and public worship at facilities near Denver, Colorado. Its facilities include meeting rooms, lodging, and recreational facilities for religious-related group conferences.

The Camp/Conference Center is incorporated under the laws of the State of Colorado to operate as a charitable religious organization within the meaning of Section 501(c)(3) of the Internal Revenue Code. It is exempt from federal and state income taxes, and contributions by the public are deductible for income tax purposes.

2. Summary of Significant Accounting Policies:

The financial statements of the Sample Camp/Conference Center have been prepared on the accrual basis. The preparation of financial statements in conformity with generally accepted accounting principles requires management to make estimates and assumptions that affect the reported amounts and disclosures. Actual results could differ from these estimates. The fair value of financial instruments approximates their carrying value. The significant accounting policies followed are described below to enhance the usefulness of the financial statements to the reader.

The financial statements include certain prior-year summarized comparative information in total but not by net asset class. Such information does not include sufficient detail to constitute a presentation in conformity with generally accepted accounting principles. Accordingly, such information should be read in conjunction with the financial statements for the year ended June 30, 20x1, from which the summarized information was derived.*

* This paragraph would be included only if using the prior-year summary alternative.

Classes of Net Assets

The financial statements report amounts separately by class of funds or net assets.

a) **Unrestricted** amounts are those currently available at the discretion of the board for use in the organization's operations and those resources invested in equipment.

b) **Temporarily restricted** amounts are those which are stipulated by donors for specific operating purposes or for the acquisition of equipment.

c) **Permanently restricted** amounts are those which represent permanent endowments where it is stipulated by donors that the principal remain in perpetuity and only the income is available as unrestricted or temporarily restricted, as per endowment agreements.

All contributions are considered available for unrestricted use, unless specifically restricted by the donor or subject to other legal restrictions.

Cash and Cash Equivalents

Cash and cash equivalents include cash, checking, and savings accounts and certificates of deposit with original maturities of 90 days or less.

Inventory

Inventories represent books, music and tapes for resale, and food, craft and maintenance supplies for camp and conference operations. Food inventory is priced on the specific identification method. Bookstore inventory is priced on the weighted average method. The remaining inventory is stated at the lower of cost or market on the first-in, first-out method.

Investments

Investments in equity securities with readily determinable fair values and all debt securities are reported at fair value with gains and losses included in the statement of activities. All other investments (such as real property) are reported at the lower of cost or fair value.

Land, Buildings, Equipment and Depreciation

Expenditures for land, buildings, and equipment after January 1, 1980 are capitalized at cost. Donated assets to be used in the ministry are capitalized at their fair market value on the date of the gift. Costs of several individual land and building additions prior to 1980 are not determinable due to age, method of acquisition and other related factors. Land, buildings, and equipment are valued at estimated replacement cost, net of accumulated depreciation from date of acquisition.

The organization reports gifts of land, buildings, and equipment as unrestricted support unless explicit donor stipulations specify how the donated assets must be used. Gifts of long-lived assets with explicit restrictions that specify how the assets are to be used, and gifts of cash or other assets that must be used to acquire long-lived assets are reported as restricted support. Absent explicit donor stipulations about how long those long-lived assets must be maintained, the organization reports expirations of donor restrictions when the donated or acquired long-lived assets are placed in service.

Depreciation is computed on the straight-line method over the estimated useful lives of the related assets.

Income and Expenses

Contributions are recorded as income when promises or cash is received or ownership of donated assets is transferred to Sample Camp/Conference Center. Contributions designated by donors for specified projects or purposes are recorded as temporarily restricted contributions and the related net assets are reclassified to unrestricted net assets.

Other income is recorded as earned.

Expenses are recorded when incurred, in accordance with the accrual basis of accounting.

3. Investments:

Investments in equity securities with readily determinable fair values and all debt securities are reported at fair value, with gains and losses included in the statements of activities. All other investments (such as real property) are reported at the lower of cost or fair value.

4. Accounts and Accrued Interest Receivable:

Accounts and accrued interest receivable consist of the following:

	June 30,	
	20x2	20x1
Registration and fees	$ 104,200	$ 116,900
Employee	10,800	24,300
Accrued interest	-	600
	$ 115,000	$ 141,800

5. Inventory:

Inventory consists of the following:

	June 30,	
	20x2	20x1
Books, music, and tapes	$ 194,900	$ 201,200
Food supplies	96,500	79,600
Craft supplies	23,300	25,800
Maintenance supplies	50,700	46,700
	$ 365,400	$ 353,300

6. Land, Buildings and Equipment:

Land, buildings, and equipment consist of the following:

	June 30,	
	20x2	20x1
Land	$ 1,070,100	$ 1,070,100
Buildings and improvements	9,500,200	9,373,800
Equipment	2,570,100	2,233,600
Construction in progress	510,400	446,200
	13,650,800	13,123,700
Less accumulated depreciation	(6,213,900)	(5,718,500)
	$ 7,436,900	$ 7,405,200

Depreciation charged to operations for the years ended June 30, 20x2 and 20x1, was $509,400 and $467,100, respectively.

7. Pension Plan:

The Sample Camp/Conference Center sponsors a noncontributory defined contribution pension plan for all qualified employees. The Sample Camp/Conference Center annually contributes an amount equivalent to 6% of the total covered compensation received by all participants of the plan. Contributions to the plan for the years ended June 30, 20x2 and 20x1, amounted to $85,900 and $97,200, respectively.

8. Charitable Trusts:

As trustee, the Sample Camp/Conference Center administers revocable life income agreements that provide for a beneficial interest to the Sample Camp/Conference Center at the grantor's death. Because the agreements are revocable at the discretion of the grantor, the trust amounts are recorded as liabilities. All income is reportable by the grantors for tax purposes. At the grantor's death, the remaining assets will be recorded as contribution income.

At June 30, 20x2 and 20x1, charitable trusts amounted to $63,600 and $63,400, respectively, and are funded by certificates of deposit restricted for these agreements.

9. Endowment:

The endowment fund is subject to restriction of gift instrument requiring in perpetuity that the principal be invested and the income only be used for various purposes.

During 20x1, a donor gifted $100,000 for a permanent endowment fund, and in 20x2 the organization received other endowment gifts totaling $900,000. Endowment agreements stipulate that 42% of endowment income is to be used for camper scholarships and 58% for operating needs. During 20x2, $120,000 of endowment investment income was recognized with $50,000 and $70,000 recognized as temporarily restricted and unrestricted income, respectively.

In addition, certain agreements stipulate that realized and unrealized gains must be kept in perpetuity. The governing board has determined that for endowments which do not explicitly govern net appreciation, all realized and unrealized gains and losses will be used to create a quasi-endowment, which will be used for maintenance purposes when the principal reaches $100,000. For the year ending June 30, 20x2, $5,000 of net realized and unrealized gains were added to unrestricted net assets in the endowment fund, and $48,600 pertained to net realized and unrealized gains for endowments, which explicitly stated that realized and unrealized gains must be kept in perpetuity.

Exhibit 5—Sample Church

Statement of Financial Position

	December 31,	
ASSETS	20x2	20x1
Current Assets:		
Cash and cash equivalents (Note 2)	$ 386,100	$ 376,800
Restricted—special building project (Note 3)	128,500	3,500
Contributions receivable	30,000	30,000
	544,600	410,300
Land, Buildings, and Equipment:		
Land	1,322,400	1,474,900
Buildings	4,030,600	3,939,800
Equipment	850,500	644,100
	6,203,500	6,058,800
Less accumulated depreciation	(618,900)	(411,900)
	5,584,600	5,646,900
Other Assets:		
Gift property held for sale	15,000	15,000
Note receivable (Note 4)	49,100	54,500
Restricted—bond sinking fund (Note 5)	426,500	116,000
Deferred bond costs—net of accumulated amortization of $18,400 and $18,500 in 19x3 and 19x2, respectively.	228,500	247,000
Total Assets	$ 6,848,300	$ 6,489,700
LIABILITIES AND NET ASSETS		
Current Liabilities:		
Accounts payable and accrued liabilities	$ 122,300	$ 130,200
Current maturities of long-term debt (Note 5)	162,000	149,000
	284,300	279,200
Long-term Debt—less current maturities (Note 5)	3,445,000	3,631,000
Total liabilities	3,729,300	3,910,200
Net Assets:		
Temporarily restricted:		
Scholarship fund	153,600	132,700
Special building project	158,500	33,500
Bond sinking fund	426,500	116,000
	738,600	282,200
Unrestricted:		
Net investment in property and equipment	2,206,100	2,080,400
Undesignated	174,300	216,900
	2,380,400	2,297,300
Total net assets	3,119,000	2,579,500
Total Liabilities and Net Assets	$ 6,848,300	$ 6,489,700

See notes to financial statements

Exhibit 5—Sample Church

Statement of Activities

	Years Ended December 31,					
	20x2			20x1		
	Unrestricted	Temporarily Restricted	Total	Unrestricted	Temporarily Restricted	Total
Support and Revenue:						
Tithes and offerings	$ 2,470,900	$ -	$ 2,470,900	$ 2,103,700	$ -	$ 2,103,700
Restricted contributions	-	458,700	458,700	-	161,000	161,000
Contributed skilled services	25,500	-	25,500	-	-	-
Special project	-	125,000	125,000	-	-	-
Special events	15,000	-	15,000	18,500	-	18,500
Other income	89,900	-	89,900	63,000	-	63,000
Interest income	23,800	-	23,800	26,500	-	26,500
Loss on sale of assets	(46,200)	-	(46,200)	(1,500)	-	(1,500)
Net assets released from restrictions:						
Satisfaction of program restrictions	50,000	(50,000)	-	35,000	(35,000)	-
Satisfaction of equipment acquisition restrictions	21,600	(21,600)	-	-	-	-
Expiration of time restrictions	9,800	(9,800)	-	-	-	-
Assessments against restricted gifts	45,900	(45,900)	-	16,100	(16,100)	-
Total Support and Revenue	2,706,200	456,400	3,162,600	2,261,300	109,900	2,371,200
Expenses:						
Program services:						
Missions	774,000		774,000	494,400		494,400
Ministry	1,340,000		1,340,000	1,057,000		1,057,000
	2,114,000	-	2,114,000	1,551,400	-	1,551,400
Management	345,900	-	345,900	306,700	-	306,700
Fund-raising	163,200	-	163,200	139,000	-	139,000
Total Expenses	2,623,100	-	2,623,100	1,997,100	-	1,997,100
Change in Net Assets	83,100	456,400	539,500	264,200	109,900	374,100
Net Assets, Beginning of Year	2,297,300	282,200	2,579,500	2,033,100	172,300	2,205,400
Net Assets, End of Year	$ 2,380,400	$ 738,600	$ 3,119,000	$ 2,297,300	$ 282,200	$ 2,579,500

See notes to financial statements

Exhibit 5—Sample Church

Schedule of Functional Expenses

Year Ended December 31, 20x2

	Missions	Ministry	Management	Fund-Raising	Total
Grants and support	$774,000	$ -	$ -	$ -	$774,000
Salaries and benefits	-	532,300	85,200	42,600	660,100
Depreciation and amortization	-	218,400	41,300	4,200	263,900
Facilities	-	89,000	32,400	7,800	129,200
Interest	-	250,400	95,800	22,100	368,300
Printing	-	46,300	6,500	8,600	61,400
Professional services	-	-	24,200	40,000	64,200
Office expense	-	69,800	26,100	15,600	111,500
Telephone	-	24,300	12,400	8,800	45,500
Travel	-	60,200	7,900	6,500	74,600
Other	-	49,300	14,100	7,000	70,400
Totals	$ 774,000	$ 1,340,000	$ 345,900	$ 163,200	$2,623,100

Year Ended December 31, 20x1

	Missions	Ministry	Management	Fund-Raising	Total
Grants and support	$494,400	$ -	$ -	$ -	$494,400
Salaries and benefits	-	323,500	78,600	38,500	440,600
Depreciation and amortization	-	188,700	38,600	4,200	231,500
Facilities	-	98,300	30,300	7,600	136,200
Interest	-	262,400	84,000	18,300	364,700
Printing	-	32,500	5,600	10,400	48,500
Professional services	-	-	19,000	22,500	41,500
Office expense	-	52,500	16,900	12,300	81,700
Telephone	-	20,200	9,400	11,400	41,000
Travel	-	49,500	4,900	7,200	61,600
Other	-	29,400	19,400	6,600	55,400
Totals	$ 494,400	$ 1,057,000	$ 306,700	$ 39,000	$1,997,100

See notes to financial statements

Exhibit 5—Sample Church

Statement of Cash Flows

| | Years Ended December 31, | | | | | |
| | 20x2 | | | 20x1 | | |
	Unrestricted	Temporarily Restricted	Total	Unrestricted	Temporarily Restricted	Total
Cash Flows from Operating Activities:						
Change in net assets	$ 83,100	$ 456,400	$ 539,500	$ 264,200	$ 109,900	$ 374,100
Adjustments to reconcile change in net assets to net cash provided by operating activities:						
Depreciation and amortization	263,900	-	263,900	231,500	-	231,500
Loss on sale of asset	46,200	-	46,200	1,500	-	1,500
Increase in gift property held for sale	-	-	-	(15,000)	-	(15,000)
Increase in special project	-	(125,000)	(125,000)	-	(3,500)	(3,500)
Increase in contributions receivable	-	-	-	-	(30,000)	(30,000)
Increase (Decrease) in accounts payable and accrued liabilities	(7,900)	-	(7,900)	1,700	-	1,700
Assessments against restricted gifts	45,900	(45,900)	-	16,100	(16,100)	-
Expiration of time restrictions	9,800	(9,800)	-	-	-	-
Satisfaction of program restrictions	50,000	(50,000)	-	35,000	(35,000)	-
Other—net	183,200	(183,200)	-	-	-	-
Net Cash Provided by Operating Activities	674,200	42,500	716,700	535,000	25,300	560,300

(continued on next page)

Exhibit 5—Sample Church

Statement of Cash Flows— *Continued*

| | Years Ended December 31, | | | | | |
| | 20x2 | | | 20x1 | | |
	Unrestricted	Temporarily Restricted	Total	Unrestricted	Temporarily Restricted	Total
Cash Flows from Investing Activities:						
Proceeds from sale of property and equipment	276,500		276,500	14,300		14,300
Acquisition of land, building, and equipment	(505,700)		(505,700)	(901,900)		(901,900)
Principal payments on note receivable	5,300		5,300	5,900		5,900
Net Cash Used by Investing Activities	(223,900)	-	(223,900)	(881,700)	-	(881,700)
Cash Flows from Financing Activities:						
Increase in bond sinking fund	(310,500)	-	(310,500)	-		
Satisfaction of equipment acquisition restrictions	21,600	(21,600)	-	(6,600)		(6,600)
Decrease in bond proceeds held in trust for future construction	-	-	-	507,900		507,900
Principal payments on long-term debt	(173,000)	-	(173,000)	(70,000)		(70,000)
Net Cash Provided (Used) by Financing Activities	(461,900)	(21,600)	(483,500)	431,300	-	431,300
Increase (Decrease) in Cash and Cash Equivalents	(11,600)	20,900	9,300	84,600	25,300	109,900
Cash and Cash Equivalents:						
Beginning of year	244,100	132,700	376,800	159,500	107,400	266,900
End of year	$ 232,500	$ 153,600	$ 386,100	$ 244,100	$ 132,700	$ 376,800

See notes to financial statements

Exhibit 5—Sample Church

Notes to Financial Statements
December 31, 20x2

1. Nature of Organization:

The Sample Church (church) was incorporated as a not-for-profit corporation under the laws of the State of Colorado in 1985 and began conducting services in February 1986. The five-fold purpose of the church is to exalt Christ (worship), to bring people to Christ (evangelism), to bond people in Christ (community and fellowship), to build people in Christ (discipleship), and to send people into ministry for Christ (missions).

In addition to weekly services, the church provides Bible study classes and various activities for attendees. The church operates a school (grades kindergarten through eight), a children's day out and preschool program, and a bookstore.

2. Summary of Accounting Policies:

The financial statements have been prepared on the accrual basis. The preparation of financial statements in conformity with generally accepted accounting principles requires management to make estimates and assumptions that affect the reported amounts and disclosures. Actual results could differ from these estimates. The fair value of financial instruments approximates their carrying value. The significant accounting policies followed are described as follows:

Cash and Cash Equivalents

For purposes of the statement of cash flows, cash and cash equivalents are defined as actual currency, demand deposits and highly liquid investments with original maturities of three months or less.

As of December 31, 20x2 and 20x1, cash and cash equivalents include $153,600 and $132,700, respectively, which is restricted for the scholarship endowment fund.

Land, Buildings and Equipment

Land, buildings, and equipment are stated at cost, or, if donated, at the estimated fair market value at the date of donation. Depreciation is recorded using the straight-line method at various rates calculated to allocate the cost of the respective items over their estimated useful lives.

Estimated useful lives are:

Buildings (sanctuary and fellowship hall)	30 years
Equipment	5 - 10 years

Deferred Bond Costs

Issuance costs of $276,300, related to the First Mortgage Bonds, 19x1 Series (Note 5), have been capitalized and are being amortized over the term of the bonds using the straight-line method.

Contributed Services

A substantial number of unpaid volunteers have made significant contributions of their time to perform clerical work in the organization's offices. In addition, the organization received approximately 700 hours of contributed services with a fair value of $35 per hour from a bookkeeper.

3.   Special Building Project

The organization is conducting a capital campaign to build a new church. In December 20x1, a donor unconditionally promised to give $30,000 restricted for the church building, payable when the church building is halfway completed. At the time the organization received the contribution, it expected the church building to be halfway completed by June 30, 20x2, and recorded the contribution receivable at its estimated net realizable value of $30,000. Due to unexpected construction delays, the church building was not halfway completed until January 20x3, at which time the donor paid the $30,000.

4.   Note Receivable:

As of June 30, 20x2 and 20x1, the unsecured note receivable is from an individual, with interest at 9% due annually each February 28 until February 28, 20x4, at which time principal payments of $5,000 plus interest shall be payable annually until maturity on February 28, 20x9. Additional principal payments may be made at any time during the term of the note. Principal payments of $5,300 and $5,900 were made during 20x2 and 20x1, respectively.

5. Long-Term Debt:

Long-term debt consists of the following:

| | December 31, | |
	20x2	20x1
First Mortgage Bonds, 19x1 Series, interest payable semiannually on May 1 and November 1 at rates ranging from 8.5% to 10.0%, maturing in amounts ranging from $70,000 in 20x1 to $244,000 in 20x6, secured by the church's land, buildings and equipment	$ 3,607,000	$ 3,780,000
Less current maturities	(162,000)	(149,000)
	$ 3,445,000	$ 3,631,000

At the option of the church and upon not less than fifteen days written notice to bondholders of record, the First Mortgage Bonds, 19x1 Series, may be redeemed in whole or in part on February 1, May 1, August 1, or November 1, by the payment of principal and accrued interest, except that the bonds may not be redeemed with borrowed funds prior to May 1, 20x3. The church covenants and agrees that, so long as any bonds issued under the indenture or any supplement thereto are outstanding, it will periodically pay into a bond sinking fund held by a trustee sufficient to pay the principal and interest as it becomes due and payable on all bonds outstanding. The church shall make weekly deposits into the bond sinking fund in the amount of $7,200, commencing May 22, 20x0 through and including April 29, 20x1, and in the amount of $9,875, commencing May 6, 20x1 and thereafter while any bonds are outstanding.

Future maturities of long-term debt consist of the following:

Year ending December 31,

20x3	$ 162,000
20x4	176,000
20x5	192,000
20x6	210,000
20x7	112,000
Thereafter	2,755,000
	$ 3,607,000

On February 1, 19x4, the church transferred $300,000 from the bond sinking fund and redeemed bonds scheduled to mature May 1, 20x5.

6. Interest Expense:

Interest expense for 20x2 and 20x1 is primarily for church property, and is allocated on the same basis as depreciation and amortization.

7. Subsequent Event:

On January 10, 20x3, the church sold the Bronson parsonage for $147,300. The book value of the parsonage was $162,200 at December 31, 20x2. Accordingly, the church recorded a loss of approximately $15,000 in January 20x3.

Exhibit 6—Sample Rescue Mission

Balance Sheet

ASSETS	June 30, 20x2	June 30, 20x1
Current Assets:		
Cash and cash equivalents	$ 323,600	$ 237,700
Temporary investments	21,200	13,600
Gift-in-kind inventory (Note 4)	215,800	371,100
Total current assets	560,600	622,400
Land, Buildings, and Equipment:		
Land	213,400	213,400
Buildings and improvements	2,057,500	2,050,100
Furniture and fixtures	69,200	91,600
Machinery and equipment	177,900	176,300
Vehicles	97,400	114,100
	2,615,400	2,645,500
Less Accumulated Depreciation and Amortization	(511,800)	(468,400)
Land, buildings, and equipment—net	2,103,600	2,177,100
Total Assets	$ 2,664,200	$ 2,799,500
LIABILITIES AND NET ASSETS		
Current Liabilities:		
Accounts payable and other accrued liabilities	$ 110,600	$ 67,500
Annuities payable	46,500	32,100
Total liabilities	157,100	99,600
Net Assets:		
Unrestricted:		
Land, buildings, and equipment	2,103,600	2,177,100
Gift-in-kind inventory	215,800	371,100
Operating	136,900	146,700
Total unrestricted net assets	2,456,300	2,694,900
Temporarily restricted	50,800	5,000
Total net assets	2,507,100	2,699,900
Total Liabilities and Net Assets	$ 2,664,200	$ 2,799,500

See notes to financial statements

Exhibit 6—Sample Rescue Mission

Statement of Activities

Years Ended June 30,

	20x2			20x1		
	Unrestricted	Temporarily Restricted	Total	Unrestricted	Temporarily Restricted	Total
Support and Revenue:						
Contributions:						
Individuals, businesses, and other	$ 1,635,500	$ 215,100	$ 1,850,600	$ 1,561,800	$ 15,000	$ 1,576,800
Gifts-in-kind (Note 4)	1,335,100	-	1,335,100	1,503,200	-	1,503,200
Clothing sales	775,800	-	775,800	615,200	-	615,200
Land and building (Note 5)	-	-	-	814,000	-	814,000
Contributed skilled services	37,600	-	37,600	84,100	-	84,100
	3,784,000	215,100	3,999,100	4,578,300	15,000	4,593,300
Investment income	11,900	-	11,900	14,800	-	14,800
Other	12,800	-	12,800	5,200	-	5,200
Net Assets Released from Restrictions:						
Satisfaction of program restrictions	116,800	(116,800)	-	10,000	(10,000)	-
Expiration of time restrictions	8,500	(8,500)	-	-	-	-
Assessments against restricted gifts	14,000	(14,000)	-	-	-	-
Satisfaction of equipment acquisition restrictions	30,000	(30,000)	-	-	-	-
Total Support and Revenue	3,978,000	45,800	4,023,800	4,608,300	5,000	4,613,300

(continued on next page)

Exhibit 6—Sample Rescue Mission

Statement of Activities— *Continued*

Years Ended June 30,

	20x2			20x1		
	Unrestricted	Temporarily Restricted	Total	Unrestricted	Temporarily Restricted	Total
Expenses:						
Program services:						
Mission and Outreach Services	695,900		695,900	539,800		539,800
Rehab Farm	292,800		292,800	216,400		216,400
Dental and medical	278,300		278,300	178,700		178,700
Literacy and Education Center	88,100		88,100	78,100		78,100
Food, clothing, and other distributions (Note 4)	1,528,000		1,528,000	1,461,400		1,461,400
Public awareness and education	231,500	-	231,500	138,600	-	138,600
	3,114,600	-	3,114,600	2,613,000	-	2,613,000
Supporting activities:						
General and administrative	343,700	-	343,700	402,200	-	402,200
Fund-raising	758,300	-	758,300	594,600	-	594,600
	1,102,000	-	1,102,000	996,800	-	996,800
Total Expenses	4,216,600	-	4,216,600	3,609,800	-	3,609,800
Change in Net Assets	(238,600)	45,800	(192,800)	998,500	5,000	1,003,500
Net Assets, Beginning of Year	2,694,900	5,000	2,699,900	1,696,400	-	1,696,400
Net Assets, End of Year	$ 2,456,300	$ 50,800	$ 2,507,100	$ 2,694,900	$ 5,000	$ 2,699,900

See notes to financial statements

Exhibit 6—Sample Rescue Mission

Statement of Functional Expenses

Year ended June 30, 20x2

With Comparative Totals for Year Ended June 30, 20x1

	Program Services							Supporting Activities				
	Mission and Outreach Services	Rehab Farm	Dental and Medical	Literacy and Education	Food, Clothing, and Other Distributions	Public Awareness and Education	Program Services Total	General and Administrative	Fund-Raising	Supporting Activities Total	20x2 Total	20x1 Total
Multimedia and telemarketing	$ -	$ -	$ -	$ -	$ -	$ 36,700	$ 36,700	$ -	$ 129,600	$ 129,600	$ 166,300	$ 96,000
Repairs and maintenance	60,600	11,300	3,600	200	-	-	75,700	8,500	800	9,300	85,000	74,300
Office	37,600	29,600	23,200	4,300	-	600	95,300	64,500	26,600	91,100	186,400	201,700
Professional and contract services	24,200	11,900	10,800	5,100	-	24,500	76,500	33,700	66,400	100,100	176,600	173,500
Gift-in-kind distributions	-	-	-	-	755,700	-	755,700	-	-	-	755,700	842,400
Gifts-in-kind goods sold	-	-	-	-	772,300	-	772,300	-	-	-	772,300	619,000
Salaries and benefits	359,900	128,600	171,900	59,200	-	-	719,600	171,100	167,700	338,800	1,058,400	824,800
Telephone and utilities	48,300	43,500	12,900	9,200	-	-	113,900	15,700	5,500	21,200	135,100	109,500
Donor letters	-	-	-	-	-	94,300	94,300	-	288,900	288,900	383,200	257,600
Printed materials	-	-	-	-	-	75,400	75,400	-	72,200	103,500	178,900	156,300
Depreciation	45,900	39,300	32,800	-	-	-	118,000	31,300	-	13,100	131,100	110,100
Ministry and other expenses	119,400	28,600	23,100	10,100	-	-	181,200	13,100	600	6,400	187,600	144,600
Total Expenses	$ 695,900	$ 292,800	$ 278,300	$ 88,100	$1,528,000	$ 231,500	$3,114,600	$ 343,700	$ 758,300	$1,102,000	$ 4,216,600	$ 3,609,800
Percent of Total Expenses	17%	7%	7%	2%	36%	5%	74%	8%	18%	26%	100%	100%
20x1: Total Expenses	$ 539,800	$ 216,400	$ 178,700	$ 78,100	$1,461,400	$ 138,600	$2,613,000	$ 402,200	$ 594,600	$ 996,800		
Percent of Total Expenses	15%	6%	5%	2%	40%	4%	72%	11%	17%	28%		

See notes to financial statements

Exhibit 6—Sample Rescue Mission

Statement of Cash Flows

	Years Ended June 30,	
	20x2	20x1
Cash Flows from Operating Activities:		
Change in net assets	$ (192,800)	$ 1,003,500
Adjustments to reconcile change in net assets to net cash provided by operating activities:		
Depreciation and amortization	131,000	110,100
Net decrease (increase) in gifts-in-kind inventory (Note 4)	155,300	(125,900)
Contribution of land and building (Note 5)	-	(814,000)
Increase (decrease) in payables	43,100	(8,300)
Net Cash Provided by Operating Activities	136,600	165,400
Cash Flows from Investing Activities:		
Sales of investments	13,600	-
Purchases of investments	(21,200)	-
Purchases of land, buildings, and equipment	(57,500)	(129,200)
Net Cash Used by Investing Activities	(65,100)	(129,200)
Cash Flows from Financing Activities:		
Proceeds from annuity agreements	14,400	32,100
Net Cash Provided by Financing Activities	14,400	32,100
Increase in Cash and Cash Equivalents	85,900	68,300
Cash and Cash Equivalents, Beginning of Year	237,700	169,400
Cash and Cash Equivalents, End of Year	$ 323,600	$ 237,700

See notes to financial statements

Exhibit 6—Sample Rescue Mission

Notes to Financial Statements
June 30, 20x2

1. Nature of Organization:

Founded in 19x5, The Sample Mission (mission) is a corporation exempt from federal income tax under Section 501(c)(3) of the Internal Revenue Code of 1986, as amended.

The purpose of the mission is to meet people at their point of need, physical and spiritual. Through practical programs of public awareness and education, shelter, food, and clothing distribution, and through Christian teaching and work discipling, the mission aims to return the poor, needy, and homeless to society as self-sufficient, productive citizens.

2. Summary of Significant Accounting Policies:

The financial statements have been prepared on the accrual basis. The preparation of financial statements in conformity with generally accepted accounting principles requires management to make estimates and assumptions that affect the reported amounts and disclosures. Actual results could differ from these estimates. The fair value of financial instruments approximates their carrying value. The significant accounting policies followed are described as follows:

Basis of Accounting

The financial statements of the mission are prepared in accordance with the principles of fund accounting to ensure the observance of limitations and restrictions placed on the use of resources available to the mission. Under these principles, resources for various purposes are classified for reporting purposes into funds established according to their nature. Separate accounts are maintained for each fund; however, in the accompanying financial statements, funds that have similar characteristics have been combined. Temporarily restricted net assets consist of unexpended donor-restricted contributions.

Cash and Cash Equivalents

Cash includes checking, savings, and money market accounts. Certificates of deposit with a maturity of three months or less when purchased are considered to be cash equivalents.

Temporary Investments

Temporary investments include marketable equity securities and mutual funds. These investment securities are recorded at the lower of cost or fair value. At June 30, 20x2 and 20x1, cost approximated fair value.

Gifts-in-Kind Inventory

Gifts-in-kind inventory consists of donated merchandise such as food, clothing and miscellaneous items used in the operation of the mission's programs, including the used clothing thrift store. The value of clothing donated within the community or to other agencies cannot be substantiated and, thus, is unrecorded. All other inventory is recorded at its estimated fair value at the date of donation.

Land, Buildings, and Equipment

Land, buildings, and equipment are recorded at cost when purchased or, if donated, at estimated fair value at the date of receipt. Depreciation and amortization is provided using the straight-line method over the following estimated useful lives:

Buildings and improvements	10 - 30 years
Furniture and fixtures	5 - 10 years
Machinery and equipment	5 - 10 years
Vehicles	3 - 5 years

Depreciation expense for the years ended June 30, 20x2 and 20x1 was $131,000 and $110,100, respectively.

The organization reports gifts of land, buildings, and equipment as unrestricted support, unless explicit donor stipulations specify how the donated assets must be used. Gifts of long-lived assets with explicit restrictions that specify how the assets are to be used, and gifts of cash or other assets that must be used to acquire long-lived assets are reported as restricted support. Absent explicit donor stipulations about how long those long-lived assets must be maintained, the organization reports expirations of donor restrictions when the donated or acquired long-lived assets are placed in service.

Annuities Payable

The mission has established a gift annuity plan whereby donors may contribute assets to the organization, in exchange for the right to receive a fixed dollar annual return during their lifetimes. This transaction provides for a portion of the transfer to be considered a charitable contribution for income tax purposes. The difference between the amount of the annuity and the liability for future payments, determined on an actuarial basis, is recognized as income at the date of the gift. Upon the death of the annuitant (or the last joint annuitant), income distributions cease. The actuarial liability for annuities payable is evaluated annually (giving effect to investment income and payments to annuitants) and any surplus or deficiency is recognized as unrestricted investment income or expense.

Contributions

Donation income is recorded when promises are made, cash is received, or ownership of donated assets is transferred to the mission. During fiscal years 20x2 and 20x1, the mission obtained contributions that were restricted by the donor for specified purposes. Donor-restricted contributions are recorded as revenue in the temporarily restricted class of net assets until the funds have been expended by the mission for the purposes specified, at which time the net assets are reclassified to the unrestricted class of net assets. Donated materials, including gifts-in-kind, are recorded at estimated fair value. The mission records income and expense for contributed medical services valued at the healthcare provider's standard hourly rate for the number of hours contributed in the mission's medical programs. Clothing contributed to the mission, in excess of requirements for the mission's internal programs, is distributed to other relief organizations.

Functional Allocation of Expenses

The costs of providing various program services and supporting activities have been summarized on a functional basis in the statement of activities. Accordingly, certain costs, such as depreciation and payroll, have been allocated among the pro- grams services and supporting activities benefited.

During the fiscal year ended June 30, 20x2, the organization conducted activities that included fund-raising appeals, as well as program and management and general components. These materials included direct mail letters and newsletters. Of the costs of those activities, $841,700 of joint costs were allocated as follows: $610,200 was allocated to fund-raising and $231,500 was allocated to public awareness and education.

During the fiscal year ended June 30, 20x1, the organization conducted activities that included fund-raising appeals, as well as program and management and general components. These materials included direct mail letters and newsletters. Of those costs, $621,800 of joint costs were allocated as fol- lows: $447,700 was allocated to fund-raising, $138,600 was allocated to public awareness and education, and $35,500 was allocated to general administrative.

3. Summarized Comparative Information

The statement of functional expenses includes certain prior- year summarized comparative information in total, but not by functional classification. Such information does not include sufficient detail to constitute a presentation in conformity with generally accepted accounting principles. Accordingly, such information should be read in conjunction with the financial statements for the year ended June 30, 20x1, from which the summarized information was derived.

4. Gifts-in-Kind Program:

The Mission operates a substantial gifts-in-kind program. Activity for fiscal years 20x2 and 20x1 is summarized as follows:

	Beginning Inventory	Add Contributions	Subtract Distributions	Ending Inventory
20x2:				
Clothing (for resale)	$ 222,500	$ 654,600	$ 772,300	$ 104,800
Food	68,600	426,800	458,400	37,000
Furniture and equipment	61,200	237,500	250,900	47,800
Medical supplies	18,800	16,200	8,800	26,200
Volunteer medical services	-	37,600	37,600	-
	$ 371,100	$ 1,372,700	$ 1,528,000	$ 215,800
20x1:				
Clothing (for resale)	$ 104,500	$ 737,000	$ 619,000	$ 222,500
Food	42,300	629,300	603,100	68,600
Furniture and equipment	98,400	118,100	155,200	61,200
Medical supplies	-	18,800	-	18,800
Volunteer medical services	-	84,100	84,100	-
	$ 245,200	$ 1,587,300	$ 1,461,400	$ 371,100

5. Contribution of Land and Building:

During the fiscal year ended June 30, 20x1, the mission received a donation of the land and building they utilize as their administrative headquarters. The land and building were recorded as contribution income of $814,000 which was based on the appraised value of the property at the date of receipt.

Exhibit 7—Sample School

Statement of Cash Receipts, Cash Disbursements, and Cash Balance

Year Ended June 30, 20x2
(With Summarized Information for the Year Ended June 30, 20x1)

	Unrestricted	Temporarily Restricted	Permanently Restricted	Total	Comparative Totals for 20x1
Cash Receipts:					
Registration fees	$ 55,000	$ -	$	$ 55,000	$ 51,600
Tuition	959,200	-		959,200	923,500
Tuition received in advance (Note 6)	-	256,600		256,600	224,600
Interest and dividend income (Note 8)	4,950	750		5,700	4,300
Day care	21,400	-		21,400	18,200
Contributions:					
Through church	9,000	-		9,000	7,300
Through church—restricted (Note 7)	-	7,500		7,500	2,400
Through sample school	71,900	-		71,900	72,400
Lunchroom	14,400	-		14,400	12,600
State auxiliary fund	35,900	-		35,900	34,000
Fund-raising revenue	101,900	-		101,900	63,700
Other	20,600	-		20,600	14,200
Less Discounts	(94,200)	-	-	(94,200)	(86,200)
Total cash receipts	1,200,050	264,850	-	1,464,900	1,342,600
Net Assets Released from Restrictions	224,600	(224,600)	-	-	-
	1,424,650	40,250	-	1,464,900	1,342,600
Cash Disbursements (see schedule attached)	(1,441,200)	-	-	(1,441,200)	(1,311,200)
Excess (Deficit) of Cash Receipts over Cash Disbursements	(16,550)	40,250	-	23,700	31,400
Cash Balance, Beginning of Year	45,100	227,000	10,000	282,100	250,700
Cash Balance, End of Year (Note 3)	$ 28,550	$ 267,250	$ 10,000	$ 305,800	$ 282,100

See notes to financial statements

Exhibit 7—Sample School

Notes to Financial Statements
June 30, 20x2

1. Nature of Organization:

The Sample School (school) is an Illinois corporation exempt from federal income tax under Section 501(c)(3) of the Internal Revenue Code.

The school is a coeducational, preschool through grade twelve, predominantly college preparatory day school, serving primarily Christian families. Governed by a board of directors, the school is a nonprofit, nondenominational ministry of the church.

The financial statement does not include assets, liabilities, revenue and expenses of the church. The church is a separate Illinois corporation which is also exempt from federal income tax under Section 501(c)(3) of the Internal Revenue Code. The school is under common control of the church and is included in the audited financial statements of the church.

2. Summary of Significant Accounting Policies:

The financial statement of the school has been prepared on the cash basis; consequently, certain revenues are recognized when received rather than when earned, and certain expenses are recognized when paid rather than when the obligation is incurred.

The financial statements include certain prior-year summarized comparative information in total, but not by net asset class. Such information does not include sufficient detail to constitute a presentation in conformity with generally accepted accounting principles. Accordingly, such information should be read in conjunction with the financial statements for the year ended June 30, 20x1, from which the summarized information was derived.

3. Cash:

Cash balance as of June 30, 20x2 is as follows:

Unrestricted	$	28,550
Restricted:		
Sutton Scholarship Fund—permanent		10,000
Sutton Scholarship—temporarily (see Note 8)		750
Other scholarship fund—temporarily (See Note 7)		7,500
Kitchen equipment fund—temporarily		2,400
Tuition received in advance—temporarily		256,600
	$	305,800

Cash and cash equivalents on deposit at Fidelity Savings & Trust exceeded federally insured limits by $125,000.

4. Marketable Securities:

Marketable securities acquired by gift are not reflected on the accompanying cash basis financial statement. At June 30, 20x2, the school owned 446 shares of a marketable security with an estimated fair value at the date of the gift of $6,200. At June 30, 20x2, the estimated current value is $14,800.

5. Related Parties:

The school paid $125,794—for janitorial, maintenance, utilities, computer services, administrative services, and for the licensing of a church employee as the school's administrator—to the church for the year ended June 30, 20x2.

6. Tuition Received in Advance:

A 5% discount of the annual tuition was allowed if the total payment was received by the school by June 15, 20x2, or within two weeks after acceptance of a new student. A 4% discount was allowed if the total payment was received by July 15, 20x2.

7. Donor Restricted Contribution:

The school received $7,500 from an individual in June 20x2. This was designated by the donor to be used for future scholarships. See also Note 3.

8. Donor-Restricted Income:

Interest earned of $750 on the Sutton Scholarship Fund is temporarily restricted by donor stipulation for scholarships for Native American students.

9. Note Payable:

Note payable is as follows:

Note payable bank, secured by a school bus, bearing interest at prime plus 1%, currently 7%, payable in monthly principal installments of $462.91 plus interest. Remaining principal and accrued interest are due on note's maturity date of November 30, 20x5.	$ 11,600
Less current portion	(5,600)
	$ 6,000

The note payable matures as follows:

Fiscal year ending June 30,	
20x3	$ 5,600
20x4	5,600
20x5	400
	$ 11,600

10. Operating Leases:

Lease with ABC Rental, Inc. for copier equipment, payable in annual installments of $1,300, due August 20x4.

Fiscal year ending June 30,	
20x3	$ 1,300
20x4	1,300
	$ 2,600

11. Employee Benefit Plan:

Tax-Deferred Annuity Plan

The school has established a tax-deferred annuity plan for its full-time employees. All full-time employees are eligible to participate in the TDA upon completion of age twenty-one and one year of service at the school.

Subject to the limitations imposed under Section 403(b) of the Internal Revenue Code, the school made annuity purchase payments at a rate equal to 100% of the amounts that employees had contributed through a salary reduction agreement with the school, plus a matching contribution which is periodically determined by the school and the church. Contributions totaled $15,900 for the year ended June 30, 20x2.

12. Uncertainties:

As of June 30, 20x2, a lawsuit was pending related to an accident in 20x1 that involved the school's bus. As of August 24, 20x2, the case was still in the process of discovery. Based on a review of the facts in the case, management believes that the likelihood of a material loss from this litigation is remote.

Exhibit 7—Sample School

Schedule of Cash Disbursements

Year Ended June 30, 20x2

	Program	Adminis- trative	Fund- Raising	Total
Advertising	$ -	$ 1,600	$ -	$ 1,600
Books	9,200	-	-	9,200
Conferences	3,800	-	-	3,800
Dues and Subscriptions	4,800	-	-	4,800
Equipment	9,400	1,100	3,600	14,100
Fund-raising Fees	-	-	42,000	42,000
Insurance:				
Accident	4,900	-	-	4,900
Group	1,800	-	-	1,800
Hospitalization	59,700	-	2,100	61,800
Student	3,400	-	-	3,400
Workers' compensation	12,500	-	300	12,800
Interest Expense	600	500	-	1,100
Library	8,900	-	-	8,900
Lunchroom Expenses	10,100	-	-	10,100
Maintenance and Repairs	1,400	7,100	-	8,500
Other	3,300	5,900	3,600	12,800
Postage	2,100	400	1,000	3,500
Principal Payments on Chattel				
Note Payable	-	6,600	-	6,600
Professional Development	7,900	-	-	7,900
Professional Services	-	6,400	-	6,400
Salaries and Wages:				
Administrative	-	115,800	-	115,800
Regular contract	903,300	-	34,100	937,400
Supplemental contract and bonuses	19,100	-	-	19,100
Substitutes	6,500	-	-	6,500
Scholarship	2,300	-	-	2,300
Social Security and Medicare Tax	74,400	10,000	2,400	86,800
Supplies:				
School	18,600	-	-	18,600
Office	-	500	700	1,200
Publications	3,000	400	200	3,600
Tax-Deferred Annuity	14,100	1,800	-	15,900
Telephone	1,400	6,200	400	8,000
	$ 1,186,500	$ 164,300	$ 90,400	$ 1,441,200

Appendix D — Illustrations of an Investment Pool

Example A

Three funds (Funds A, B, and C) combined their cash some years ago into an investment pool by simultaneous investments totaling $100,000 in the proportions indicated below. These assets were received and invested on December 31, 19x0. On December 31, 20x2, the pooled investments on a cost basis were carried at $120,000, which is the amount of the original contributions plus $20,000 representing net realized gains retained by the investment pool.

The market value at December 31, 20x2, of the pooled assets was calculated to be $150,000. On that basis, the unrealized net gains were $30,000.

A new fund (Fund D) invested $100,000 of cash in the investment pool at December 31, 20x2.

The following table presents the transactions set forth above and illustrates the calculation of the resulting equity percentages:

Fund	Cash Contributions to Pool	Original Equity Percentage	Value of Pool December 31, 20x2 Cost	Value of Pool December 31, 20x2 Market	Value After Entry of Fund D	New Equity Percentage
A	$40,000	40.0 %	$48,000	$60,000	$60,000	24.0 %
B	35,000	35.0	42,000	52,500	52,500	21.0
C	25,000	25.0	30,000	37,500	37,500	15.0
D	-	-	-	-	100,000	40.0
	$100,000	100.0 %	$120,000	$150,000	$250,000	100.0 %

If Fund A were to withdraw from the investment pool at December 31, 20x2, it would be entitled to 24.0% or $60,000, rather than $48,000.

The equity percentages to be utilized for entries to determine the with-drawals from the pool are based on market values.

Example B

A simpler approach to pooling of monies is used by some organizations. This approach presumes that there is no variance between the cost and market value of invested assets such as is true of bank money market investment accounts. All income and gains/losses are currently distributed as part of income. The assets may all come from within the sponsoring organization or, as frequently occurs, from related ministries and affiliated field entities. The amount owed to each participant in the pool is maintained in a separate liability account. To maintain stability in the rate earned by participants, an undistributed reserve may be maintained so that fluctuations in earnings can be absorbed. Earnings are maintained in a separate account to track income accurately. Distributions of earnings are charged to another account. The monthly earnings are distributed (i.e., added to) amounts owed to each participant. Should the participant desire to withdraw part of its investment or only the earnings amount, that cash amount may be paid from the pooled funds by the organization managing the pool. Each participant records its investment in the pool in the asset section of its ledger. Earnings are recorded by the various entities as earned. All pool accounts—assets, liabilities, net assets, income, and expenses—may be segregated in the liability section of the corporation holding the pool or in a separate custodial fund.

At least one organization has expanded this concept to use the currently available zero-based banking services. It has issued checks to all the participants so that each can withdraw money directly as needed in its operations. An internal system is then used to calculate average daily balances and to calculate and distribute each participant's portion monthly.

Booking for the various entities would be as follows (only affected accounts are shown):

Earnings for this example are calculated at 10%. Earnings were distributed at 10% for the month January of 20x2; however, for the year 20x2, distributions average 9%, with 1% maintained as a stability reserve.

	December 31, 20x1	January 31, 20x2	December 31, 20x2
Organization A (entity managing the pool):			
*Invested Pool Accounts:			
Investments	$100,000 Dr	$100,830 Dr	$210,000 Dr
Owed to Organization A	$ 40,000 Cr	$ 40,332 Cr	$ 43,600 Cr
Owed to Organization B	35,000 Cr	35,290 Cr	38,150Cr
Owed to Organization C	25,000 Cr	25,208 Cr	27,250 Cr
Owed to Organization D	-	-	100,000 Cr
	100,000 Cr	100,830 Cr	209,000 Cr
Net assets (after closing)	-	-	1,000 Cr
Total amounts owed and net pool assets	$100,000 Cr	$100,830 Cr	$210,000 Cr
Investment income	$ -	$ 830 Cr	$ 10,000 Cr
Earnings distributed		830 Dr	9,000 Dr
Net excess retained for pool stability	$ -	$ -	$ 1,000 Cr
Organization Accounts:			
Investments in pool	$ 40,000 Dr	$ 40,332 Dr	$ 43,600 Dr
Investment income	-	332 Cr	3,600 Cr
Organization B:			
Investments in pool	$ 35,000 Dr	$ 35,290 Dr	$ 38,150 Dr
Investment income	-	290 Cr	3,150 Cr
Organization C:			
Investments in pool	$ 25,000 Dr	$ 25,208 Dr	$ 27,250 Dr
Investment income	-	208 Cr	2,250 Cr
Organization D:			
Investments in pool	$ -	$ -	$100,000 Dr
Investment income	-	-	- Cr

Appendix E—Internal Controls

As part of its fiduciary responsibility, the governing board of every organization is responsible for seeing that adequate internal controls are in effect.

Internal control is a system of policies and procedures intended to provide reasonable assurance that the objectives of the entity will be achieved. Only some of these policies and procedures relate to accounting and reporting. For example, those concerning the effectiveness of management decision-making processes such as whether to invest more money in mailing lists or in development of computer programs, although important, don't ordinarily relate to accounting and reporting.

The objectives of internal accounting control for not-for-profit organizations are generally the same as those for profit-oriented organizations. Some characteristics of not-for-profit organizations that may influence internal accounting control include:

- A volunteer governing board, many of whose members may have limited financial backgrounds.

- A limited number of staff personnel, sometimes too few to provide the appropriate segregation of duties.

- A mixture of volunteers and employees participating in operations. Depending on the size and other features of the organization, day-to-day operations sometimes are conducted by volunteers instead of employees. Persons involved with not-for-profit organizations, especially volunteers, are more likely to become frustrated with what they view as onerous control procedures and attempt to ignore or circumvent the procedures.

- The manner in which responsibility and authority are delegated varies among organizations. This may affect control over financial transactions, particularly with respect to authorization.

- A budget, usually approved by the governing board. The budget normally serves as authorization for the activities to be carried out by management in attaining the organization's program objectives.

- The existence, or absence, of expenditure limits on management through the use of spending authority limits, capital budgets, etc.

For the most part, internal control does not itself prevent embezzlement but should ensure that if committed (and collusion is not present), it will be discovered within a reasonable period of time and the person responsible identified. This possibility of discovery helps persuade most people not to allow temptation to get the better of them. Therefore, in addition to preventing potential misstatements of financial information and safeguarding the ministry's assets, fraud prevention is a significant objective—although not an overriding one—of an internal control structure.

BASIC CONTROLS

Policies and Procedures

The organization should establish clear definitions of authority and responsibility, including operating policies and accounting procedures for executing and recording transactions. This information should be clearly communicated (in written form) to all affected personnel, including volunteers, and should be updated regularly. All personnel should receive adequate training about the organization's policies.

On the other hand, required procedures should be no more burdensome than is necessary to accomplish the desired objectives. A cost-benefit analysis should be done to ensure that procedures generate benefits which exceed their costs, both in terms of dollars and staff morale.

Budgets

A budget is one of the most effective internal controls, if the budget is soundly conceived and compared to actual amounts on a monthly basis. If deviations from the budget are carefully followed up by the controller or executive director, the likelihood of a large misstatement (intentional or unintentional) or misappropriation taking place without being detected fairly quickly is reduced considerably. This type of overall review of the financial statements is very important, and every member of the board or its delegated committee should ask questions about any item which appears to be significantly out of line, either with the budget or with what he/she would have expected to have been the actual figures. Many times this type of probing into deviations from the expected has uncovered actual or potential problems.

Control Over Cash and Other Receipts

The basic objective of internal control over receipts is to ensure that all amounts to which the organization is entitled, or for which it has responsibility, are deposited in the organization's bank account or are otherwise brought under proper control and accountability. Small organizations must be particularly diligent because of the limited number of persons usually involved. Some basic procedures are:

1. Prenumbered receipts should be issued immediately for all cash and checks at the time first received. A duplicate copy should be accounted for and a comparison eventually made between the total of the amounts shown on the receipts issued and the amount deposited in the bank. If merchandise or premiums are given in exchange for gifts, the receipt should indicate the total amount received and the fair value of any merchandise or premium. (Tax regulations relating to gifts are discussed in paragraph 4-88 and 4-89.)

2. For the protection of both the cash collected and the reputations of those who handle it, care should be taken that cash collections are always under the control of at least two people.

    Although no procedure will absolutely guard against an usher skimming cash from a church or other offering before it is initially locked up and counted, the cumulative risk can be lowered by rotating the ushers' duties, always keeping the cash visible to two people, and locking it up promptly until the collection can be counted by at least two people together who should both sign the cash collection report. This report should be given to the treasurer or business manager for subsequent comparison with the deposit on the bank statement. The offerings should be promptly deposited intact.

Control over cash receipts may be especially difficult when part or all of a cash offering is given directly to a missionary or other visitor. Churches and other organizations sponsoring such offerings should remit checks directly to the visitor's organization rather than presenting the gift or honorarium directly to the visitor.

3. Two persons should open all mail and list all amounts received for each day. This list should subsequently be compared to the bank deposit by someone not handling money. Checks should be restrictively endorsed promptly upon receipt.

4. All amounts received should be deposited in the bank— intact and on a timely basis. No part of any "cash" receipts should be put in the petty cash fund or used directly to pay bills. Rather, checks should be issued to pay expenses. In this way, bank statements will show a complete record of all receipts and expenditures of the organization.

5. Receipts should be issued for all noncash gifts received, with a detailed description of the item. The organization should not, however, value the gift for the donor. In the case of commodities or other large gifts from producers, wholesalers, or retailers, to determine the amount to be recorded as a contribution, the ministry should request that the donor value the goods at fair value, giving consideration to quantities and condition.

Control Over Cash Disbursements

The basic objective of internal controls over cash disbursements is to reduce the risk of misappropriation by ensuring that a record of all disbursements is made and that only authorized persons are in a position to disburse funds. Specific procedures to help accomplish this include:

1. All disbursements should be made by check with approved supporting documentation retained for each disbursement. No amounts should be paid by cash with the exception of minor petty cash items. Checks should always be payable to a specific person (not "cash"), including checks for petty cash reimbursement. This makes it more difficult to fraudulently disburse funds.

2. Persons authorized to sign checks should not also make accounting entries. Two signatures should be required on checks over a minimum amount. Note: Two signatures on a check provide additional control only if *both* check signers carefully examine the invoices or other supporting documentation behind the disbursement before signing the check. A risk of having dual signatures is that each check signer will rely on the other and will review the supporting bills in a perfunctory manner which results in less control than if only one person signed but realized he/she had full responsibility.

3. A person other than the person making accounting entries should receive bank statements directly from the bank and should reconcile them regularly. This procedure helps prevent the bookkeeper from fraudulently issuing a check and covering up the disbursement in the books.

Control Over Investments

The basic objective of internal controls over investments is to ensure that assets are properly recorded, adequately safeguarded, and managed in accordance with any related restrictions and prudent investment management practices, and that all investment income due is promptly collected, deposited, and properly recorded. Specific procedures to accomplish this include:

1. *Segregation of Duties*
   The receipt, recording, custody, transaction authorization,

and performance monitoring functions should be clearly segregated.

2. *Recording of Investments*
Endowments should be recorded in separate accounts and restrictions on investment principal and investment income documented. Endowments should be recorded in the investment ledger by a person independent of initial receipt or custody of endowment securities. The investment ledger should be reconciled with the general ledger by a person independent of the initial receipt, custody, or recording of endowment securities.

3. *Custody of Investments*
Endowment securities should be deposited with an independent custodian or in a bank safe deposit box.

   - If deposited with an independent custodian, accounting and custodial functions should be segregated. The custodian should issue periodic reports to the organization and carry sufficient fidelity insurance.

   - If deposited in a bank safe deposit box, access should be limited to two or more authorized persons and all visits recorded.

4. *Authorization and Monitoring of Investments*
Security transactions, including purchases, sales, renewals, and exchanges, should be approved by authorized non-accounting personnel (usually the investment committee of the board or an appropriate financial officer). The basis of valuation of investment securities should be periodically reviewed, and the write-down and write-off of endowment securities limited to authorized nonaccounting personnel.

5. *Investment Income*
The disbursement of restricted investment income should be reviewed by appropriate personnel to determine whether the disbursement is in conformity with donor or board-imposed restrictions. Any restrictions on and proposed uses of investment income should be reviewed prior to disbursement. Investment income received should be periodically compared

with investment revenue estimates in the operating budget. The promptness and accuracy of investment income payments by underlying companies and investment counselors should be reviewed.

If securities are "pooled" for investment purposes, the allocation formula and the computation and distribution of investment income and realized and unrealized gains or losses should be periodically reviewed. Investment income and realized and unrealized gains should be distinguished.

Other Areas of Control

1. Someone other than the person responsible for making entries to the general ledger should authorize any write-offs of accounts receivable or other assets.

   This control helps to ensure that if the bookkeeper has embezzled accounts receivable or some other asset, he/she will not be able to cover up the theft by writing off the receivable or other asset on the books.

   Negotiable assets such as marketable securities should be kept in a bank safe deposit box (with two signatures required for entry), held by a bank or other independent custodian, or in "street name" by a major, well-known broker.

   This control is to ensure that securities are protected against loss by fire or theft in the organization's office or from bankruptcy of a broker-dealer.

3. Fixed asset records should be maintained and an inventory taken periodically.

   This is to ensure that the organization has a complete, permanent record of its assets, which should contain information such as a description of the asset, cost, date acquired, location, serial number, and similar information. This information will provide a record of the assets for which employees are responsible, as well as provide important records for insurance purposes.

FIDELITY INSURANCE

An organization should consider the need for fidelity insurance. Fidelity insurance provides that if a loss from embezzlement occurs, the organization will recover the loss (up to the amount of the policy). This insurance does not cover theft or burglary by an outside person. It provides protection only against an employee's or volunteer's dishonesty. Note: A fidelity insurance company may not reimburse for a loss if it believes adequate internal controls were not in place to help prevent the loss from happening.

FOREIGN OPERATIONS

Internal controls are important not only at home, but also in foreign operations, where local business practice, cultural differences, and geographical distance often make the establishment of internal controls more difficult.

Obviously, procedures vary depending on whether the ministry is carrying out its mission directly by its own employees or through other entities, including foreign ministries. The following control procedures, among others, should be considered.

1. site visits by management and/or internal audit personnel

2. periodic financial statements (should be required in all cases)

3. remission of funds only upon receipt of a statement showing disbursements made (imprest accounting)

4. audits by independent auditing firms

The controls discussed above are basic and should not be considered all inclusive. A complete system of internal controls encompasses all of the procedures of the organization. The board should regularly review the adequacy of the controls in effect and may want to retain the services of a professional to help set up and monitor the effectiveness of internal control systems, especially if the organization is a large or complex one or if it has peculiar problems or procedures.

Appendix F—Functional Allocations

The following are examples of methods that may be used to allocate expenses:

- A study of the organization's activities may be made periodically to determine the best practicable allocation methods. The study should include an evaluation of the preceding year's time records or activity reports of key personnel, the use of space, the consumption of supplies and postage, and so forth. Allocation methods should be revised, if necessary, to reflect significant changes in the nature or level of the organization's current activities.

- Periodic time records may be kept by employees who spend time on more than one function as a basis for allocating salaries and related employment costs. The records should indicate the nature of the activities in which the employee is involved. If the functions do not vary significantly from period to period, the preparation of time reports for selected test periods during the year may be sufficient. (These methods should be used for all workers, regardless of status; e.g., full-time, part-time, intern, paid, or volunteer.)

- Automobile, travel, and other costs incurred by employees may be allocated on the basis of the expense or time reports of the employees involved.

- Telephone expense may be allocated in the same way as the salary of the employee using each extension, after making direct charges for the long-distance calls or other services attributable to specific functions.

- Stationery, supplies, and postage costs may be allocated based on a study of their use.

- Occupancy costs may be allocated based on a study of the activities (by function) of the personnel using the space involved.

- Depreciation and rental of equipment may be allocated based on asset usage.

- Interest on loans to acquire capital assets; (e.g., building mortgage, capital lease, and similar transactions), may be allocated based on asset usage.

- Interest on "working capital" loans, such as under a line of credit, would normally be allocated to management and general unless a specific program or fund-raising use of the loan can be identified.

In order to promote uniformity in reporting, EJAC recommends that Christian ministries report their program services, as much as possible, in categories selected from the list on the following page.

Large or diverse organizations might report their program services under two or more of the major categories in this list. Smaller or more focused organizations—whose program services are encompassed by one major category—might report their expenses under two or more subcategories; for example, a relief agency might report expenses under "Agriculture training" and "Food distribution."

TYPICAL CATEGORIES OF PROGRAM SERVICES

Schools, Bible Schools, and Seminaries

Bible Schools
Correspondence Schools
Christian Training Institutes
Extension Programs
Seminaries
Seminars/Conferences
Education
Other

Churches, Church Growth, and Evangelism

Bible Classes
Camps
Church Ministry
Church Planting
Church Relations
Christian Education,
   Sunday School,
   Vacation Bible Schools
Prison Ministries
Fellowship
Youth Clubs, Youth
   Centers, Hostels
Evangelism
Evangelistic Crusades
Military Ministry
Counseling
Music
Missions
Worship
Other

Education/Training Ministry (other than Bible Schools and Seminaries)

Adult Literacy
Candidate Training Schools
Children's Schools
Day-Care Centers
Elementary Schools
Kindergartens
Orphanages
Colleges
Preschools
Retreat Centers
Schools for the Handicapped
Secondary Schools
Seminars
Teacher Training
Libraries
Music
Arts
Sports
Other

Linguistics Ministry

Anthropology
Linguistics
Literacy Materials
Specialized Training Schools
Translation
Other

Camps

Food Service
Horse Ranches
Adult Conferences
Day Trips
Youth Camps
Other

Media Ministry

Bookstores and Distribution
Cassettes
Films (not used for recruiting
 or fund-raising)
Printing
Publications

Radio
Tape Ministry
Television
Tracts
Other

Medical Ministry

Dental Clinics
Hospitals
Medical Training Schools
Pharmacies

Primary Health Care Medical
 Clinics
Public Health
Crisis Pregnancy Centers
Other

Ministry to Constituency (other than fund-raising activities)

Furlough Ministries
Home Service Ministries
Magazine and Media Reports

Prayer Bulletins and Reporting
Spiritual Counseling
Other

Relief, Rehabilitation, and Community Development Ministry

Agriculture Training
Clothing Distribution
Community Planning
Food Distribution
Food Production

Industrial Training
Medical Services
Resettlement
Water Development
Other

Services to Missions/Churches

Aviation
Computers
Construction
Development and Maintenance

Radio
Retirement Facilities
Vehicles
Other

Rescue Missions

Medical Clinics
Food Service
Housing
Public Education

Rehabilitation
Thrift Stores
Other

TYPICAL FUNCTIONAL ALLOCATIONS

As a guide to the more common expenses of a Christian ministry, the following indicate typical allocations to program services and supporting activities.[1]

Type of Expense	Typical Allocations
1. Missionary appointee	—Fund-raising (securing support to serve for the first time) —Program (for ministry to constituency or specific preparation for field service)
2. Furlough expenses (includes salary allowances)	—Fund-raising (for support development portion)
3. Travel and shipping to and from work location	—Specific program (including ministry to constituency) —Specific programs —Management and general —Fund-raising (based on the personnel cost allocation)
4. Mission home representatives	—Fund-raising —Ministry to constituency program
5. Maintenance of mailing lists	—Fund-raising —Management and general
6. Literature and videos, direct mail	—Fund-raising —Ministry to constituency or literature program
7. Recruitment of paid workers	—Specific program benefited —Management and general —Fund-raising (based on functions of recruit) (EJAC believes this reporting is appropriate, although GAAP is unclear and some may believe all costs should be charged to general & administrative.)

Type of Expense	Typical Allocations
8. Recruitment of volunteers	—Fund-raising
9. Overall administration, including administration of deferred gifts	—Management and general
10. Orientation and candidate school	—Management and general —Specific program
11. Dinner rallies	—Fund-raising —Direct benefit costs, offset against contributions
12. Publications, magazines, books, advertising	—Specific program —Fund-raising —Management and general (for advertising and reporting on ministry accomplishments)
13. Radio and TV programs	—Fund-raising —Specific program for ongoing ministries
14. Letters to constituents	—Specific program —Fund-raising —Management and general
15. Development, including deferred-giving solicitations and activities	—Fund-raising
16. Retirement benefits (This allocation should be consistent with that used during the individual's active service; i.e., charging the activity[ies] which primarily benefited from the person's service. Only those benefits paid or accrued by the organization should be reported.)	—Specific programs —Fund-raising —Management and general

Type of Expense	Typical Allocations
17. Administrators: Executive	—Specific program(s) (based on direct participation) —Fund-raising —Management and general
Program administrator	—Specific program —Fund-raising —Management and general (for participation in overall administrative functions)

[1] All allocations are subject to the constraints of SOP 98-2, *Accounting for Costs of Activities of Not-for-Profit Organizations and State and Local Governmental Entities That Include Fund-raising*

Appendix G—AICPA Flowcharts for Reporting of Related Entities

The following flowcharts are excerpts from SOP 94-3, *Reporting of Related Entities by Not-for-Profit Organizations*. Refer to Chapter 8 for more specific information regarding related entities.

RELATIONSHIP WITH ANOTHER NOT-FOR-PROFIT ORGANIZATION

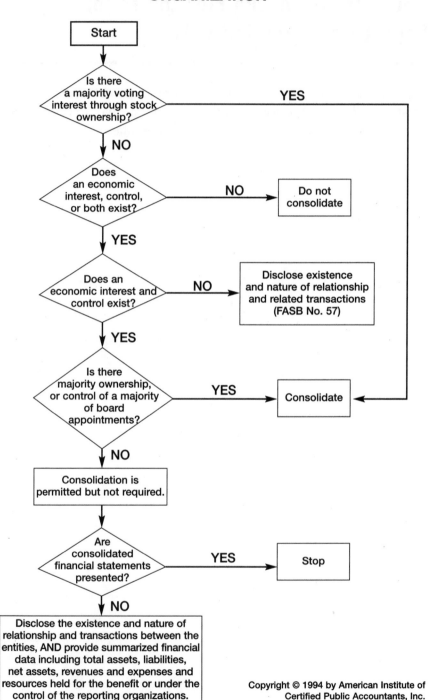

RELATIONSHIP WITH ANOTHER NOT-FOR-PROFIT ORGANIZATION

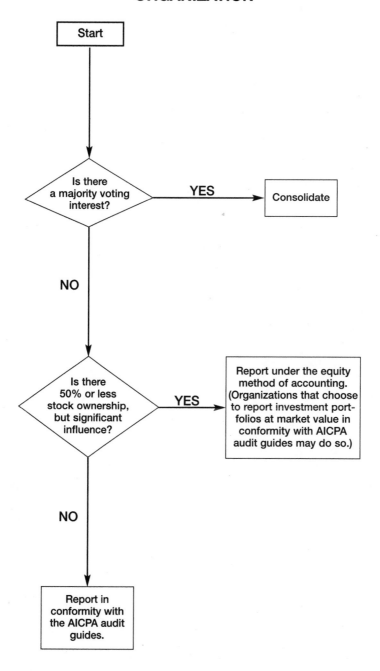

Appendix H—Sample Joint Ministries Agreement

This sample joint ministries agreement is provided for illustrative purposes only. Such agreements are commonly used between Canadian and U.S. Christian ministries.

Agreements should only be entered into following the engagement of competent legal counsel to consider applicable laws, regulations, and organizational provisions that impact and must be considered in preparing such documents.

EJAC cautions readers to consult competent legal counsel in considering and preparing such agreements.

Sample Joint Ministries Agreement

THIS AGREEMENT, made as of the ____ day of _____ , 20__.

B E T W E E N:
Canadian Charity, a non-profit corporation incorporated pursuant to the laws of the [the appropriate jurisdiction] (hereinafter referred to as "Canadian")

A N D
U.S. Charity, a non-profit corporation incorporated pursuant to the laws of the [the appropriate jurisdiction] (hereinafter referred to as "U.S.")

WHEREAS   Canadian is a charitable organization and a registered charity within the meaning of such terms in the Income Tax Act (Canada);

AND WHEREAS U.S. is classified as a tax-exempt, religious non-profit organization under Section 501(c)(3) of the Internal Revenue Code (U.S.);

AND WHEREAS the parties hereto share certain doctrinal distinctives and have similar charitable objects and interests;

AND WHEREAS the parties hereto have concluded that certain of the ministries which are carried on by each organization could be more effectively and economically carried on by pooling the resources which each of the parties is willing to devote to such ministries for the purpose of carrying on these ministries jointly;

AND WHEREAS it is the intent of the parties hereto that this agreement be entered into for the sole purpose of establishing a meaningful structure for regulating and overseeing the ministry activity or activities which are co-funded by the parties hereto;

AND WHEREAS each of the parties hereto is an autonomous organization and each party acknowledges that it shall continue to be a distinct entity from the other parties to this agreement and each party shall determine from time to time in consultation with the other party the ministries which will be carried on jointly.

NOW THEREFORE, in consideration of the mutual covenants hereinafter contained, the parties agree as follows:

ARTICLE I: PURPOSE

1.1   Joint Activity
The parties shall collectively carry on the ministry activities which are mutually agreed upon by each of the parties hereto from time to time and which are in compliance with the terms and provisions of this Agreement. Such ministry activities shall not be inconsistent with those activities which are permitted or authorized by the objects or purposes of each of the parties.

1.2   Jurisdiction
This agreement shall be interpreted according to the laws of the _____(the jurisdiction of one of the parties to this Agreement)

1.3   Name
In carrying out the joint ministry activities pursuant to the provisions

of this Agreement, such activities shall be conducted under the name (hereinafter called the _____) provided that the name may be modified in the various countries in which the ministry activities are carried on

(a) to meet the specific legal requirements of such country, and

(b) such modification is first approved by the Management Committee.

1.4   Retention of Records

All records required to be kept pursuant to this Agreement, all financial information and books of account and all other documentation shall be retained at _____ or at such other location as the parties shall determine from time to time. The parties hereto shall have full access to such records and all copies of same shall be provided to either party upon written request.

ARTICLE II: ORGANIZATION

2.1   Management Committee

The ministry activities carried on pursuant to this Agreement shall be managed by a Management Committee composed of five (5) persons. Two (2) of such persons shall be appointed by Canadian and shall be designated as voting members. Three (3) of such persons shall be appointed by U.S. and shall also be designated as voting members. Any change in the number of persons who shall constitute the Management Committee shall require the approval of all parties whereupon such change shall immediately become effective. A first and second alternative voting member may be designated to take the place of any voting member of the Management Committee.

The appointment of each person and the designation of voting members shall be for a term of three (3) years, ending at the third annual meeting of the Management Committee following the initial appointment of such appointee or appointees. Nothing herein shall prevent a party from designating another appointee or voting member in the place and stead of its representative throughout the term.

2.2   The Management Committee shall meet annually or more frequently as the interests of the joint ministry activities may require, at [identify the place of meeting]. A meeting of the members of the Management Committee may be called by the chairperson at any time. The secretary shall convene a meeting of the members of the Management Committee pursuant to a written request therefor from the chairperson or any two members, and a quorum at any meeting of the management Committee shall be determined in accordance with Article 2.6.

2.3   Notice of any meeting of the Management Committee shall be given in writing stating the time, date and place, and mailed to each member at the last address thereof as shown on the records maintained for the joint ministry activities. Such notice may be faxed to any member where the member has so requested and has provided the secretary with a fax number. In the event of mailing, postage shall be prepaid and the notice deposited in the post office or post box at least 20 days (exclusive of the day of mailing and of the day of the meeting for which notice is given) before the day for which the meeting is called. The same notice period shall be required for a notice provided by fax. Meetings of the Management Committee may be held at any time without formal notice if all the members are present or those members who are absent have waived notice and have signified in writing their consent to the meeting being held in their absence.

2.4   Where all the members have consented thereto, any member may participate in a meeting of the Management Committee by means of a conference telephone or other communications equipment by means of which all persons participating in such a meeting can hear each other, and a member participating in such a meeting by means of a conference telephone or other communicating equipment shall be deemed to be present in person at the meeting. Any consent given hereunder shall be effective whether given before or after the meeting to which it relates. Notice of any meeting or any irregularity in any meeting, or the notice thereof, may be waived by any member.

2.5   The number of votes to be exercised by any voting member of the Management Committee shall be determined in the following manner:

(a) following the preparation of the financial statements of the joint ministry activities and prior to the annual meeting of the Management Committee, each year the financial contribution of each party to such joint ministry activities for the immediately preceding fiscal period shall be determined as a percentage of the aggregate of all financial contributions to the joint ministry activities by parties to this Agreement for the immediately preceding fiscal period. In determining such contributions, a reasonable value shall be assigned to any resource input contributed to the joint ministry activities by any party to this Agreement, and such value shall be deemed to be a financial contribution and be included in such calculations.

(b) upon the determination of the percentage contribution by each party to this Agreement, the total number of votes to be cast by each party's voting members shall be equal to one vote for each full percentage point of such party's financial contribution determined in accordance with Article 2.5(a). Where a party to this Agreement has more than one Appointee to the Management Committee, the total number of votes which such party's appointees are entitled to cast shall be divided among such party's appointees.

2.6   A Quorum at any meeting of the Management Committee shall be four (4) members present in person or by teleconference.

2.7   Votes

At all meetings of the Management Committee, every question shall be decided by the majority of the votes cast. Each voting member shall have such number of votes on any question before the Management Committee, as determined pursuant to the provisions of Article 2.5. The Chairperson of the meeting shall not have a second or casting vote in the case of an equality of votes.

2.8   Budget Process

(a) At its last meeting in each fiscal year during the term of this Agreement, the Management Committee shall approve a budget setting out the estimated costs and the funding required for all proposed ministry activities to be carried on jointly by the parties hereto for the ensuing fiscal year. Such budget shall be forwarded to the parties for their consideration and approval. If such budget meets with the approval of all parties, with or without change, the budget or amended budget, as the case may be, shall become the budget for joint ministry activities for the ensuing year.

(b) Each party shall contribute such funds as agreed to by that party during the budget approval process, and such funds shall be used to carry out the joint ministry activities as set out in the budget.

2.9 Powers and Duties

The Management Committee shall oversee the ministry activities which are carried on jointly by the parties hereto. In doing so, the Management Committee shall exercise such rights, powers, and privileges as assigned to them by the parties, which shall include the following:

(a) the Management Committee may establish policies, which are not inconsistent with the charter, bylaws and policies of each of the parties, as it considers necessary or advisable for the general conduct and management of the activities which are carried on jointly;

(b) the Management Committee shall elect one of its members to be chairperson and one of its members to be secretary;

(c) the members of the Management Committee may establish a single joint bank account in the name of all parties to this Agreement, to which all funds to be used in the joint ministry activities shall be deposited. The Management Committee shall designate the individuals who shall have signing authority for such account.

(d) the Management Committee may establish such committees as it deems appropriate for the general conduct and management of the activities which are carried on jointly, and may determine the duties and responsibilities of such committee;

(e) the Management Committee may, from time to time, appoint such officers and employ such persons as it considers to be necessary to carry out the functions described therein.

(f) the Management Committee shall provide regular reports to the parties hereto and act within the authority given to it by the parties from time to time.

2.10 Remuneration

(a) No member of the Management Committee shall receive any

remuneration for acting as a member of such committee. However, expenses incurred in attending meetings or fulfilling duties specifically assigned by the Management Committee may be paid out of the funds received from the parties for the joint ministry activities.

(b) In the event the services of an individual or individuals are required to carry out functions in connection with the ministry activities which are carried on jointly, a party to this Agreement may employ such individual or individuals and then make the services of such employee or employees available to the Management Committee to carry on the ministry activities carried on jointly by the parties. The compensation paid to such employee or employees shall be included in the financial contributions by such party to fund the joint ministry activities in determining the number of votes to be cast by such party, pursuant to the provisions of Article 2.5 of this Agreement. While performing their services, such individual or individuals shall be under the direction of the Management Committee with respect to the manner in which such services are to be provided. With the approval of the parties hereto, the parties may jointly employ persons for the purposes of the joint ministry activities in such capacities, at such remuneration, and upon such terms as the Management Committee determine.

ARTICLE III: TERM AND TERMINATION

3.1   Term

The parties hereto shall commence to carry on the joint ministry activities in accordance with the provisions of this Agreement upon the signing of the Agreement by each of such parties. The parties shall continue to carry on the joint ministry activities until terminated by the agreement of the parties hereto.

3.2   Termination

(a) Upon the termination of this Agreement, a complete accounting of all property held in connection with the joint ministry activities shall be made to the parties herein and, subject to the provisions of Article 5.2, such property shall be distributed among the parties in proportion to the contributions made by them to such joint ministry activities. Such distribution shall take place no later than sixty (60) days following the completion of the said accounting.

(b) Upon the distribution of the property to the parties, each party hereto shall cease to have the right to use and shall discontinue the use of names, marks, designs and logos which are the names, marks, designs and logos of or similar to those owned by the other party to this Agreement.

ARTICLE IV: MANAGEMENT

4.1   Records of the Joint Ministry
Records of the joint ministry activities shall be maintained as required by law, as well as minutes of all meetings of the Management Committee. Copies of all minutes and annual reports of the joint ministry activities shall be promptly forwarded to each party.

4.2   Annual Reports
Within sixty (60) days after the end of each fiscal period, the Management Committee shall submit an annual report of the ministry that is carried on jointly by the parties hereto during such fiscal year to each party.

ARTICLE V: FINANCIAL ARRANGEMENTS

5.1   Financial Support
Each of the parties hereto agrees to provide funds for the joint ministry activities to meet the financial commitments made in connection with the joint ministry activities established in accordance with the budget approved pursuant to article 2.8, or as otherwise mutually agreed upon from time to time by the parties.

5.2   Capital Acquisitions
(a) To the greatest extent possible, any real property required in carrying out the joint ministry activities shall be acquired or leased by one party to the Agreement who shall then contribute the use of such real property for the joint ministry

activities. For the purposes of Article 2.5, the fair rental value related to the use of real property in ministry activities that are carried on jointly shall be deemed to be that party's financial contribution. Such party shall retain the title to the property and shall be entitled to retain such property upon the termination of this Agreement.

(b) In the event that real property is acquired or leased for use in the joint ministry activities and is not acquired by one party, such real property will be acquired from the funds made available for the joint ministry activities, in accordance with the budget approved pursuant to Article 2.8. Title to such property shall be held by one of the parties hereto, but such party shall hold such property in trust for the parties to this Agreement in proportion to their contributions to the joint ministry activities. Upon the termination of this Agreement where such property is not disposed of prior to termination, the real property so held in trust shall be conveyed to the parties in accordance with their respective interests. If the real property is necessary to effectively carry on the joint ministry activities, and one of the parties hereto desires to so carry on such activities, the party withdrawing shall offer to sell, rent or lease to the remaining party its interest in the real property at the fair market value of the selling price, rental rate or lease rate of such interest. If the parties are unable to mutually agree to the terms and conditions of such sale, rental or lease within ninety (90) days, such asset shall be sold and the net sale proceeds distributed to the parties in accordance with their proportional interests.

5.3   Financial Statements

The Management Committee shall furnish to each party within sixty (60) days of the fiscal year-end set out in Article 5.5 statements of the financial condition of the ministry activities which are carried on jointly by the parties at the end of such fiscal year. Such statements shall be signed by two (2) members of the Management Committee on behalf of the Committee and shall include an opinion on such statements from an independent auditor approved by the parties hereto. Such auditor's opinion shall confirm that it is an audit of the activities carried on jointly by the parties pursuant to this agreement.

5.4   Fiscal Policies

The Management Committee shall establish and maintain fiscal policies, accounting systems and procedures compatible with the policies, accounting systems and procedures adopted by the parties hereto.

5.5   Fiscal Year

The fiscal year used to report on the joint ministry activities of the parties shall end on December 31 of each calendar year.

ARTICLE VI: MISCELLANEOUS

6.1   Scope of Agreement

This Agreement shall govern and define the respective rights, benefits, liabilities, obligations, interests and powers of the parties with respect to the creation and operation of the joint ministry activities.

6.2   Relationship of the Parties

Each party acknowledges that its relationship in participating in the ministry activities which are carried on jointly is that of a joint participant in such activities pursuant to the terms and provisions of this Agreement, and expressly disclaims any intention to create a partnership. Nothing in this Agreement shall constitute any such party the partner, agent or representative of any other party, or create any trust of one in favor of any other party or render one party liable for the debts or obligations of any other party, except as specifically provided for in this Agreement.

6.3   Amendment

This Agreement may not be modified or amended except with the written consent of all the parties hereto.

6.4   Assignment

Except as otherwise provided to the contrary, this Agreement shall be binding upon and inure to the benefit of the parties and their respective successors and permitted assigns. No party may assign its rights hereunder except as herein expressly provided.

6.5   Further Assistance

The parties hereto agree that they will, from time to time at the reasonable request of any of them, execute and deliver such instruments, conveyances and assignments and take such further action as may be required pursuant to the terms hereof to accomplish the intent of this Agreement.

6.6   Time of the Essence
Time shall be deemed to be of the essence with respect to all time limits mentioned in this Agreement.

6.7   Entire Agreement
This Agreement constitutes the entire Agreement between the parties hereto pertaining to the subject matter hereof, and supersedes all prior and contemporaneous agreements, understandings, negotiations and discussions whether oral or written of the parties, and there are no warranties, representations or other agreements between the parties in connection with the subject matter hereof except as specifically set forth herein.

6.8   Notice
Except as otherwise herein set forth, any notice contemplated or required to be given hereunder shall be in writing and either delivered personally, sent by prepaid mail or reproduced electronically addressed as follows:

In the case of Canadian:

_____

_____

_____

In the case of U.S.:

_____

_____

_____

6.9   Severable Covenants
If any covenant or obligation set forth in this Agreement or the application of it to any party or the particular circumstances shall, to any extent, be invalid or unenforceable, the remainder of this Agreement or the application of such obligation to the parties or circumstances

other than those to which it is held invalid or unenforceable shall not be effected thereby, and each such obligation shall be separately valid and enforceable to the fullest extent permitted by law.

6.10   Headings
All headings in this Agreement are inserted for convenience and reference only and are not to be considered in the construction or interpretation of any provisions of this Agreement.

6.11   Gender
Words used herein which refer to male persons shall include female persons.

IN WITNESS WHEREOF the parties hereto have executed this Agreement and have hereunto affixed their corporate seals attested to by their duly authorized officers in that behalf this   day of   , 20__.

```
SIGNED, SEALED AND DELIVERED )
            In the presence of        ) Canadian
                                      )
                                      )
                                      ) Per:_____
                                      )
                                      ) U.S.
                                      )
                                      )
                                      ) Per:_____
                                      )
```

Appendix I—Cash Basis Financial Statements

Some organizations prepare their financial statements only on the basis of cash receipts and disbursements. Use of the cash basis may be appropriate if financial statements in conformity with generally accepted accounting principles are not required (i.e., cash basis information is sufficiently informative to satisfy the needs of the various internal and external users of the organization's financial statements).

The cash basis of accounting and acceptable modifications of the cash basis are not discussed in a formal way in accounting literature. Reporting on cash basis financial statements is governed by SAS 62/AU 623, which also discusses reporting on cash basis financial statements modified to reflect accrual basis accounting where modifications have "substantial support." Generally, modifications may be considered to have "substantial support" if (1) the method is equivalent to the accrual basis of accounting for the particular item, and (2) their application is not illogical (e.g., recognition of assets and revenues on the accrual basis while liabilities and expenses are accounted for on the cash basis would be illogical). Modifications given as examples in SAS 62/AU 623 as having "substantial support" are recording depreciation on fixed assets and accruing income taxes. EJAC believes there is also substantial support for modifying the cash basis financial statements of not-for-profit organizations to account for investments at fair market value in conformity with generally accepted accounting principles.

When cash basis financial statements are modified to reflect accrual basis accounting in areas having substantial support, appropriate disclosures required by generally accepted accounting principles should accompany the statements. However, it is generally not necessary to modify the wording of the standard report on cash basis financial statements presented as SAS 62/AU 623.08. Other appropriate GAAP disclosures relating to these areas should also be made (e.g., the basis for capitalizing or expensing fixed assets expenditures, the methods used to depreciate fixed assets, and the disclosures required by FASB Statement No. 124).

SPECIFIC ASPECTS OF CASH BASIS REPORTING

Fixed Assets and Depreciation

Many not-for-profit organizations that prepare their financial statements on the cash basis capitalize significant expenditures for fixed assets. Under FASB Statement No. 93, depreciation is mandatory for all exhaustible fixed assets of not-for-profit organizations. EJAC believes that the capitalization and depreciation of exhaustible fixed assets is preferable for all not-for-profit organizations, including those otherwise on the cash basis.

Investments

Investments are initially recorded by not-for-profit organizations at cost when purchased, or at fair value when received as donations or transferred from one class of net assets to another. The appropriate GAAP method of accounting for investments after they have been acquired is discussed in FASB Statement No. 124.

While EJAC believes that investments carried as assets should be reflected in cash basis financial statements in conformity with FASB Statement No. 124, since the cash basis does not purport to conform to GAAP, it technically cannot object if an entity wishes to continue to state its investments at cost. In any event, the basis of accounting for investments and the disclosures required by FASB Statement No. 107 (as amended by FASB Statement No. 126), including the aggregate amounts of realized and unrealized gains and losses, should be appropriately disclosed.

SOP 94-3 (reprinted at paragraph 8.29 of the *AICPA NPO Guide*) also provides guidance on accounting for investments in related for-profit entities.

Other Modifications

When reporting on an examination of modified cash basis financial statements, problems may arise in that there may not be "substantial support" for one or more of the modifications, or the modifications may be so extensive that the statements are tantamount to accrual basis statements. In the former circumstance, the auditor's report should be appropriately modified and include a middle paragraph explaining the situation. In the latter case, it would not be appropriate to report on the financial statements as prescribed by SAS 62/AU 623.05 for cash basis financial statements. Rather, the auditor should use the standard form of report (see SAS 58/AU 508), appropriately modified for the departures from generally accepted accounting principles (i.e., for the items accounted for on the cash basis).

Statement of Cash Flows

Another issue is whether a cash basis organization must present a statement of cash flows. In many cases, the information in this statement, if prepared, would largely duplicate information already in the statement of activities (cash receipts and disbursements). If this is the case, preparation of the statement of cash flows in the format of FAS 95 would seem to serve little purpose, and would not be required. If, however, an organization has numerous or significant transactions which would be reported as investing or financing cash flows in that statement (e.g., borrowing, purchase, and sale of long-term assets) and which are not reported in the statement of activities, EJAC strongly recommends presentation of the statement of cash flows.

Other Footnote Disclosures in Cash Basis Statements

SAS 62/AU 623.09 provides that OCBOA financial statements should include all informative disclosures that are appropriate for the basis of accounting used. As discussed in paragraph 1-20 of this Guide, AICPA Auditing Interpretation No. 14 of Section 623, *Evaluating the Adequacy of Disclosure in Financial Statements Prepared on the Cash, Modified Cash, or Income Tax Basis of Accounting,* (AU section 623.88), states as follows:

> .90 If cash, modified cash, or income tax basis financial statements contain elements, accounts, or items for which GAAP would require disclosure, the statements should either provide the relevant disclosure that would be required for those items in a GAAP presentation or provide information that communicates the substance of that disclosure. That may result in substituting qualitative information for some of the quantitative information required for GAAP presentations....

.91   If GAAP sets forth requirements that apply to the presentation of financial statements, then cash, modified cash,
and income tax basis statements should either comply with
those requirements or provide information that communicates
the substance of those requirements. The substance of GAAP
presentation requirements may be communicated using qualitative information and without modifying the financial statement format. For example:

a.   Information about the effects of accounting changes,
     discontinued operations, and extraordinary items
     could be disclosed in a note to the financial state-
     ments without following the GAAP presentation
     requirements in the statement of results of operations,
     using those terms, or disclosing net-of-tax effects.

b.   Instead of showing expenses by their functional clas-
     sifications, the income tax basis statement of activi-
     ties of a trade organization could present expenses
     according to their natural classifications, and a note
     to the statement could use estimated percentages to
     communicate information about expenses incurred
     by the major program and supporting services. A vol-
     untary health and welfare organization could take
     such an approach instead of presenting the matrix of
     natural and functional expense classifications that
     would be required for a GAAP presentation, or, if
     information has been gathered for the Form 990
     matrix required for such organizations, it could be
     presented either in the form of a separate statement
     or in a note to the financial statements.

c.   Instead of showing the amounts of, and changes in,
     the unrestricted, temporarily and permanently
     restricted classes of net assets, which would be
     required for a GAAP presentation, the income tax
     basis statement of position of a voluntary health and
     welfare organization could report total net assets or
     fund balances; the related statement of activities
     could report changes in those totals; and a note to the
     financial statements could provide information—using

estimated or actual amounts or percentages—about the restrictions on those amounts and on any deferred restricted amounts, describe the major restrictions, and provide information about significant changes in restricted amounts.

.93   If GAAP would require disclosure of other matters, the auditor should consider the need for that same disclosure or similar disclosure that communicates the substance of those requirements...

EJAC believes there are certain footnote and other disclosures which should be made, so that the statements are not misleading. These include:

- significant accounting policies and any changes therein (APB 22 and 20), including the policy regarding collections discussed in FASB Statement No. 116

- language relating to the use of estimates in preparation of the statements (per SOP 94-6), if the statements include any modifications such as depreciation or market value of investments which may involve estimates

- information regarding significant related parties (FASB Statement No. 57, SOP 94-3) (whether or not consolidated)

- significant commitments and contingencies (FASB Statement No. 5); EJAC also believes that application of this statement requires disclosure of material unrecorded liabilities and obligations, such as those described in FASB Statement Nos. 13, 43, 47, 87, 106, and 112, and unconditional promises to make contributions to others (per FASB Statement No. 116)

- foreign currency gain/loss (FASB Statement No. 52) (This could be omitted.)

- interest paid, if significant (FASB Statement No. 95) (This could be omitted.)

- value, concentration of risk, and possible impairment of financial instruments and other assets (FASB Statement Nos. 105, 107, 119, 121, and 124)

- FASB Statement No. 117 disclosures and presentation:

  - classes of net assets (revenue, net assets, and change in net assets by class)

  - totals of: assets, liabilities, net assets, and change in net assets

  - all expenses and unrestricted investment return reported in the unrestricted class

- disclosures relating to joint costs of multipurpose activities (SOP 98-2)

EJAC also believes that the limitations on the use of extraordinary items and prior period adjustments contained in APB 9 and 30 and FASB Statement No. 16 should be observed.

Appendix J—Flowchart for Distinguishing Contributions from Agency Transactions

The following information and flowchart from FASB No. 136 are helpful for distinguishing the nature of various types of resource inflows for reporting purposes. Refer to chapter 4 for more specific information regarding contributions, agency, and exchange transactions.

ILLUSTRATIVE GUIDANCE

Introduction

This appendix provides a diagram to assist entities in the application of this Statement and examples that illustrate the application of the standards in specific situations. The diagram is a visual supplement to the written standards section. It should not be interpreted to alter any requirements of this Statement, nor should it be considered a substitute for those requirements. The relevant paragraphs of the standards section of this Statement and of FASB Statement No. 116, *Accounting for Contributions Received and Contributions Made,* are identified in the parenthetical notes. The examples do not address all possible situations or applications of this Statement.

Diagram

The diagram depicts the process for determining the appropriate accounting for a transfer of assets from a donor to a recipient organization that accepts the assets and agrees to use those assets on behalf of a beneficiary specified by the donor, or transfer those assets, the return on investment of those assets, or both to a beneficiary specified by the donor. (For additional information about how a beneficiary is specified, refer to FASB No. 136, paragraphs 68 and 69.) The diagram also depicts the process for determining the appropriate accounting for a transfer from a resource provider that takes place in a similar manner but is not a contribution because the transfer is revocable, repayable, or reciprocal.

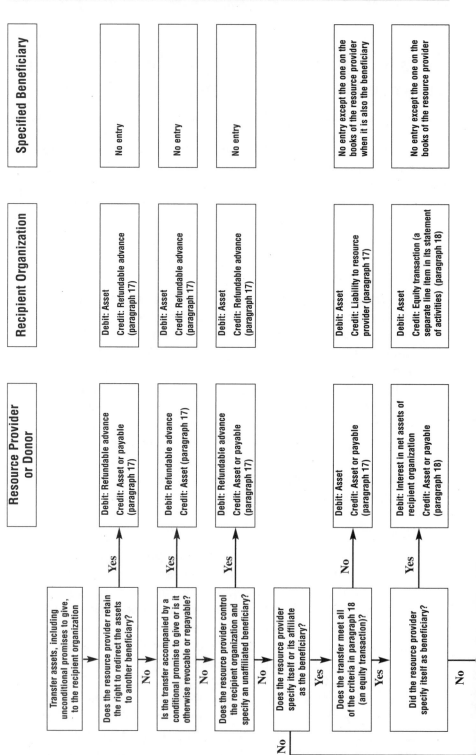

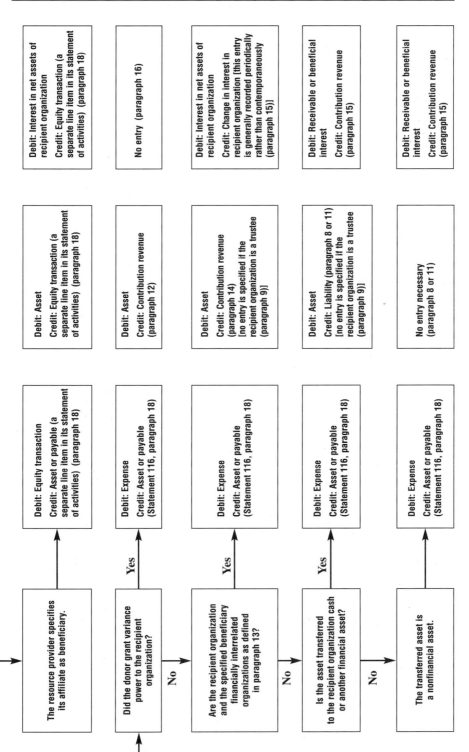

Appendix K—Flowchart for Accounting for Split-Interest Gifts

The following flowchart is helpful for distinguishing and accounting for various types of split-interest gifts. Refer to chapter 7 for more specific information regarding split-interest gifts.

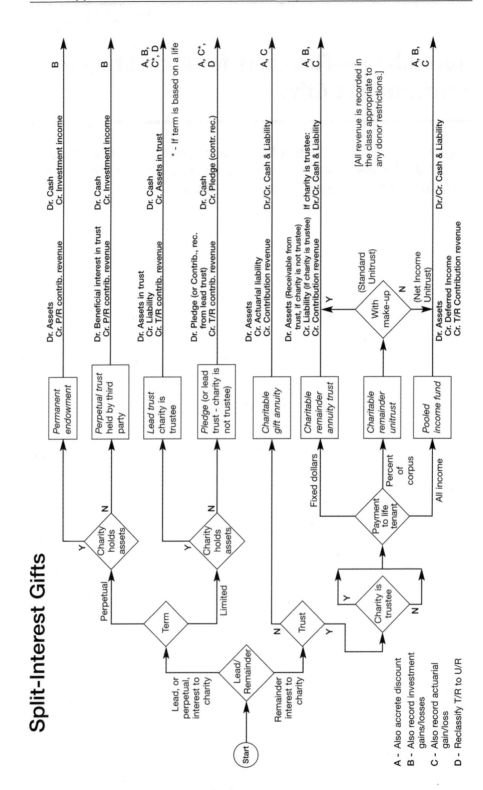

Split-Interest Gifts

A - Also accrete discount
B - Also record investment gains/losses
C - Also record actuarial gain/loss
D - Reclassify T/R to U/R

Significant Changes in the 2001 Edition

The following is a brief summary of the major changes in this Guide from the 1997 edition:

Chapter	Description of Changes	Reference
Chapter 1 Accounting for Christian Ministries	1. Clarifies the auditor's responsibility pertaining to communications, including information other than general purpose audited financial statements	1-3
	2. Expands discussion of materiality	1-12
	3. Discusses AICPA Auditing Interpretation No. 14 of Section AU 623 on OCBOA disclosures	1-20
Chapter 2 Financial Statements and Reporting	1. Includes examples of factors to consider in determining whether donor-imposed restrictions exist	2-5
	2. Clarifies that the Guide includes EJAC's recommendation on a display issue that is not explicitly addressed by GAAP for restrictions on specific assets	2-6
	3. Clarifies that GAAP requires that totals be reported for assets, liabilities, and net assets	2-7
	4. Expands discussion of GAAP requirements pertaining to functional reporting	2-11
	5. EJAC recommends that organizations use the direct method of reporting net cash flows from operating activities	2-15

Chapter	Description of Changes	Reference
Chapter 3 Net Assets	1. Clarifies example of permanently restricted annuity gift	3-8
	2. Clarifies FASB Statement No. 117 disclosure requirements pertaining to temporarily restricted net assets	3-10
	3. Clarifies FASB Statement No. 116 provisions pertaining to accounting polices for recognizing temporary restrictions that are satisfied on or before the end of the fiscal year in which the gifts are received	3-11
	4. Clarifies that the Guide includes EJAC's recommendation on a display issue that is not explicitly addressed by GAAP for reporting unrestricted net assets	3-14
	5. Deletes EJAC's recommendation on an issue that is explicitly addressed by GAAP for contribution refunds	3-24
Chapter 4 Revenue	1. Clarifies that the guidance pertaining to trusts refers to split-interest trusts	4-13
	2. Clarifies that the Guide includes EJAC's recommendation on a display issue that is not explicitly addressed by GAAP for disclosures about the components of changes in the value of split-interest agreements	4-13
	3. Clarifies GAAP pertaining to accounting for costs of soliciting and administering split-interest agreements	4-14
	4. Expands discussion of transactions and events that result in reclassifications from temporarily restricted net assets to unrestricted net assets	4-23

Chapter	Description of Changes	Reference
Chapter 4 **Revenue** *(continued)*	5. Clarifies that the Guide includes EJAC's recommendation on a display issue that is not explicitly addressed by GAAP for custodial funds for unremitted personal amounts held on behalf of members	4-28
	6. Clarifies that the guidance on special events pertains to intangible, as well as tangible, benefits	4-29
	7. Clarifies GAAP for reporting special events	4-30
	8. Discusses FASB Statement No. 136, *Transfers of Assets to a Not-for-Profit Organization or Charitable Trust That Raises or Holds Contributions for Others*	4-31
	9. Discusses FASB Statement No. 136	4-32
	10. Discusses FASB Statement No. 136	4-33
	11. Discusses FASB Statement No. 136	4-34
	12. Discusses FASB Statement No. 136	4-35
	13. Discusses FASB Statement No. 136	4-36
	14. Notes that accounting for faith promises may require subjective judgments	4-38
	15. Discusses intentions to give	4-39
	16. Discusses conditional promises	4-40
	17. Discusses unconditional promises	4-41
	18. Discusses EJAC's recommendations on characteristics that determine intentions to give, conditional promises, and unconditional promises	4-42

Chapter	Description of Changes	Reference
Chapter 4 **Revenue** *(continued)*	19. New examples relating to guidance to help determining whether a communication is an expression of an intention to give, a conditional promise, or an unconditional promise	4-44
	20. Discusses determining the amount to be reported for unconditional promises and the considerations pertaining to open-ended promises	4-45
	21. Expands discussion of measuring fair value for promises to give	4-45
	22. Expands discussion of oral promises	4-47
	23. Clarifies GAAP for reporting promises to give, particularly that such promises need not be legally enforceable to be recognized as contributions	4-48
	24. Clarifies the discussion of affiliated and related entities as it pertains to discounting receivables and payables	4-53
	25. Clarifies GAAP for recognizing contributed services	4-58
	26. Clarifies GAAP for recognizing contributed services	4-59
	27. Clarifies GAAP for recognizing contributed services	4-60
	28. Clarifies GAAP for recognizing contributed services in circumstances in which more than one organization is involved	4-61
	29. Clarifies GAAP for recognizing contributed services	4-62
	30. Discusses EJAC's recommendations on issues that are not explicitly addressed by GAAP for disclosing the methods used to measure recognized contributed services	4-65

Chapter	Description of Changes	Reference
Chapter 4 **Revenue** *(continued)*	31. Discusses EJAC's recommendations on issues that are not explicitly addressed by GAAP for disclosing contributed services that do not meet the FASB Statement No. 116 recognition criteria	4-65
	32. Clarifies GAAP for contributed facilities	4-67
	33. Clarifies GAAP for gifts-in-kind which are intended to be sold at auctions in fund-raising events by transferring them to another resource provider	4-68
	34. Discusses nonfinancial assets received, particularly as "pass-through relief items"	4-71
	35. Clarifies GAAP for contributions of inventory	4-72
	36. Deletes the discussion from the paragraph previously numbered as 4-62, which stated that contributions of facilities more lavish than would otherwise be rented by the organization should be reported at the value that the organization would otherwise pay for facilities fulfilling that same purpose, because GAAP does not explicitly address this issue	4-74
	37. Clarifies GAAP for contributed facilities through long-term leases	4-74
	38. Clarifies GAAP for accounting for provision by an individual or organization of free use of living or working facilities to a missionary in the field or while on home leave	4-75
	39. Clarifies GAAP for expenses which will benefit the reporting organization and that are paid for by another organization	4-76
	40. Discusses below-market rate loans	4-77

Chapter	Description of Changes	Reference
Chapter 5 Expenses	1. Clarifies GAAP for reporting and disclosing the components of program expense	5-12
	2. Clarifies that activities that are undertaken with the hope of receiving contributions are fund-raising activities, even if the activities do not explicitly ask for contributions	5-16
	3. Clarifies that fund-raising includes encouraging potential donors to contribute their services and time, so costs related to recruiting volunteers (unpaid workers) should be included in fund-raising expenses, regardless of whether the services contributed by those volunteers meet the recognition criteria for contributed services	5-19
	4. Clarifies that a supply of brochures or production costs of fund-raising broadcasts not yet aired should be expensed, even though the brochures have not yet been distributed or the broadcast has not aired	5-21
	5. Clarifies GAAP for reporting membership development activities	5-22
	6. Expands discussion on cost allocations	5-24
	7. Clarifies GAAP for disclosing cost allocations	5-26
	8. Discusses AICPA SOP 98-2, *Accounting for Costs of Activities of Not-for-Profit Organizations and State and Local Governmental Entities That Include Fund Raising*	5-28
	9. Discusses AICPA SOP 98-2	5-29
	10. Clarifies that grants may be either contributions or exchange transactions	5-36

Chapter	Description of Changes	Reference
	11. Clarifies GAAP for reporting promises to give, particularly that such promises do not need to be legally enforceable to be recognized as contributions	5-37
	12. Clarifies the discussion of parent and subsidiary relationships as it pertains to discounting receivable and payables	5-38
	13. Discusses AICPA SOP 98-5, *Reporting on the Costs of Start-Up Activities*	5-48
	14. Discusses AICPA SOP 98-5	5-49
	15. Discusses AICPA SOP 98-5	5-50
	16. Discusses AICPA SOP 98-1, *Accounting for the Costs of Computer Software Developed or Obtained for Internal Use*	5-51
Chapter 6 Accounting for Investments and Property and Equipment	1. Clarifies the disclosure requirements of FASB Statement No. 107, *Disclosures about Fair Value of Financial Instruments*	6-5
	2. Clarifies GAAP for reporting investments other than those with readily determinable fair values and debt securities	6-5
	3. Clarifies that the Guide includes EJAC's recommendation on an issue that is not explicitly addressed by GAAP for disclosures about fair values of investments carried at other than fair value	6-6
	4. Clarifies that property, plant and equipment should be recorded at cost, net of accumulated depreciation, except in the absence of historical cost records and when initially adopting GAAP Standards, in which case other bases may be used to determine "estimated historical cost."	6-14

Chapter	Description of Changes	Reference
	5. Clarifies GAAP for reporting foreign property, plant and equipment to which the organization has title	6-15
Chapter 7 **Annuities,** **Trusts, and** **Similar Gifts**	1. Clarifies journal entries and GAAP for reporting split-interest agreements	7-1
	2. Refers to FASB Concepts Statement No. 7, *Using Cash Flow Information and Present Value in Accounting Measurements,* for a detailed discussion of present value and its use in accounting measurements	7-10
	3. Clarifies journal entries and GAAP for reporting split-interest agreements	7-23
	4. Clarifies GAAP for legally mandated reserves pertaining to split-interest agreements	7-24
	5. Includes EJAC's recommendation on an issue that is not explicitly addressed by GAAP for circumstances in which legally required or voluntary reserves for split-interest arrangements exist and the balance sheet is disaggregated	7-24
Chapter 8 **Related** **Organizations**	1. Clarifies GAAP disclosures pertaining to related parties	8-1
	2. Includes EJAC's recommended disclosures pertaining to related parties	8-1
	3. Clarifies the provisions of AICPA SOP 94-3, *Reporting of Related Entities by Not-for-Profit Organizations*	8-4
	4. Clarifies the provisions of AICPA SOP 94-3	8-5
	5. Clarifies the provisions of AICPA SOP 94-3	8-6
	6. Clarifies the provisions of AICPA SOP 94-3	8-7

Chapter	Description of Changes	Reference
Chapter 8 Related Organizations *(continued)*	7. Clarifies the provisions of AICPA SOP 94-3	8-8
	8. Clarifies GAAP pertaining to subsidiary-only and parent-only financial statements	8-9
	9. Clarifies the provisions of AICPA SOP 94-3 pertaining to affiliated ministries	8-11
	10. Clarifies the provisions of AICPA SOP 94-3 pertaining to developing organizations	8-13
	11. Clarifies the provisions of AICPA SOP 94-3 and FASB Statement No. 57, *Related Party Disclosures* pertaining to revenue producing operations	8-14
	12. Clarifies the provisions of SOP 94-3 pertaining to organizations under common control	8-15
	13. Clarifies the provisions of the *AICPA NPO Guide* pertaining to accounting for combinations	8-22
	14. Discusses accounting for separations (reverse mergers) and related GAAP considerations including reporting accounting changes.	8-23
Chapter 9 Canadian Principles and Practices	This new chapter summarizes Canadian tax and accounting principles and compares and contrasts them with U.S. standards.	
Appendix A	1. Includes a definition of *exchange transaction*	
Appendix B	1. Deleted the Exhibit previously numbered 3	
Appendix C	1. Exhibit 1, Note 1— Clarifies that temporary restrictions include time restrictions	

Chapter	Description of Changes
Appendix C *(continued)*	2. Exhibit 1, Note 2—Adds a disclosure pertaining to the accounting policy for purpose restrictions fulfilled in the same period in which the contribution is received
	3. Exhibit 1, Note 2—Revised to reflect AICPA SOP 98-2
	4. Exhibit 2A, Note 3— Clarifies the disclosure of contributions receivable collected
	5. Exhibit 2A, Note 5— Clarifies the reason for not recognizing contributed services
	6. Exhibit 3, Statement of Financial Position—Includes contributions receivable
	7. Exhibit 3, Statement of Cash Flows—Includes change in contributions receivable
	8. Exhibit 3, Notes to Financial Statements, Note 2— Clarifies that temporary restrictions include time restrictions
	9. Exhibit 3, Notes to Financial Statements, Note 2— Clarifies disclosure of the recognition policy for contributions receivable
	10. Exhibit 3, Notes to Financial Statements, Note 2— Deletes the disclosure saying that faith promises are not recognized
	11. Exhibit 3, Notes to Financial Statements, Note 2— Adds disclosure pertaining to contributed services
	12. Exhibit 3, Notes to Financial Statements, Note 2—Adds disclosure pertaining to AICPA SOP 98-2
	13. Exhibit 4, Notes to Financial Statements, Note 2— Clarifies disclosure of the recognition policy for contributions receivable
	14. Exhibit 5, Statement of Financial Position—Includes contributions receivable

Chapter	Description of Changes
Appendix C *(continued)*	15. Exhibit 5, Statement of Cash Flows—Includes contributions receivable
	16. Exhibit 5, Notes to Financial Statements, Note 2—Adds disclosure pertaining to contributed services
	17. Exhibit 5, Notes to Financial Statements, Note 3—Adds disclosure of special building project
	18. Exhibit 6, Notes to Financial Statements, Note 2—Clarifies disclosure of the recognition policy for contributions receivable
	19. Exhibit 6, Notes to Financial Statements, Note 2—Adds disclosure pertaining to AICPA SOP 98-2
	20. Exhibit 6, Notes to Financial Statements, Note 3—Adds disclosure pertaining to summarized comparative information
Appendix F	1. Table of Typical Functional Allocations— Clarifies that all allocations are subject to the constraints of AICPA SOP 98-2
	2. Table of Typical Functional Allocations—Includes EJAC's recommendation on an issue that is not explicitly addressed by GAAP for reporting the costs of recruiting employees
Appendix I	1. Discusses AICPA Auditing Interpretation No. 14 of Section AU 623 on OCBOA disclosures
Appendix J	1. Replaces Chart 1 with flowchart from FASB Statement No. 136

Index

A

Accounting changes, *44-46*

Accounting Changes (APB–20), *197*

Accounting for Certain Investments Held by Not-for-Profit Organizations (FAS-124), *89-90, 408, 412*

Accounting for charitable gift annuities, *176-77*

Accounting for Contingencies (FAS-5), *194, 411*

Accounting for Contributions Received and Contributions Made (FAS-116), *51-52, 53, 54, 56, 60, 68, 75, 76, 77, 78, 79-80, 81-82, 83, 134, 159, 168, 169, 193, 253, 257, 261, 411, 413-15*

Accounting for costs involving fund-raising, *119*

Accounting for joint activities, *119*

Accounting for Costs of Activities of Not-for-Profit Organizations and State and Local Governmental Entities That Include Fund-Raising (SOP 98-2), *62, 114, 116, 119-29, 412*

Accounting for the Costs of Computer Software Developed or Obtained for Internal Use (SOP 98-1), *141-43*

Accounting for Derivative Instruments and Hedging Activities (FAS-133), *148, 149*

Accounting for lead interests, *166-69*

Accounting for Leases (FAS-13), *86-87, 411*

Accounting for Nonmonetary Transactions (APB–29), *84*

Accounting for perpetual trusts held by a third party, *170-71*

Accounting for pooled income funds and net income unitrusts, *178-79*

Accounting for remainder interests, *174-75*

Accounting for split-interest gifts, *164-79*

Accounting for Web Site Development Costs (EITF 00-2), *143*

Accounting practices, Canadian, *203-18*

Accounting principles, Contributions, *51*

Accounting Principles and Reporting Practices for Certain Nonprofit Organizations (SOP 78-10), *191*

Accounting Principles Board (APB) Opinions,
    No. 9, *44*
    No. 16, *196-97*
    No. 17, *197*
    No. 20, *44, 197-98*
    No. 21, *78, 168*
    No. 29, *84*
    No. 30, *44*

Accrual basis of accounting, *6-8*
    Definition, *223*
    Examples, *268-95, 296-302, 314-19, 320-30*
    In general, *6-8*
    When cash basis meets GAAP requirements, *7*

Activities statement,
    Examples,
        Detailed example, *333-35*

Activities statement,
    Examples, *(continued)*
      Multicolumn, *274-76, 321-22,*
      333-35, 337-38, 347, 356-57
      Single column, *297*
    Functional classification, *19-20*
    In general, *18-20*
    Use of multiple columns, *19*
Administered revenue, Canada,
    212-13
Advertising costs, *138-39*
AERDO, *84*
Affiliated organization support,
    133-37
Agency funds, *180*
Agency transactions and contribu-
    tions distinguished, *413-15*
Agent, definition of, *223*
AICPA Audit Interpretation No. 14,
    10-11
AICPA, definition of, *223*
AICPA Audit and Accounting Guide,
    Not-for-Profit Organizations (NPO
    Guide 2000), *17-18, 20, 23, 83,*
    84, 92, 107-8, 111-12, 114, 118,
    139, 149, 150-52, 153, 155-56,
    157-58, 165
AICPA Statement on Auditing
    Standards No. 78, Consideration
    of Internal Control in a Financial
    Statement Audit, *25-26*
Allocation of expenses, *109-10,*
    117-32, also see Statement of
    functional expenses
    Allocation methods, *128*
    Audience criterion, *126-27*
    Content criterion, *127-28*
    Disclosures, *129-31*
    Functional, *383-84*
    Fund-raising costs, *119-31*
    Furloughs, *131-32*
    In general, *117-19*

    Incidental activities, *128-29*
    Joint activities, *119*
    Notes to financial statements,
    285
    Program functions, *120-21*
    Purpose criterion, *119-26*
    Sabbaticals, *131-32*
    Study leaves, *131-32*
American Institute of Certified
    Public Accountants (AICPA) publi-
    cations,
    AICPA Audit and Accounting
      Guide, Not-for-Profit Organiza-
      tions (NPO Guide 2000), *6, 8,*
      17-18, 20, 23, 83, 84, 92, 107-
      8, 111-12, 114, 118, 138, 150-
      52, 153, 155-56, 157-58, 165
    AICPA Statement on Auditing
      Standards No. 78, *25-26*
    Auditing Interpretation No. 14 of
      Section 623, Evaluating the
      Adequacy of Disclosure in
      Financial Statements Prepared
      on the Cash, Modified Cash,
      or Income Tax Basis of
      Accounting, *10-11*
    EITF Issue 00-2, *143*
    SOP 78-10, *191*
    SOP 93-7, *138*
    SOP 94-3, *78, 186-88, 135,*
      189-90, 191, 195, 391-93,
      408, 411
    SOP 94-6, *411*
    SOP 98-1, *141-43*
    SOP 98-2, *62, 114, 116,*
      119-29, 412
    SOP 98-5, *141*
    Technical Practice Aid No. 1,
      6140.05, *89*
Annuity gift, definition of, *223,* see
    Charitable gift annuities

Annuity trust, definition of, *223*
Audience criterion, *126-27*
Auxiliary activity, definition of, *224*

B

Balance sheet, see Statement of
  financial position
Bargain sale, definition of, *224*
Below-market rate loans, *89*
Bequests, *78-79*
Bible schools, categories of program
  services, *385*
Board designated funds, see
  Designated net assets
Borrowing from restricted funds,
  27-28
Broadcasters, sample financial
  statements, *320-30*
Budgets, *376-77*

C

Calls to prayer, *131*
Camps,
  Categories of program services,
    385
  Sample financial statements,
    331-45
Canadian accounting principles and
  practices,
  Accounting for revenue, *208-10*
  Accounting practices, *203-4*
  Administered revenue, *212-13*
  Charitable gifts, *202-3, 209-10*
  Consolidation of special trusts,
    206-8
  Contingent beneficial interest in
    special trust, *205-6*
  Contributions, types of, *209-10*
  Endowment funds, *210-12*

Fund accounting, *214-16*
Gifts-in-kind, *217*
Inter-fund transfers, *216-17*
Life insurance, *218*
Notional revenues, *217-18*
Pledges, *217*
Registered charities, *201-2*
Sources of revenue of a regis-
  tered charity, *208-9*
Special trust funds, *204-5*
Unrestricted revenue, *212*
Canadian Institute of Chartered
  Accountants, definition of, *224*
Capitalization of property and
  equipment, *156*
Cash basis financial statements,
  Examples, *309-12, 314-19*
  Footnote disclosures, *409-12*
  In general, *9-12, 407-12*
Cash basis, when it meets GAAP
  requirements, *7*
Cash disbursements, control over,
  378-79
Cash flows, see Statement of cash
  flows
Cash management, *27-28*
Cash receipts, control over, *377-78*
Cash surrender value, *181*
Charitable business, *99*
Charitable gift annuities, *163-64,
  176, 284, 288-89*
  Accounting for, *176-77*
Charitable gifts, Canada, *202-3,
  209-10*
Charitable gifts, tax rules, *93-94*
  Quid pro quo, *61-62, 93*
Charitable lead trusts, definition of,
  224
Charitable remainder,
  Annuity trusts, *163-64, 171-76*
  Unitrusts, *173, 177-79*

Churches,
  Categories of program services,
    385-86
  Sample financial statements,
    346-54
CICA, definition of, 224
Classes, definition of, 224
Classes of net assets, 33-37
Classification of expenses
  Functional, 109-32
  Natural, 21, 108, 132-33
Classification of property, equip-
  ment and depreciation, 159
Community development ministry,
  Categories of program services,
    386
Comparative financial statements,
  22-24
Conditional promise to give, 74, 224
Conference centers,
  Sample of financial statements,
    331-45
Consolidated financial statements,
  definition of, 224
Consolidation of All Majority-owned
  Subsidiaries (FAS-94), 195
Consolidation of financial data,
  190-92, 195-96
Consolidation of special trusts,
  Canada, 206-8
Content criterion, 127-28
Contingencies, accounting for, 194
Contingent beneficial interest in a
  special trust, Canada, 205-6
Contributions,
  Accounting principles, 51
  Agency transactions distin-
    guished, 413-15
  Below-market rate loans, 89
  Change in temporarily restricted
    net assets, 58-60

Contributed services,
  In general, 79-82
  Valuing, 82-83
Contributions made, 53
Contributions received, 53
Controls,
  Budgets, 376-77
  Cash, 377-79
  Cash disbursements, 378-79
  Contributions, 49-50
  Investments, 379-81
  Policies and procedures, 376
Corpus, definition of, 224
Deferred gifts, 78, 163-64, 224
Definition of, 224
Direct and other designated gifts,
  Honoraria and expense reim-
    bursement, 60
  Personal gifts, 61
  Special fund-raising events,
    61-63
Discounting of pledges, 77-78
Donor restricted support, 54-55
Endowments, see Endowments
Gifts-in-kind, 83-88
Legacies and bequests, 78-79
"Pass-through" gifts and gifts-
  in-kind, 63-68
Permanently restricted support,
  55-56
Promises to give,
  Conditional promises, 69-70
  Intentions to give, 69
  Pledges, 68-69
  Unconditional promises,
    70-71
Purchases/sales transactions
  distinguished, 51-52
Return of, 46, 58
Services, 81-83

Contributions, *(continued)*
    Special fund-raising events, *61-63*
    Tax rules, *93, 94-96*
    Temporarily restricted support, *56-58*
    Unrestricted support, *54*
    Valuing contributed services, *82-83*
Costs related to sales of goods and services, *137-38*
Currency translation, *46*
Custodian funds, *61, 180, 224*
Cy pres, *171*

D
Debt-financed income,
    Exceptions, *101*
Deferred gifts,
    Definition, *224*
    Endowments, *79*
    In general, *78, 163-64*
    Legacies and trusts, *79*
    Trusts, *78*
Deferred revenue, definition of, *225*
Depreciation, *154-55, 157-58*
Deputized fund-raising, see Support-raising
Derivative instruments, *148, 149*
Designated net assets, *225*
Designated gifts,
    Expense reimbursed, *60, 91*
    Staff honoraria, *60*
Developing organizations, *193*
Disclosure of Information about Financial Instruments With Off-Balance-Sheet Risk and Financial Instruments with Concentrations of Credit Risk (FAS-105), *77, 412*

Disclosures About Fair Value of Financial Instruments (FAS-107), *149, 408, 411, 412*
Disclosures, joint costs, *129-31*
Disclosure of property and equipment, *154-55*
Discounting of pledges, *77-78*
Donated and contributed services,
    Below-market rate loans, *88-89*
    Canada, *217*
    Determining who is the recipient, *253-55*
    Facilities, *83-88*
    In general, *79-81*
    Inventory, *86*
    Long-term lease of property, *86-87*
    Materials, *83-88*
    Need to purchase services, *261-65*
    Requiring specialized skills, *257-59*
    Thrift shops, *86*
    Valuing services, *82-83*
Donor restricted support, *54-55, 163-82, 237-40*
Donor restricted endowment funds, *151*
Dues, see Membership dues

E
Earned Income,
    Gains and losses on investments, *89-91*
    Income earned on investments, *89*
    Revenue from sales of goods and services, *91-92*
Economic interest, *189-90*

Education/training ministry (other than Bible Schools and Seminaries), Categories of program services, *385*

Elements of Financial Statements (FASB Concepts Statement No. 6), *5-6, 7-8, 20, 34, 35, 37-38, 42-43, 58-59, 143, 157, 264*

Employers' Accounting for Pensions (FAS-87), *139, 140, 141, 411*

Employers' Accounting for Post-employment Benefits (FAS-112), *140, 141, 411*

Employers' Accounting for Post-retirement Benefits Other Than Pensions (FAS-106), *140, 141, 411*

Employers' Disclosures about Pensions and Other Postretirement Benefits (FAS-132), *140*

Encumbrances, *225*

Endowments,
    Accounting for, *151*
    Canada, *210-12*
    Definition of, *225*
    Donor restricted, *151*
    In general, *79*
    Permanent, *165-66, 171*
    Pure, definition of, *229*
    Quasi, definition of, *229*
    Term, *59*

Equity, see Net assets

Estates, life, *181-82*

Evangelism, categories of program services, *385*

Events, fund-raising, *61-63*

Exchange transactions, *52, 226*

Expendable net assets, *226*

Expenses,
    Advertising costs, *138-39*
    Costs related to goods and services, *137-38*
    Functional classification, *108, 109-10*
    Grants, *133-37*
    Investment, *139*
    Losses, *143-44*
    Natural classifications, *108*
    Post-employment, *139-41*
    Program Services, *110-11*
    Supporting activities, *111-16*

Expense allocations, see Allocation of expenses

Expense reimbursements, *60, 91*

Extraordinary items, *44-45, 226*

F

Facilities, donated, *83-88*

Faith promises, *69, 71-73, 226*

FASB, *226* , also see Financial Accounting Standards Board Technical Bulletins

Fidelity insurance, *382*

Field ministry, definition of, *226*

Financial Accounting Standards Board (FASB) Technical Bulletins,
    Business Combinations and Intangible Assets, *196*
    Consolidated Financial Statements: Purpose and Policy—Revision of Exposure, Draft issued October 16, 1995, *192*
    Definition of, *226*
    FAS 5, *194, 411*
    FAS 7, *77, 166*
    FAS 13, *87, 411*
    FAS 43, *411*
    FAS 47, *411*
    FAS 52, *46, 156, 411*
    FAS 57, *188, 191, 192, 196, 411*
    FAS 87, *140, 141, 411*

FAS 93, *154-55, 157, 408*
FAS 94, *187, 192, 195*
FAS 95, *21-22, 411*
FAS 105, *77, 412*
FAS 106, *140, 141, 411*
FAS 107, *149, 408, 412, 411*
FAS 112, *140, 141, 411*
FAS 116, *51-52, 53, 54, 56, 60, 68, 75, 76, 77, 78, 79-80, 81, 83, 134, 159, 168, 169, 193, 253, 257, 261, 411, 413-15*
FAS 117, *4, 6, 15, 16, 18-19, 21, 22, 33, 35-37, 39, 41-42, 51, 55, 62, 89, 90, 107, 108, 109, 110, 111, 116, 132-33, 151, 175, 193, 197, 412*
FAS 119, *412*
FAS 121, *142-43, 158, 412*
FAS 124, *89-90, 151-52, 407, 408, 411, 412*
FAS 132, *140*
FAS 133, *148, 149*
FAS 136, *61, 63-68, 85-86, 179, 413*
FASB Concepts Statement No. 6, *5-6, 7-8, 20, 34, 35, 37-38, 42-43, 58-59, 143, 157, 264*
Financial management, *24-29*
   Cash management, *27-28*
   Internal control, *25-26*
   Ratios, *28-29*
Financial statements,
   Cash basis,
      In general, *9-12, 407-12*
      Examples, *309-12, 314-19*
      When it meets GAAP requirements, *7*
   Comparative, *22-24*
   Consolidated, *195-96, 224*
   Notes to financial statements, *22, 76-77*

Purpose of, *3-4*
Required, *15-22*
Sample of camp/conference, *331-45*
Sample of cash basis, *407-12*
Sample of church, *346-54*
Sample of large ministry, *268-94*
Sample of religious broadcaster, *324-30*
Sample of rescue mission, *355-65*
Sample of small ministry, *296-319*
Sample of school, *365-70*
Statement of activities, *18-20*
Statement of cash flows, *21-22*
Statement of financial position, *15-18*
Statement of functional expenses, in general, *20-21*
Financial Statements of Not-for-Profit Organizations (FAS-117), *4, 6, 15, 16, 18-19, 21, 22, 33, 35-37, 39, 41-42, 51, 55, 62, 89, 90, 107, 108, 109, 110, 111, 116, 132-33, 151, 175, 193, 197, 412*
Footnote disclosures,
   Cash basis financial statements, *409-12*
For-profit entities, *195*
Foreign Currency Translation (FAS-52), *46*
Foreign operations, *285, 382*
Form 990, *233*
Form 990-T, *102*
Form 1041, *103*
Functional allocations, *383-84*
Functional classification of expenses, also see Statement of functional expenses,
   Definition of, *226*

Functional classification of
expenses, *(continued)*
Fund-raising activities, *114-16*
In general, *109-10*
Investments, *139*
Losses, *144*
Management and general
activities, *112-14*
Membership development
activities, *116*
Program services, *110-11*
Statement of functional
expenses,
Examples, *293-94, 302, 308,
313, 319, 348, 358*
In general, *20-21*
Supporting activities, *111-16*
Typical functional allocations,
387-89
Fund, definition of, *226*
Fund accounting,
Canada, *214-16*
In general, *8-9*
Fund balance, definition of, *226*
Fund group, definition of, *226*
Fund-raising,
Activities, *114-16, 227*
Allocation of costs, *117-32*
Special events, *61-63*
Funds,
Agency, *180*
Custodian, *180*
Held in trust by others, *227*
Pooled income, *171-73, 177-79,
229*
Furlough expenses, definition of, *227*
Furloughs, *131-32*

G
GAAP, *3, 227*

Gains and losses on investments,
Recording, *89-90*
Unrestricted, *90*
Generally Accepted Accounting
Practice (GAAP), *3, 227*
Gift annuity, see Charitable gift
annuities
Gifts,
Deferred, *78, 163-82*
"Pass-through," *63-68*
Personal, *61*
Split-interest, *164-69*
Gifts-in-kind,
Canada, *217*
Donated facilities, *83-88*
In general, *79-81*
Inventory, *86*
Long-term lease of property,
86-87
Materials, *83-88*
Thrift shops, *86*
Valuing services, *81-83*
Goods or services, sales of, *137-38*
Grants,
Governmental, *52*
Restricted, *223-36*
To other organizations, *133-37*

H
Hedging activities, *148, 149*
Honoraria, staff, *60*

I
Incidental activities, *128-29*
Income,
Charitable business, *99*
Debt-financed, *100-102*
Passive, *99-100*

Pooled income, *171-73, 177-79, 229*

Unrelated business, *97-98*

Insurance,

Canada, *218*

Fidelity, *382*

Life, *181*

Intangible Assets (APB–17), *197*

Intention to give, *74-75*

Inter-fund transfers, Canada, *216-17*

Interest on Receivables and Payables (APB–21), *78, 168*

Internal controls,

In general, *25-27*

Influencing factors, *375-76*

Components of, *376-81*

Internal use of software, *141-43*

International currency transactions, *46*

Investments,

Accounting for, *147-53*

Carrying value, *148-49*

Control over, *379-81*

Earned income, *89*

Expenses, *139*

Gains and losses on, *89-91*

Notes to financial statements, *286*

Pools, *153, 227, 371-73*

Realized gains and losses, *149-52*

Unrealized gains and losses, *149-52*

Irrevocable trusts, *171-75, 177-79*

IRS Publications,

No. 526, *135*

No. 598, *97*

No. 1391, *93*

No. 1771, *93*

J

Joint activities, *119*

Audience criterion, *126-27*

Content criterion, *127-28*

Purpose criterion, *119-26*

Joint ministries agreement, *192*

Sample of, *395-406*

L

Lead interests, *165-66*

Accounting for, *166-69*

In general, *165-66*

Lease of property, *87*

Legacies and bequests, *79*

Life estates, *181-82*

Life income agreement, definition of, *227*

Linguistics ministry, categories of program services, *385*

Loans, below-market rate, *89*

Losses, *143-44*

M

Management and general activities, *112-14*

Materiality, *8*

Media ministry, categories of program services, *386*

Medical ministry, categories of program services, *386*

Membership development activities, *116*

Membership dues, *92*

Mergers, *196-98*

Ministry accomplishments, *5-6*

Ministry to constituents, definition of, *228*

Modified cash basis,

Examples, *303-8, 314-19*

In general, *9-12*

N

Natural expense classification, *21,
    108, 132-33*
Net assets,
    Accounting changes, *44-45*
    Classes, *33-37*
    Designated, *225*
    In general, *33*
Net assets, *(continued)*
    International currency transac-
        tions, *46, 228*
    Other changes in, *44-46*
    Permanently restricted, *37-38*
    Prior period adjustments, *45-46*
    Return of contributions, *46, 58*
    Temporarily restricted, *38-39*
    Transfer of, *41-44*
    Reclassification of, *41-44*
    Unrestricted, *40-41*
Net income unitrusts, *177-79*
Net investments, definition of, *228*
Nonreciprocal transfer, *228*
Notes to financial statements,
    In general, *22, 76-77*
    Joint costs disclosures, *129-31*
    Related entities, *195-96*
Notional revenues, Canada, *217-18*

O

Object classification of expenses,
    228
Operations in other locations and
    countries, *194-95*
Other comprehensive bases of
    accounting, *9-12*

P

"Pass-through gifts," *63-68*
Passive income, *99-100*

Pensions, accounting for,
    In general, *139, 140*
    Notes to financial statements,
        291-92
Permanent endowment, *165-66, 171*
Permanent restrictions, definition of,
    228
Permanently restricted support,
    In general, *55-56*
    Irrevocable trusts, *171-79*
    Net assets, *37-38, 228*
Perpetual trusts, *169-71*
Personal gifts,
    Custodian (agency funds), *61,
        180*
    Definition of, *61, 228*
Pledges, see Promises to give,
Pooled fund-raising, *229*
Pooled income funds, *171-73,
    177-79, 229*
Pools, investment, *153, 371-73*
Postemployment expenses, *139-41*
Prior period adjustments, *45-46*
Private foundation status, *103-4*
Program services,
    By country, *295*
    Definition of, *229*
    Examples of categories, *385-86*
    In general, *110-11*
Promises to give,
    Canada, *217*
    Conditional or restricted, *247-52*
    Conditional promises, *69-70, 74*
    Definition of, *229*
    Discounting of, *77-78*
    Examples,
        Conditional promise, *69-70,
            74*
        Intention to give, *69, 74-75*
        Unconditional promise, *70,
            71-74*

Factors to consider, *69-75*
Intentions to give, *69, 74-75*
Noncash items, *84*
Notes to financial statements, *76-77, 287*
Oral pledges, *76*
Pledges, *68-69*
Recording of, *68-69*
Unconditional, *70, 71-74*
Property and equipment,
Capitalization policy, *156*
Classification, *159*
Depreciation, *157-58*
Held in other countries, *159*
In general, *154-55*
Lease of, *87*
Recognition and disclosure, *154*
Reporting, *155-56*
Purchase of services if not donated, *261-65*
Purchases distinguished from restricted grants, *233-36*
Purchases distinguished from contributions, *51-52*
Pure endowment, definition of, *229*
Purpose criterion, *119-26*
Purpose-restricted gifts, factors to consider, *237-40*

Q
Quasi-endowment, *55-56, 229*
Quid pro quo transactions, *61-62, 93*

R
Ratios, *28-29*
Realized gains and losses, *149-52*
Reclassification of net assets, *41-43, 59-60, 229*

Recognition and disclosure of property and equipment, *154-55*
Recognition of Depreciation by Not-for-Profit Organizations (FAS-93), *154-55, 157, 408*
Registered charities, Canada, *201-2*
Rehabilitation ministry, categories of program services, *386*
Related organizations,
Consolidation of financial data, *190-92*
Disclosures, *195-96*
In general, *185-90*
Flowchart, *392-93*
For-profit entities, *195*
Mergers, *196-98*
Operations in other locations and countries, *194-95*
Related Party Disclosures (FAS-57), *188, 191, 192, 196, 411*
Relief ministry, categories of program services, *386*
Religious broadcasters, see Broadcasters
Remainder,
Interests, *171-73, 174-75*
Trusts, *174-76, 224*
Remainderman, definition of, *229*
Reporting of property and equipment, *155-56*
Reporting of Related Entities by Not-for-Profit Organizations (SOP 94-3), *78, 135, 186-89, 189-90, 191, 195, 391-93, 408, 411*
Reporting on Advertising Costs (SOP 93-7), *138*
Reporting on the Costs of Start-Up Activities (SOP 98-5), *141*
Reporting the Results of Operations (APB-9), *44*

Reporting the Results of
Operations—Reporting the Effects
of Disposal of a Segment of a
Business, and Extraordinary,
Unusual and Infrequently
Occurring Events and
Transactions (APB–30), *44*
Rescue missions,
Categories of program services,
386
Rescue missions, *(continued)*
Sample financial statements,
355-64
Restricted grants,
In general, *233-36*
Distinguished from contributions,
51-52
Restricted net assets, definition of,
229
Restricted support, *54-55*
Restriction, definition of, *230*
Return of contributions, *46, 58*
Revenue, (also see Contributions)
Accounting principles, Canada,
208
Administered, Canada, *212-13*
In general, *49, 230*
Unrestricted, Canada, *212*
Revenue producing operations,
193-94
Revocable trusts, *180*
Revolving loan funds, *230*

S

Sabbaticals, *131-32*
Sales of good and services,
Distinguished from contributions,
51-52
Membership dues, *92*
Recording, *91-92*

Reductions in amounts charged,
137-38
Sales tax, *103*
Samples of financial statements,
see Financial statements
Schedule of cash disbursements,
370
Schools,
Categories of program services,
385
Sample financial statements,
365-70
Seminaries, categories of program
services, *385*
Services, contributed, see Donated
and contributed services
Significant changes in editions of
the Guide, *419-25*
Software, internal use, *141-43*
SOP 78-10, *191*
SOP 93-7, *138*
SOP 94-3, *78, 186-88, 135, 189-90,
191, 195, 391-93, 408, 411*
SOP 94-6, *411*
SOP 98-1, *141-43*
SOP 98-2, *62, 114, 116, 119-29, 412*
SOP 98-5, *141*
Special events, *61-63, 290*
Special trust funds,
Canada, *204-5*
Consolidation, *206-8*
Contingent beneficial interest,
205-6
In general, *204-5*
Specialized skills of volunteers,
257-59
Split interest agreement, definition of,
230
Split interest gifts,
Flow chart, *418*
In general, *164-79*

Staff honoraria, *60*
Start-up activities, *141*
Statement of activities, see
  Activities statement
Statement of assets, liabilities, and
  net assets,
    Examples,
      Cash basis, *309-13*
      Modified cash basis, *303-8*
Statement of cash flows,
    Cash basis, *409*
    Direct method, *21*
    Examples,
      Direct method, *277-80*
      Indirect method, *281*
      Multicolumn, *277-80, 349-50*
      Single column, *281, 298,*
        323, 339, 359
    In general, *21-22*
    Indirect method, *21*
    Use of multiple columns, *22*
Statement of Cash Flows (FAS-95),
  21-22
Statement of cash receipts, cash
  disbursements, and cash
  balance, *365*
Statement of financial position,
    Examples,
      Detailed, *270-73, 331-32*
      Multicolumn, *270-73, 331-32,*
        336, 346, 355
      Single column, *268-69, 296,*
        320
    In general, *15-18*
    Liquidity, *16*
    Use of multiple columns, *18*
Statement of functional expenses,
  also see Functional allocation of
  expenses,
    Examples, *293-94, 302, 308,*
      313, 319, 348, 358
    In general, *20-21*

Statement of Position, see SOP
Statement of revenues and
  expenses, see Activities statement
Statement of revenues, expenditures,
  and net assets,
    Examples,
      Cash basis, *310*
      Modified cash basis, *304*
Stipulation, definition of, *230*
Study leaves, *131-32*
Support, definition of, *230*
Support to affiliated organizations,
  133-37
Support-raising,
    Conditional promise example, *74*
    Definition of, *225*
    In general, *94-97*
    Intention to give example, *74-75*
    Revenue recorded, *56-57*
    Unconditional promise example,
      73-74
    When a supported person
      leaves the organization, *57*
Supporting activities, *111-12, 230*
    Fund-raising activities, *114-116*
    Management and general
      activities, *112-14*
    Membership development
      activities, *116*

T

Tax-deductible contributions,
Tax matters,
    Charitable giving, *93-94*
      Disclosure of value of gift to
        donor, *93-94*
      Receipting donor for gifts
        over $250, *94*
      Rules relating to charitable
        giving, *93-94*
      Support-raising, *94-97*

Tax matters, *(continued)*
  Debt-financed income, *100-2*
  Remittances to personnel, *97*
  Unrelated business activity,
    98-100
  Unrelated business income,
    97-98
Temporarily restricted,
  Basis of classifying temporarily
    vs. permanently restricted,
    55-58
  Changes in temporarily
    restricted net assets, *58-60*
  Definition of, *230*
  Net assets, *38-41*
  Redirecting contributions, *58*
  Reclassifying temporarily
    restricted net assets, *59-60*
Term endowment, *59, 230*
Thrift shops, *86*
Transfer of net assets, *41-43, 230*
Transfers of Assets to a Not-for-Profit
  Organization or Charitable Trust
  That Raises or Holds Contributions
  for Others (FAS-136), *61, 63-68,*
  85-86, 179, 413
Trusts,
  Annuity trust, *223*
  In general, *163-64*
  Irrevocable, *171-75, 177-79*
  Lead, *165-169*
  Notes to financial statements,
    284, 289-90
  Remainder trust, *171-73*
  Revocable, *180*
  Third party perpetual, *169-71*
  Unitrusts, *171-73, 177-79, 230*

U

Unconditional promise to give, *70-77*
Unrealized gains and losses, *149-52*
Unrelated business activity,
  Charitable business exemption,
    99
  Debt financed income, *100-1*
  In general, *98-100*
  Managing, *102-3*
  Not related to exempt purposes,
    98-99
  Passive income exemption,
    99-100
  Regularly carried on activity, *98*
  Trade or business income, *98*
Unrelated business income, *97-98*
Unrestricted net assets, *40-41, 220*
Unrestricted revenue, Canada, *212*
Unrestricted support, *54*
Using Cash Flow Information and
  Present Value in Accounting
  Measurements (FAS-7), *77, 166*

V

Valuing contributed services, *82-83*
Voluntary health and welfare organi-
  zations, *231*
Volunteer services,
  Determining the true recipient,
    253-55
  Requiring specialized skills,
    257-59

W

Web site development costs, *143*